BROTHERHOOD OF CORRUPTION

★ ★ ★

A Cop Breaks the Silence
on Police Abuse, Brutality,
and Racial Profiling

Juan Antonio Juarez

CHICAGO
REVIEW
PRESS

Library of Congress Cataloging-in-Publication Data

Juarez, Juan Antonio, 1966–

    Brotherhood of corruption : a cop breaks the silence on police abuse, brutality, and racial profiling / Juan Antonio Juarez.— 1st ed.

       p.   cm.

    Includes bibliographical references.

    ISBN 1-55652-536-2

    1. Chicago (Ill.). Police Dept.   2. Police corruption—Illinois—Chicago.   3. Police brutality—Illinois—Chicago.   4. Racial profiling in law enforcement—Illinois—Chicago.   5. Juarez, Juan Antonio, 1966–.   6. Ex-police officers—Illinois—Chicago—Biography.   I. Title: Police abuse, brutality, and racial profiling. II. Title.

HV8148.C4J83   2004

364.1'323'0977311—dc22   2003028193

Cover design: Arc Group Ltd.

Interior design: Pamela Juarez

Published by Chicago Review Press, Incorporated

814 North Franklin Street

Chicago, Illinois 60610

ISBN 1-55652-536-2

Printed in the United States of America

5 4 3 2 1

To the great city of Chicago

AUTHOR'S NOTE

*The life which is unexamined
is not worth living.*
— PLATO

I SPENT SEVEN YEARS as one of the thirteen thousand police officers who patrolled Chicago. Since my departure many police practices have changed, such as wanton and indiscriminant beatings and the closed-eyes approach once taken by the administration. Yet many questionable practices remain, such as the willingness to let rogue cops escape punishment and the prevalence of racial profiling in the name of the War on Drugs.

While I was a cop I saw injustices that developed into patterns, patterns ill suited to those who were sworn to serve and protect the public. After I resigned from the Police Department and years later after finishing my second master's degree, I had time to reflect, dig deeper, and look at my career. When I talked to my former supervisors I found more disturbing trends. While I never questioned anything when I was a cop, I can no longer remain silent.

This book may never have materialized if I hadn't kept my FOP (Fraternal Order of Police) handbook from my rookie year, which informed me that one of my best friends today was the very first person I arrested. He was also the first citizen I ever witnessed receiving a beating by a Chicago police officer. In 1999, I began having vivid recollections about my first arrest that left me a bit puzzled. The arrestee's image vaguely resembled a friend I had met in 1997, so I looked in my handbook and was mortified to find my friend's name in my book. I called him to verify that he had been arrested in 1990. He told me he had and began telling me his side of the story. Discovering this amazing coincidence started me on a path that produced the book you now hold.

This is my story, an attempt to detail the events that shaped and changed my life, for better and worse. To protect those who are a part of my story, all names have been changed except my own. Other than that, this is a work of nonfiction, based on conversations, interviews, public records, and personal recollection. Finally, it is my hope that the information contained in this book will raise public awareness about societal injustices and empower people to seek the truth. This is why I am sharing my story with you.

CONTENTS

ACKNOWLEDGMENTS

I WOULD LIKE TO THANK Josiah Olson, Elaine O'Sullivan, Sheila Dunlap, Dave Mitchell, Maurice Thornton, José Rivera, Nick Maiella, Kenneth Saltman, Eddie, Robert, Stephen A. Perkins, and J.Q.R. Thanks to Steven R. Lowy for his expert bargaining. I also want like to thank Shaunna for her love, support, and understanding. Thanks also to my family; my publisher; my acquisitions editor and first editor, Cynthia Sherry; my substantive editor, Lisa Rosenthal; and most of all, the Great Creator.

1

A TASTE OF AUTHORITY

"HEY, MOTHERFUCKER! Open the goddamn door before I kick it in!" Steve bellowed, bringing the ropelike vein in his neck to life as his face turned crimson. "I'm gonna give you 'bout two seconds."

The pounding hard-core punk music rattled Steve and shook the door as we stood on the front porch of 13— North Greenview Avenue for five minutes ringing the bell. We'd been called to a noise disturbance; the complainant was a neighbor. It was clear that this was a bona fide incident and should be settled with a simple radio code of 4 (noise disturbance)—either Paul (peace restored) or Frank (some other police action taken). At least that's what I'd learned at the academy.

"Hey!" yelled Steve. "Open this motherfuckin' door!"

This is what other cops loved about Steve; he didn't take shit from anyone. He was a cop's cop—hardworking and diligent with a penchant for aggressiveness. My father had met him when they worked the Chicago Housing Authority (CHA) Public Housing North detail in the 1980s. Over the years they kept in touch. When I got out of the police academy, my father pulled some strings to get me assigned to the 14th District with Steve as field training officer (FTO). He was a Caucasian veteran of three decades. In his midfifties and short, he nonetheless had a vice-grip handshake and a jawline that perfectly matched his sharp military haircut. I was to pull on his coattails for the next sixty days.

Hundreds of cops had learned from him, and many adopted his police mentality. "If you wanna be a good cop," my father told me, "you gotta have a great FTO." I considered myself lucky and was excited to have such a respected elder showing me the ropes.

Steve brought his knee up to his chest and thrust his foot into the door just as it began to open. The force of his foot meeting the door sent the person inside flying back about ten feet, landing on his ass.

"Hey, stupid! I'm a cop!" Steve straddled the chest of this scrawny white kid as soon as the door was open. "You do what I say, when I say! Understand!" The kid, dazed and trying to recover from the impact of the door, had a gash on his forehead. There was blood streaming down the bridge of his nose as he looked up at Steve. I remained standing at the threshold, frozen by the sudden and bloody violence, but the mixture of Steve's power and authority sent a thrill down my spine.

"Can you fuckin' hear me?" Steve demanded, grabbing a fistful of the kid's long brown hair. "Or is the music too fuckin' loud? Cuz it is to me!" The kid's face was a blur as Steve yanked his hair and shook his head as if it were a toy in the jaws of a rottweiler. Meanwhile, the blood kept pouring from the kid's forehead.

"I can hear you. I can hear you," the kid pleaded. "Let go of my hair. C'mon man, let go of my hair."

This kid was what Steve referred to as an "urban pioneer." These kids had money, or at least their parents did, but chose to live in the sketchy parts of Chicago where drugs, gangs, violence, poverty, and cheap rents flourish. Steve didn't care for these types at all. "These kids," he had told me on the way to the call, "are friggin' slackers. Who the fuck do they think they are? They come to live in the shit; they deserve to be treated like shit. Their parents are loaded, so they can afford to be art fucks. Escaping responsibility, if you ask me. They remind me of those friggin' long-haired hippies. I was at the convention in '68. I know how to handle these spineless twats."

The surrounding neighborhood—Wicker Park, once primarily a poor, working-class Puerto Rican and Mexican neighborhood—was changing. A number of street gangs still clung to it, but gentrification was slowly sweeping them away—boarded-up brownstones with graffiti-covered exteriors were being replaced by rapidly constructed three-story single-family houses. Neighborhood families were being priced out as young professionals and "urban pioneers" staked out new territory. Times were changing, but in Steve's mind this kid, and those like him, represented the past—antiauthority, rebellious, and confrontational, just like the youth of the late 1960s and early '70s.

Steve was a stubborn bulldog of a man. Every call was calculated and solved before we arrived at the scene. He surrendered none of what he considered his personal space, and he was never one to back down or change his opinions. Once determined, he didn't bend.

"You need to turn this shit down!" Steve hollered while he sat on the kid's chest, pinning his arms to the ground. "Your fuckin' neighbor is complainin' 'bout this shit! Where you think you're at anyway?" Steve resumed pulling the kid's hair.

"Man, all you had to do was ask!" the kid shot back. "Get off me, and I'll turn it down!" Still glaring at him, Steve relented, released his hair, and got off his chest. I cautiously crossed the threshold, entered the apartment, and peered over Steve's shoulder as this sticklike kid lifted himself from the ground. Grabbing a T-shirt from the couch, he tried to slow the flow of the blood rushing from his forehead. He walked over to the receiver and lowered the volume.

"Listen! If we hafta come back here, you're gonna spend the night in jail. I'm sure the brothers would love to get their hands on a lily-white ass like yours. So don't make us come back. If you do, you'll be sorry! Understand?"

"But—"

"What don't you fuckin' understand?"

"I don't think it's against the law—"

"Oh! Now you're gonna fuckin' tell me 'bout the law!" Steve erupted. "See! That's the fuckin' problem—you're thinking!" Steve jabbed a finger into the kid's temple. "Did I ask you to think?" The kid stood silent, cemented to the spot, only flinching with each prod that punctuated Steve's demands. "Do yourself a favor and don't fuckin' think! Don't make us come back! Am I clear?"

"What about my door?" the kid asked meekly. The hinges were almost torn out.

That was enough for Steve. "You just earned yourself a ticket to jail, asshole!" He whipped out his handcuffs so fast the kid was stunned.

"Sounds like your fuckin' problem. Here's some advice—don't stand in front of flying doors." And with that, we left, my first arrest in tow.

As we walked back to the squad car, Steve said, "Code that out, rookie."

I didn't know the code for that one. It wasn't a 4—Paul or Frank—that much was sure. Wracking my brain for an appropriate response, I asked timidly, "What code do I use?"

"Tell 'em we're coming in with one arrest!" Steve instructed. Knowing he was amped up from his exchange with the kid, I wasn't about to ask him another question, but I still had no idea what the charge would be.

"What about medical attention for that kid?" I asked. I was concerned about following the protocol that required hospitalization for arrestees who were injured.

"Fuck 'em, damn hippie," Steve answered. "He deserved it."

At the station I had to ask him about the charge again once we started to fill out the paperwork. Taken aback by my naïveté, Steve gave me a look of disgust as he replied sarcastically, "Disorderly conduct. Works all the time." Then he asked, "You learn anything back there, kid?"

I had. The power, fury, and authority he had demonstrated had enthralled me. But deep down I knew something was wrong. Yet I also knew I didn't have the balls to say anything. The thought of beginning my police career by making waves, and the anxiety this provoked, silenced the little voice in the back of my head. I wanted to be a cop. My desire to join the brotherhood, to be accepted into the ranks, was greater than my need to tell the truth. Instead, I just nodded enthusiastically, "Yes, sir!"

This was my first day as a Chicago police officer.

2

SHATTERED FAMILY

I GREW UP NEAR ASHLAND AND ADDISON on the west end of Chicago's Lakeview neighborhood during the mid-1970s. It wasn't the yuppie enclave it is today, but it wasn't a ghetto area either. Instead, it was a typical working-class neighborhood filled with tough, blue-collar families.

Arriving from Mexico in 1958, my father, Juan Manuel Juarez, already had a decent command of English. He worked his way up to production manager at a mail-order wholesale company called A. C. McClurg. They sold everything under the sun, including jewelry, books, cosmetics, and automotive tools. With his athletic figure, jet-black hair, and prominent Aztecan features, my father was an exotic foreigner who took pride in his appearance. The black-framed glasses perched upon his aquiline nose made him look scholarly, and, though he didn't get beyond the eleventh grade in Mexico, he was comfortable with his intellect. He exuded confidence.

In 1961 he met my mother, Cecelia Koenig, where he worked. She was a German American second-generation Chicagoan. He was enamored of her blue eyes, long dark hair, and white skin. And she was swept off her feet by this brown-skinned, determined, and compassionate foreigner. They married in March 1962 and immediately began having kids. My oldest sister, Noreen, was conceived before my parents were married. She was born in October 1962. Another sister, Marie, followed in January 1964. Two years later in August, I entered the world and then, before the decade ended, my youngest sister, Lee, rounded out the family in March 1969.

My father was dedicated to his family. He strove to support us financially, and I believe he felt a great sense of accomplishment in being able to do so. He always surprised us with little trinkets—bubblegum-machine jewelry and dime-store toys—intending, I think, to demonstrate his love through these gifts. But emotionally he kept us at a distance. My father defined himself by what he did, and constant work was what he did. He was driven by the desire to prosper. He held down two jobs to support his growing family while attending English classes in his spare time, and he wasn't home very often. This placed the responsibility of child-rearing squarely on my mother's shoulders.

My mother, though a very busy homemaker, constantly fed our imaginations by reading to us. She chose whimsical titles, such as books by Dr. Seuss, adventure stories such as *Gulliver's Travels* and *20,000 Leagues Under the Sea*, and a litany of other books that opened us up to new worlds. She taught us how to read and write before we entered school. She seemed content in her role as our sole nurturer; she showered us with all the love and attention that my father couldn't provide. My love of adventure began with my mother.

She enjoyed toting us around the city with her sister and her female friends who also had kids. She took us to museums, the Lincoln Park Zoo, and neighborhood fire stations. She also took us to more out-of-the-way places, such as Piper's Alley and the Billy Goat Tavern, a cool restaurant mired in the green-lighted underbelly of Lower Wacker Drive where downtown workers ate their lunches. For me, the best part of these forays wasn't where we went, but how we got there. Public transportation was our ticket to adventure. Descending into the dark, cavernous tunnels of the subway system and exiting into sunshine and the chaos of downtown made my head spin. My mother made sure to provide this stimulation in our lives.

Every summer my father would take off work for two weeks to take the family on a road trip. We'd pile into the Vista Cruiser station wagon and travel to exotic places such as the Badlands in South Dakota, the Everglades in Florida, and the Merrimac Caverns in Missouri. Together my parents did incredible things to open our eyes to the world around us.

My father had one sister, Julia, who had three kids of her own. They were all a bit older than I was; they were closer to the ages of my sisters Noreen and Marie. My mother's sister, Pam, had seven kids. The oldest one, Ronnie, was my age, and we were more than a handful at family events. The connections between our families were strengthened by four doting grandparents, and both sides of my family got along amazingly well considering they came from vastly different cultures. Holidays, birthdays, summer picnics, and occasional weekends were times of great celebration. Our extended families would join together in the festivities and the kids would eat and play until we fell down from exhaustion.

But then things started to change. My parents began to have frequent heated disagreements. I was six and had no idea what these were about, but I could feel the hostility as angry words flew around me. The temperature of my family cooled. One Saturday morning Lee and I were home with our parents while Noreen and Marie were at Bible class. My mother had prepared scrambled eggs for all of us. We sat down to eat and she must have forgotten about the tortillas she had been warming on the stove. I saw flames in the reflection of the refrigerator and so did my father. The burning smell alerted my mother and she ran into the kitchen to extinguish the flames while my father sat eating his eggs. He didn't lift a finger to help her. As soon as she put the fire out and returned to the table, my father took his plate of eggs and threw it across the table into my mother's face. Then he sprang up, slamming his chair into the wall, and charged at her.

"You stupid fool!" he yelled as he pulled her hair. She feebly defended herself with weak punches. "You could have burned down the house!" He continued beating her.

Lee and I didn't want to see our mother get the shit kicked out of her. But we were afraid for our safety, wondering if our father would turn on us after he was through with her. We got up and ran into the closet of the laundry room, praying to God that the fighting would stop.

From that day on, our happy Saturday mornings were replaced by fear and anticipation of the next incident of abuse. Hiding in the closet with Lee became as much a part of my life as my parents' fights. We wouldn't come out of the closet until we heard a door slam—a signal that my father had left the house. We'd come out to find my mom crumpled on the couch, her tears mixed with blood. We knew we couldn't help her, but we'd try anyway by hugging her and trying to make her stop crying. "I'm OK," she'd say, sobbing into our necks as she hugged us. Then we'd all cry together.

During some of their fights, I'd try to be gallant and protect my mother by clinging to my father's leg. He would continue punching my mother while I desperately clung to him. I was useless.

Why wasn't my mother doing more to protect herself? I felt my resentment growing in two directions: toward my father for beating my mother and toward my mother for letting him. The greatest grudge, though, I saved for myself. I was ashamed of my inability to stop their constant fighting. I wondered if anyone could.

My mother's side of the family shied away, not wanting to get involved in the domestic disputes. My father's family did the same. Nobody was there to protect us from the hellish turn our lives had taken.

I remember the police coming to our house as my parents screamed at the top of their lungs at each other. All the cops did was tell my father he had to leave the house until he cooled off. That would only last a few hours. When even the cops proved ineffective, my mother found her own solution. She'd go out at night and get plastered.

My parents separated a few months after I turned seven. They took turns caring for us. One month my mother would be at the house taking care of us while my father roomed at the YMCA; the next month my father took over while my mother stayed at a friend's house. It went on like this for several months. Meanwhile, I felt like an emotional ping-pong ball. Both parents spoke poorly of each other when all I wanted them to do— all I *needed* them to do—was get over their differences so we could be a family again.

One night when my mother had charge of us, she left us alone to go out drinking. My father came over for a late-night visit. He found that we were alone, so he waited, seething, until my mother returned. She was plastered as usual. He beat her within an inch of her life. That was the end; my mother moved out permanently in 1974 before I turned eight.

I suddenly found myself living in a world that wasn't quite as accepting as I'd thought. Without my mother's gentle assurances, I began to feel the teasing by other kids regarding my ethnicity more acutely. "You're not white! Your name is Juan. Do you need a towel? Your back is wet," white kids taunted, while Mexican kids called me names like *pendejo* and *gringo*. I didn't understand those words because my father had always been too busy to teach us Spanish, but I knew they weren't complimentary. I was straddling two cultural worlds; I felt that neither world wanted or accepted me.

Nothing made sense to me. I wanted to know why my mother was severed from my life and how she could find it so easy to leave her kids. I thought the divorce was the fault of my sisters and myself and that our parents had separated because we had become too much of a burden. I felt discarded, abandoned by my mother and not worthy of her love or attention any longer. I craved answers, but no one took the time to explain what was going on in our world.

The next time I saw my mother, she had moved into a studio apartment in Uptown and was already living with another man. When she put her arms around me I could smell the alcohol on her breath. I was disgusted and disappointed. I had thought I'd be the central focus of my visit, but that wasn't even close to the truth. I sat alone on the couch watching television while my mother and her boyfriend giggled on the bed in plain view. It made me sick. My mother tried to use humor; she danced around my questions about when she would be coming home. I could feel she was in pain; she knew she was no longer the mother with whom I had explored Chicago.

When my father learned she had been drunk and she was living with another man, my visits to her apartment abruptly stopped. I didn't know the reasons why I saw less and less of her, but I didn't ask any questions. Instead I began creating stories in my head; I decided that my mother's boyfriend was forcing her to stay away from her kids. Meanwhile, my father painted a sordid image of my mom, telling disturbing stories of her as an unfit mother and speculating on her drinking habits and sexual practices. At first I didn't believe him, but once I'd seen the change in her, I began to take them to heart. After all, who was taking care of us? Months passed between the times I saw my mother. The months slowly turned into years.

My father tried to do the best he could to raise us, but he was stretched pretty thin. He continued working two full-time jobs to pay the bills and keep us in Catholic schools. (He thought parochial schools offered a better education.) He started one job filling candy machines at 6:00 A.M. He called us on the phone to wake us up for school. He'd finish work at 3:30 P.M. and come home to eat. Then at 5:00 P.M. he'd leave for his janitorial job at an office where he worked well into the night.

Meanwhile my oldest sister, Noreen, replaced my mother as my father's punching bag. I could no longer stand to witness his abuse. Unable to do anything about it, I made sure I was not home when he was there. And when I was home, I kept quiet and tried not to irritate him with silly questions about schoolwork. Whenever one of us brought home a test he had to sign because we failed it, he'd say, "What? Are you stupid? You'll never amount to anything!" His tongue was sharper than any knife I ever came across. When we brought home good grades, he never complimented or supported us. When it came to nurturing us or sharing his emotions, he had become even more removed.

I don't know how he managed it, but for two summers when I was ten and eleven years old, he was my baseball coach at Hamlin Park. He was a good coach, but he seemed to expect much more from me than the other players. While he would gently correct other kids' mistakes, he yelled at me in front of my teammates. I started pissing in my pants from the anxiety of getting verbally assaulted. I should have been happy to spend time with him. But I wasn't. He made a heavy sacrifice in his personal life but a warm, nurturing home life wasn't his top priority—our futures were. He was content with feeding our bodies and paying tuition, but he forgot about our hearts and minds.

By the time I was ten, he realized he needed help raising us, so we moved into a garden apartment in his sister Julia's house in early 1976. Aunt Julia became, for a little while at least, a surrogate mother. She prepared us breakfast, made sure we had lunch, and watched us after school. But she had three children of her own to care for—Angel, Maria, and Paco— and they came first. Her door was always open to us, and she did her best to help my father, but she wasn't our mother.

During the time that we were in Aunt Julia's care, Angel, who was five years my senior, started sexually abusing me. I was ten when the abuse began. I was tall and lanky, lacking confidence and self-esteem as my father's vicious words deteriorated my spirit. Without my mother in my life and my father's immediate attention, I craved two things: acceptance and love. Angel took advantage of my needs. He was an ardent devotee of the local priests—a loyal altar boy—and he sanctified his abuse with religious icons and banter. "You've been chosen for this," he assured me when I objected or questioned his actions in the attic chapel his father constructed from cardboard. I remember him telling me, "In God's eyes, you're special," as the sharp bristles on his beard rubbed the insides of my thighs. I was confused, especially when he made me promise not to tell anyone. I didn't want to reject God, so I gave in to Angel's requests and convinced myself that there was nothing wrong with what he was doing to me.

After two years of taking care of my sisters and me in addition to her own three children, Aunt Julia slowly pulled her welcome mat out from under our feet. Our visits upstairs to eat and be with her family became rare.

My family continued to deteriorate. Noreen couldn't take any more abuse from my father; she moved out to live with our mom. The relationship between my mother and myself was nearly nonexistent. And now my aunt Julia abandoned us as well. It felt as if each day another part of my heart dried up and blew away.

With no daily adult supervision in our lives, Marie, Lee, and I fended for ourselves. We cooked our own meals, washed our own clothes, ran around the neighborhood as long and as late as we wanted, and went to bed whenever we felt like it. I ended up finding and making a lot of trouble during this unsupervised time. I had friends who had as much free time as I did, so we found trouble together.

3

DREAMING OF AN ESCAPE

IN THE SUMMER OF MY THIRTEENTH YEAR, a number of events shaped the direction of my life in significant ways. I was an awkward, gangling kid with hair that couldn't be controlled and a lisp that wouldn't go away. I had just started wearing glasses. To put it mildly, I was a dork. But my neighborhood friends didn't give a shit about the way I looked. They knew I was up to doing anything they'd do, so we bonded tightly. We were a veritable rainbow coalition—a Mexican American, two Irish boys, a Hawaiian kid, and a Filipino. Our taste for teenage adventures, such as climbing factory rooftops and jumping from garage to garage and other harmless mischief, expanded with our ever-increasing ability to outrun the cops. My friends and I became thorough adventurers of our neighborhood, seeking out experiences that filled us with heart-pounding adrenaline. The more cunning and dangerous the activity, the greater the surge of adrenaline I experienced. I began to love the rush of doing shit and not getting caught, and so did my friends. We were adrenaline junkies.

"Hey, you little punks, you'll stop if you know what's good for you!" the cop behind us commanded. We had climbed up the Northwestern train tracks near Grace and Ravenswood on the Chicago's North Side just for the hell of it. We were out exploring, but now the cops wanted us. Doing what came naturally, we ran. When we stopped and turned around, we saw the cop trying to navigate the steep, gravel-strewn embankment. "I'm gonna catch you. You'll be sorry, you little shits," he yelled, pumping his fist into the air. Like hell he was. We had a good lead and knew every escape route in our neighborhood. He stood up to start running but he slipped backward and lost his balance as he slid down the gravel. We had done it again. We'd ditched the flat-footed, doughnut-eating cop. We smiled at each other and took off running as our adrenaline surged.

The times when we were caught, the cops battered our ears with profanity-laden lectures. Then they'd drive us home where we'd have to sit through the completely one-sided accounts of our "hooliganism" the cops fed our parents. I remember one time, around the Fourth of July, when I was busted for lighting firecrackers near Lincoln and Hermitage. A civilian caught me and held me until the police came and then told them that I was throwing firecrackers at his car. The police drove me home; my dad happened to be there. The cops told him the story, but then they ad-libbed and told him the civilian thought I had a gun. When I corrected them and told them it was firecrackers, they got pissed off and told my dad he should beat me until I learned some respect. My dad didn't appear to believe the cops or their stories. And he definitely didn't enjoy being told how to raise his kid. He said "yeah, yeah" to the cops. This made my dad super cool in my eyes, but it also made me realize that he had no clue whatsoever about what a troublemaker I had become. I felt I could get away with anything.

Summers were brutal. The humidity was thick and the air stagnant, and the lack of refreshing solutions sometimes forced us to venture outside our neighborhood. The only way to our summer resort—swimming in Lake Michigan—was through gang territory. All my friends knew this was a risky venture if not downright suicidal. Just to the east, near Wrigley Field, a notorious faction of the Latin Eagles called the Wilton Boys ruled with impunity. To the south, around Hamlin Park and the Lathrop Homes, the Insane Deuces and PBC (Paulina Barry Corporation) flourished. And to the north, the TJOs (Thorndale Jag Offs) and the Simon City Royals sprinkled their graffiti liberally on the walls marking their territory.

We lived in the middle of a war zone. Tom Ripley, a kid I played base-ball with at Hamlin Park, had an older brother, Scott, who was two years older than we were. Scott was an all-star third baseman for Lane Tech High School, a kid whose baseball prowess was sure to get him noticed at the college level. The kids around Hamlin idolized Scott. One day, as he sat on a friend's porch talking with some buddies, a car slowly approached and a hand, gripping a gun, took aim at the porch. Flashes erupted from the gun's barrel. Scott's baseball dreams ended as the bullet severed the nerves along his spinal cord.

Mistaken identity? Gang retaliation? It really didn't matter; the damage had been done. From that day on, I hated gangs and vowed I would do something to help society against their senseless violence.

Later that summer I witnessed the mighty force of the Chicago police for the first time—another event that helped shape the course of my life. My father dropped me off with some family friends he knew from Mexico, the Martinezes. They lived in Pilsen, a Mexican neighborhood on the South Side of Chicago. They had a son named Pablo who was my age. We were going to hang out for the weekend. As luck would have it, Fiesta del Sol was taking place. Cars and people were draped in Mexican flags, mariachis strolled up and down Eighteenth Street, and the sibilant sounds of Spanish, along with the scent of grilled steak and tamales, hung in the air. Mr. Martinez's car inched westward from Halsted Street. Heavy pedestrian and automobile traffic contributed to the visible frustration of the numerous white non-Spanish-speaking police officers assigned to the area for this event. Traffic was just about deadlocked, but no one seemed to be in a hurry. Two officers pulled a driver out of his double-parked car.

"Listen amigo, move yer fuckin' car out of da intersection!" one of the police officers ordered the driver, who responded by putting his hands up in the air and saying, "Take-it-eezee, amigo. I go away. I go, OK?"

"I'm not yer fuckin' amigo!" the other officer said and shoved the Mexican backward, causing him to stumble and fall in front of our car. The officers laughed.

I was dumbfounded. "Mr. Martinez, why did they do that?" I asked Pablo's father.

"I don't know, and I'm not gonna find out," replied Mr. Martinez. He wasn't the only one remaining silent and doing nothing. Celebrants on the sidewalk continued on their way, no doubt afraid of incurring the penalty for meddling. The traffic, however, remained at a standstill as everyone's attention turned toward the cops.

The Mexican got up, brushing his hands on his pants. "What's that for?" he asked.

"Listen, spic! Get in yer car and move dat fuckin' piece a shit! Or else I'll lock yer ass up, comprendo?" the cop said.

The Mexican shrugged, "Why you talk to me like that? I go. You a bad polizeman."

At this the cops began to shove him back and forth until he resembled a pinball getting knocked around the bumpers. I was scared, but for some reason I couldn't look away. He stumbled, tripped over his feet, and fell. As he tried to get up, one of the cops took out a small black object from his pocket and began pummeling the back of the Mexican's head and neck.

"Motherfucker!" A flashing forehand downstroke cuffed him behind his left ear. A deft backhand followed on the upstroke. "Wetback!"

The Mexican fell to his knees as blood poured from his nose. The cop's strikes rained down on him but his cries were lost in the sounds of the celebration. His hands, forearms, and triceps took the brunt of the blows as he tried to protect himself. It was futile. He was as defenseless as my mother was when my dad kicked her ass.

Mr. Martinez was transfixed by what he saw; Pablo urged him to get out of there. Drawn by the power of what I was seeing, I sat mesmerized, my mouth gaping. Fear gripped my stomach and nausea rose in my throat—I thought I was going to puke.

"You do what I say, when I say it!" screamed the cop, bringing his right hand over his head. Another forehand slashed through the air, immediately followed by an elbow to the back of the Mexican's head. "You're gonna spend the night in jail, you ignorant beaner!" The cop stood over the Mexican, who was out cold on the sidewalk in a fetal position.

Mr. Martinez awoke from his stupor, saw an opening in the traffic, and swerved around the frenzied officers. As we drove away I looked back and saw groups of open-mouthed Mexicans in cars and on the street, but no one said or did anything. The celebration continued.

That incident added to my growing confusion about cops. Was I to respect them or simply fear them? I really wasn't certain, but the power of the police had definitely caught my attention.

★ ★ ★

As a kid I was very athletic and played baseball, basketball, and hockey, which proved a great release for my mounting aggression. The physical nature of hockey allowed me to unleash my anger at opposing teams, and I led the league in both penalty minutes and fighting. My love of sports and athleticism earned me the right to tag along with my older cousin, Paco, who was three years my senior. I thought I was cool because I hung out with the older crowd. But because of my skinny frame and slight lisp, I became an easy target for his friends' violent behavior. I wanted to be accepted, but all they did was tease me and beat me up. Both my ineffectiveness and their bullying pissed me off, but, fearing rejection, I accepted their ridicule and their violence toward me and continued to hang out with them.

My father earned a GED in the winter of 1979, when I was in eighth grade. This was further proof to us that an education was important. He also introduced my sisters and me to the girlfriend he had been keeping a secret. Her name was Dale. She was a nurse at Grant Hospital. Meeting her wasn't such a shock to us because we had been receiving Christmas cards stuffed with checks from her for the last two years. She was a bit of a mystery, but I didn't care what my father was doing with his personal life, so I never asked questions about her. I was just happy to get the cash.

My mom had had three boyfriends since my parents separated. To my knowledge, Dale was my dad's first romance. She was considerably younger than my father, loved to cook and bake, had a gentle demeanor, and was willing to play a part in our lives. Accepting her was difficult for me at first because I didn't know if she wanted to replace my mom or just be with my dad. Dale kept her own apartment; she never slept at ours. She made my dad happy, and that was good. After a while I guardedly allowed her into my life.

In 1980, as I was graduating from grammar school, my father entered the police academy. One year had passed since he had earned his GED. When I asked him why he wanted to be a cop, he explained that it was a great profession in terms of financial and job security and had great perks, especially health insurance and a retirement plan. When my father became a cop, Paco's friends suddenly stopped teasing me. They feared having to deal with him. I didn't get any more shit from anyone. This tiny badge of metal bought me instant respect, and it wasn't even mine. I wanted power and respect; I decided I wanted to be a cop just like my dad.

Two years later, in 1982, Dad married Dale and they bought a house near Central Park and Montrose. Since meeting Dale, he'd mellowed quite a bit. He seemed happy now. Though they got into screaming matches on occasion, it took only one incident for him to learn that Dale wasn't going to tolerate being slapped around. On the one occasion when he hit her, she called the cops, got him in deep shit with his job, and then promptly left the house for more than a week. They reconciled before she came home. He never hit her again.

My desire to join the police force grew stronger when my cousin Paco joined in 1986. Then Dale became a cop in 1987. I wanted a badge even more when I learned about the world of privilege that came with it. Paco told me about how chicks love a man in uniform, how he could clear a corner of gangbangers just by getting out of his squad, and how he was able to get into nightclubs for free. Meanwhile, my parents told me stories of catching criminals and throwing them in jail. The power and privilege that seemed to be woven into the fabric of a cop's uniform intrigued me more and more.

Around this time, Angel's physical interest in me began to wane, leaving me with even less self-esteem. I mentally cataloged the people who had disowned or abused me. The list was long. What was wrong with me? What was I doing wrong? Why wasn't I wanted? Accepted? Loved? I couldn't come up with any answers but I knew it was my fault.

To escape the questions battering me, I bought a twelve-speed Fuji road bike for fifty bucks from a high school buddy. I began doing epic rides—twenty-five to thirty miles—late at night. The coolness of the night air made my secret voyages that much more invigorating as my bike became my great escape machine. I'd pedal until my legs burned, my lungs ached, and my head was ready to burst from the blood coursing through my body. The surge of adrenaline I experienced as I rode, testing my physical limits, helped me work through the issues of my life and gave me room to construct a better future.

4

OUT OF THE SHADOWS

I GRADUATED FROM AN ALL-MALE high school at the bottom of my class, number 450 out of 454 students, and scored a 17 on my ACT exam, slightly below the national average. Because my grades were poor, I had to petition Northeastern University in Chicago to get accepted. They put me on a strict academic contract requiring me to maintain a 2.0 average or better. It would be a challenge—my GPA in high school had been .65—but they were giving me a clean slate and I was determined to make the most of the opportunity. Plus, there were girls at Northeastern; I wanted to excel so that I could remain there.

I thought perhaps my brains would impress girls, as my looks sure didn't. I began taking my prerequisites with dreams of transferring to DePaul University, which I considered the best college in Chicago. I did well in my classes and studied extremely hard, metamorphosing into a dean's list student during the first quarter and loving the college atmosphere. Soon my classmates became my friends. We'd meet in the student activity center between classes to shoot the shit or make weekend plans. My circle of friends was getting larger and I was having fun. It was at Northeastern where I got the best advice of my life to that point, from a sexy Puerto Rican girl who saw my hazel eyes underneath my dorky, cumbersome glasses. She told me, "Get contacts."

I did get contacts and suddenly the world of women came into focus. I had no idea how to flirt, but when girls looked at me, I returned their gazes. Soon I'd find myself wanting to conquer them and have them when and *only* when I wanted them. I was especially drawn to women of color—Mexicans, blacks, and Puerto Ricans and their wondrously curvaceous bodies—but I still lacked self-confidence. I saw how my friend Cito had tons of girls hanging on him, so I asked him his secret. "Lies," he replied. "Tell them lies."

My life had been filled with pain and sorrow, but I saw that sad topics weren't going to get me anywhere with girls. I buried the old Juan deep inside and started to create a new identity for myself. My self-esteem was still pretty poor, but I learned that telling white lies made me feel better, which changed my self-perception. "Yeah, I got great plans for my future," I'd hear myself say. "I want to be a lawyer and then maybe, someday, the mayor of this city. You know the Latino race is taking over, don't you?" They'd agree and stare deep into my eyes. My ambition drew them to me, so I kept up the charade. "Yeah, I can dance. Yeah, I can get a car. Yeah, I can love you better than your man." Soon there was nothing I couldn't do—or at least nothing I'd admit I couldn't do. I seldom brought up my family because I was ashamed of where I came from. I made sure to steer the conversation toward my plans. I soon began believing every word that came out of my mouth, and so did just about every girl I came in contact with. Women seemed to adore my self-confidence.

I started dating like there was no tomorrow. I lost my virginity and found that I loved the sexual release that women gave me. Besides, it was much more fulfilling to brag about the number of women I conquered than hang my head in shame knowing that I'd spent a lot of my past getting sucked off by a guy.

My self-esteem was growing by leaps and bounds, but so were my conniving ways. I cheated on all of my girlfriends and never got caught. I lured women into my web by stretching the truth and telling white lies. Then, for the knockout punch, I'd tell them sob stories about my sexual abuse and then lie further by saying my mother was dead. Then after I got the sex I wanted, I'd drop them without a word, without remorse. I simply walked away.

My self-esteem had a strange but altogether welcome effect on my academics. As I was telling woman about my great plans and passions for my future, I was manifesting that success in school. I wanted a big brain to impress women and visualized myself being smart because that was the new identity I was creating for myself. I began to ace classes such as earth science, chemistry, criminal justice, and psychology.

I was amazing myself. When people began telling me I could be a model, I basked in their compliments. I'd certainly never heard anything like that before. I noticed the physical changes from all my late-night bike rides—my long body was now lean and sinuous, and my angular jaw and cheekbones had become more defined. I was proud of my metamorphosis.

The summer after my first year in college, my father met a high-powered attorney while on duty. The attorney phoned the police because his house had been burglarized. My father used his connection with the lawyer to get me a job at the Circuit Court of Cook County. I was assigned to traffic court as a file clerk, retrieving driving records for judges, lawyers, court clerks, and the general public. Three months after I started, I was promoted to work in the courtrooms.

My duties put me directly in the public view. I was the clerk who called the court docket, kept order in the court, and worked closely with lawyers, and at times beautiful women, to ensure their cases were called first. I was always willing to do favors for women because I never knew where it might lead—perhaps to a conversation, then a lunch or a dinner date, and maybe a conquest. But my main desire was to get to know the legal system. My inflated dreams of becoming a lawyer did not seem so far out of reach now that school was going well for me and my confidence was growing. Getting my foot in the door of the legal profession was that easy. All my dreams were being realized.

Then I met Ana.

In between court calls I liked to wander the halls, checking out the scenery. One day I spotted a Mexican girl, around five-foot-six with long, dark, curly hair, a beautiful olive complexion, and teardrop-shaped brown eyes. She had an incredibly fit and shapely form. She was standing in the cashier's line waiting to pay a ticket. I confidently strode over to her, smiled, and then nonchalantly inquired, "What are you waiting for?"

She looked at me with a quizzical glance before turning her head and kept silent.

"I'm sorry," I began. "My name is Juan. I work here and if there's anything I can help you with, I'd like to." The people ahead of her and behind her made various faces of confusion as if saying, "Hey, I'm in line, too. Can you help me?" I ignored them all as the girl told me she was there to pay some parking tickets for her boss. She showed me the tickets and I looked at them officiously. When I finished inspecting them, I said, "Follow me."

I walked back into the courtroom, told her to wait a minute, and then went to see the judge in his chambers. I told him the tickets belonged to a friend. He instructed me to put them on the docket and told me he'd dismiss them. I bounced out of the chambers and approached the girl. She was even more beautiful standing alone in the courtroom.

"I did you a pretty big favor," I began earnestly, "but before I tell you what I did for you, you have to tell me your name."

"It's Ana. Ana Nuñez," she replied. I was mesmerized as I watched her lips form every sound. "What did you do for me?" she asked coyly. Her brown eyes penetrated my heart.

"Oh, your tickets are dismissed and you can go," I said. "Hey . . . Ana. Where are you going right now?" It was 10 A.M. and the next court call didn't start for another thirty minutes, so I hoped I'd be able to talk to her for a while.

I ended up walking Ana back to work in the warm September sunshine. As we walked and talked, I noticed that her dark, brown eyes turned a light shade of caramel in the sun and that her springy curls bounced with her every step. We talked all the way to the health club where she worked. When I got back to the courtroom, a co-worker chided me and predicted that I was going to marry Ana. I brushed it off as nonsense. "We haven't even gone out yet."

"Don't matter," she said. "It's in both of y'alls' eyes."

My first date with Ana was at O'Famé, an Italian eatery on Webster Avenue near Halsted Street. It was a cute little café that had paper tablecloths and crayons to draw on them with. We colored while we learned more about each other. Ana attended St. Xavier College on the far Southwest Side. She wanted to become an accountant. I shared my dreams of becoming a lawyer with her. We were deep in conversation when the waiter came by and asked if we wanted something to drink.

"I'd like a bottle of wine, red wine," she said. Looking at me she asked, "Is that all right?"

"Sure," I replied as the waiter walked away. In fact, her request made me wince. I had some cash, but I didn't know if I had enough to cover the libation. I decided not to worry about it and just kept up the conversation.

We found out that both of us enjoyed working out, biking, running, participating in team sports, and dancing. Now I knew how she maintained her knockout figure. We also discussed our families and found that we shared similarities in that area—we both came from broken homes. She lived with her mother, two sisters, and a brother. When I told her I lived with my father, I had an instant flash that she could provide me with the female love and affection I had so sorely missed growing up. I then visualized that I could offer her the male support and strength she had missed out on.

Before the bill came, we had made plans to go to the Art Institute, a Joffrey Ballet performance, and a play. I was excited about the prospect of seeing her again, and she was obviously interested in seeing what I was about.

Shortly after our first month together, I joined Ana's health club so we could be with each other even more. I couldn't get enough of her. The sex we shared was intense and profound, making me feel things I had never felt before. Each time we made love, we'd stare into each others' eyes and I'd whisper, "I'm gonna love you for the rest of my life." These feelings were new to me.

Another thing that kept me interested in Ana was her desire to seek higher education. Most of the women I had met to that point weren't seriously interested in school, but Ana and I shared the same drives and passions. Both of us wanted to do better in life than our parents had done. Her mother, Rosita, was a laborer, and, at sixty-three, she continued to work hard to support her family. Ever since Ana started working at fifteen, she always surrendered her paychecks to her mother to help with the bills. Her father had owned a bar on Archer Avenue and abruptly left the family without a word when Ana was seven. She hadn't had any contact with her father for several years and considered him dead. When I listened to her story, I felt like I was listening to excerpts of my own life. Though our pasts were sad, they provided the motivation behind our desires to succeed.

About the same time I met Ana, I transferred to DePaul University, the school of my dreams. It was the fall of 1987 and I felt nothing could stop me. Even though I was going to be classified as a sophomore because not all my credits from Northeastern transferred, I didn't care; I was confident I would succeed in school. Ana followed my lead and transferred from St. Xavier College to Loyola University, the school of *her* dreams.

When Ana and I celebrated our one-year anniversary in 1988, it was by far the longest relationship I had ever had with a girl. Everyone in both our families thought we were destined to marry. We believed it, too. We were two Mexicans who possessed an intense desire to exceed our personal goals, and I knew that with Ana in my life, the sky was the limit.

5

FLIGHT OF THE PHOENIX

WITH LOVE IN MY LIFE, I continued to fly high. I applied at the Dirksen Federal Building for a position in bankruptcy court. I had just started my junior year at DePaul when I was hired as a file clerk.

During finals week of the winter quarter of my junior year, I came home one day to find that I'd had an urgent call from Ana. "She was crying pretty hard," my father told me when I walked in the door. "She wanted you to call her immediately when you got home."

My mind raced as I dialed Ana's number. When she answered the phone, her voice was hoarse from crying. At the sound of my voice, she began sobbing hysterically. It was the first time in our eighteen months together that I had heard her cry. "Juan," she managed between gasping breaths, "I'm pregnant." My heart dropped into my stomach as my mouth gaped, preventing a sound from escaping.

"Juan," Ana cried. "Are you still there?"

"Yeah, I'm here," I said. "I'm coming over. OK?"

I asked my father if I could use his car, and when he asked me what was wrong, I told him that Ana had hurt herself. "It's nothing bad, but I just want to visit her and make sure she's all right," I said. He gave me the keys and I started off to her house on the other side of the city.

When I got to Ana's house, she met me at the door. Her face was puffy from so much crying. "It's not the end of the world, baby," I whispered as I held her in my arms. Her chest was heaving wildly and my mind floated back to the days when Lee and I tried to console my mother after my father had beaten her.

"What are we going to do?" Ana asked.

"I don't know, Ana. What *can* we do?" I asked.

"We're too young to start a family, Juan," she said, sobbing into my neck. I wanted to offer her some guidance. I could see that she was leaning toward having an abortion. The idea made me uncomfortable, but it was one alternative that had crossed my mind on the way to her house.

"We could get married," I said.

"What would that do for our futures?" she said, raising her head from my neck and looking into my eyes.

"I don't know, Ana," I confessed.

"We don't even make enough money to take care of ourselves; how can we take care of a baby?"

"I don't know," I said. "Other people have done it. We'd just have to put off our futures for a bit."

After further discussion, we decided it would be best if she had an abortion. She arranged the appointment and I again borrowed my father's car. I called in sick to work, picked her up, and then drove her to a clinic on Grand Avenue near Clark Street. I prayed to God everything would be fine. The operation was scheduled to last an hour, so I ran to a florist and bought her two dozen roses—yellow and red. I thought they'd show her that I loved her. I put the flowers in the car and returned to the lobby.

Finally, a nurse appeared in the back of the clinic escorting Ana. She looked pale and tired. I ran to get the car, came back, and gently guided Ana into the front seat. She immediately reclined and started softly crying with her back toward me as I drove to her house. I didn't know how to console her, so I pulled out the roses from the back seat and offered them to her. She turned around, smiled briefly, touching the fragile petals, and said "Thank you." She faced away from me and continued crying. Feelings of helplessness overwhelmed me. When we got to her house, she said she wanted to be alone so I left.

She was cutting me out of her pain, her sorrow. I felt rejected and, having nowhere to go, I drove around the city, lost in my thoughts. I was overwhelmed by sadness, not for Ana or the abortion, but because I felt as if I had been beaten up by my feelings of helplessness once again. I fell into a state of deep self-pity.

I felt that the once-unconditional love Ana and I had shared was now desecrated. Ana, in my eyes and heart, had been sullied at my hands, permanently scarred because of something I did to her. I felt so guilty. I'd loved her with a freedom that now became shackled by guilt. If I'd had control of my heart and emotions, this wouldn't have happened. I vowed never to let myself lose control again. I had to control my heart, my passions, and my emotions with Ana.

The next day, I pledged my heart to her, telling her everything I thought she needed to hear. I convinced her that I loved her with all my heart, though secretly I knew that our love had changed greatly. We vowed to keep the abortion a secret from our families. On the outside, I demonstrated devotion and affection. I overwhelmed her with lavish gifts of jewelry, clothing, and accessories to show her how much I loved her. In a sense I was replicating my father's gift-giving behavior from my childhood. The extravagant purchases were also making me broke.

Making love with Ana was out of the question. I didn't want to hurt her inside or get her pregnant again. It took us a while to feel comfortable lying in bed together. As time went on I knew she wanted to be comforted with physical contact, so I began caressing her body with my hands. I couldn't let myself go any further than oral sex with her.

"It's not your fault, Ana," I told her when she asked me if something was wrong. "It's just that I can't. I can't bear the thought of getting you pregnant again."

She hugged me, started crying, and whispered, "I understand, Juan. Just hug me, let me know you still love me and care for me." I did everything she asked, but I couldn't bring myself to make love to her.

While my personal life was in turmoil, I was excelling at DePaul. As I started the fall quarter of my senior year, I seriously considered going to graduate school to study either English or education. My relationship with Ana was entering its third year, and while we continued seeing each other, I knew I was holding back. There was love for Ana in my heart, but my mind didn't give an inch—making love to her was still out of the question. I was also sick of living at home, not having a car, and not even making

$20,000 a year. I realized something had to change if I wanted to see my life differently.

Then the police department announced it was hiring police officers. This, I thought, would change things instantly.

I took the police entrance exam late in 1989. The test for police cadets was amazingly simple for me. It was multiple-choice. Questions dealt with logic and reading comprehension, but most of the test was based on common sense and deductive reasoning. In December 1989 a letter from the police department came, notifying me of my score—98.6 percent—and my acceptance into the academy. I had scored in the top 5 percent of all candidates. I was excited. Ana, however, was not.

"Ana," I began, "you have to admit it's a great opportunity to earn more cash. And they have great benefits. Just ask your brother." Mark had been in my corner and even helped me prepare for the test.

"I know," she responded, "but what good would they do me if you're killed by some drug-crazed gangbanger? Huh? That job's too dangerous. I won't be able to eat or sleep because I'll be worrying about you all the time."

"There's no need to worry about me," I reassured her. "I can take care of myself."

"Once you stop going to classes, you'll never go back. With all the money you're making, you won't have a need to finish."

"Ana, you know what's important to me—you and school," I replied. "This job will allow me to save some money, get out of debt, and then we can start a family." I thought this line would be the winner and end the discussion, but she didn't buy it. She just sneered at me.

"You'll change and I don't wanna see it," she warned. "It happened to my brother; it'll happen to you." Having to discuss and explain what I wanted to do with *my* life was frustrating. I felt she had two choices— accept my decision or let me go. In the end, she accepted my decision.

"Don't worry, *mijo*," my father assured me when I told him about Ana's concerns. He was all for me going to the academy. It was the most secure, high-paying job that had come my way. The money would allow me to move out of my father's house. I was currently making $18,000 a year as a clerk in bankruptcy court, and the cop job paid twice that. Plus, it offered great health insurance, access to high-paying side jobs, an excellent deferred-compensation program, and other perks.

"You'll graduate from DePaul and the Department'll reimburse you for your classes. Then you can quit (the Department) and do what you really want to do," my father told me. Hearing this helped me envision a future pursuing higher education, getting a graduate degree in English and a teaching certificate for secondary-school literature. I knew I'd need to be in graduate school for at least six to eight years, and I envisioned my career as a cop lasting exactly that long.

"You're gonna quit when you're done with school, right, Juan?" Ana asked.

"Yes," I assured her. That made her happy.

I begrudgingly accepted the fact that I had to put off my education. This was the first test the police department had offered in two years, and I had no idea when they'd offer another one. When my father guaranteed that I'd benefit from the connections he had cemented during his ten years on the force—such as pulling strings to get me into the district of my choice and making sure I'd get an FTO who would show me how to be a good police officer—the idea of putting off school became tolerable. I wasn't about to pass up this opportunity.

On March 26, 1990, while I was completing the winter quarter at DePaul University, leaving me just three classes short of my bachelor's in English, I entered the police academy. Eager to become a cop and sure that I could improve society, I thought about Scott Ripley, the brother of my childhood friend, who had been gunned down by gangbangers. I knew I could make a difference in the world. Plus, the thrill and excitement of the job—dealing with unknown circumstances with every call—would require me to be on my toes, mentally and physically, every day. I welcomed that challenge. When I entered the academy, I found that the department had a rule barring a police academy cadet from attending outside classes. This bothered me momentarily because it meant I'd have to wait until my year of probation was over to resume my studies.

★ ★ ★

The classes at the police academy—civic law, Illinois statutes, and arrest procedures—were easy for me because I already knew how to study and take tests. Veterans from around the city taught these classes and some of them glamorized the role of a cop by telling anecdotal stories of grisly crimes, instant respect, the uncommonly strong brotherhood of cops, the power of the pen, and cop groupies who doted on officers from the moment the badge was pinned and the gun holstered. We also did a lot of role-playing, responding to hypothetical situations we might encounter on the streets. The scenarios pumped up my adrenaline like nothing I had ever experienced before. My eagerness to be a cop grew into an unbridled passion.

The St. Jude's Parade, which involves all the police in the Chicago metropolitan area, marked the end of my first month in the academy. The parade honors all police personnel who have died in the line of duty as well as St. Jude, the patron saint of police officers. My academy class, 1990–91, was required to participate in the organized march north down Michigan Avenue. This was my true initiation into the police brotherhood.

Police officers from all over the city were expected to march with their respective districts or units in a show of camaraderie and strength. It was a time to make new friends, see old buddies, and show pride in our chosen profession. I saw my father and stepmother with the 23rd District, my cousin with the 13th District, and Mark with his unit before we stepped off near the Wrigley Building. I felt honored to be included in this display of brotherhood.

Many politicians, including the mayor and dignitaries from other cities, were on hand in the reviewing grandstand. Each district had to march down Michigan Avenue, turn west on Chicago Avenue and pass the Emerald Society—the time-honored bagpipe players—before saluting the dignitaries. It's an awesome display of unity. The friendships I forged in the academy and at the parade fueled my desire to be accepted into the brotherhood.

I began hanging out more and more with cops. Unfortunately, my friendships put a strain on my relationship with Ana. I noticed a change in my attitude toward her. She noticed it too.

★ ★ ★

One Friday night, I had forgotten about plans I had made with Ana and instead went out for drinks with some cadets from the academy. When I went to see Ana the next day, she laid into me. "Where the fuck were you last night?" she demanded. I was taken aback. Ana usually refrained from using profanity. The attack made me respond in kind.

"I was out with the boys having a fuckin' drink! Is that all right with you?" I yelled. "I had a hard week at the academy and just wanted to relax."

"Did you forget we had fuckin' plans?" she shot back.

"I must have! Gimme a fuckin' break, we can go out tonight," I said.

"I can't. I already have plans."

"Who the fuck with?" I said, but I didn't wait for an answer. "Whatever! Now that you ruined my day, I'm leaving."

"Wait, Juan. Can't we talk about this?"

"See ya. I'll call you later when you're in a better mood."

From that point on whenever Ana asked me about what I was doing during my free time, I'd get irate. I became inflexible; my decisions were final, and I didn't leave much room for consideration. The academy and my friends there became a safe harbor for me. With them, I found acceptance for the person I was becoming.

In July we were assigned traffic-control duty for the fireworks extravaganza along the lakefront. After being in cadet khakis for three months we were finally permitted to wear the blue police uniforms. It was the first time we would be working with the public. I was detailed with a partner to work the corner of Wabash and Roosevelt. It was utter chaos as waves of people and cars came from every direction after the fireworks ended. Trying to control traffic was useless, so my partner and I stayed on the northeast corner of the intersection checking out the scenery. I began to notice how women looked at me in my uniform, checking me out from head to toe. I made eye contact with each of them. One woman stopped abruptly in the intersection to gaze at me while her boyfriend continued walking, unaware of her obvious fixation. When her boyfriend finally realized she wasn't by his side, he followed her gaze and then yelled at her. She instantly snapped out of it. Shaking her head, she smiled in my direction. I had to laugh. It was fun to flirt like this; it reminded me of my days at Northeastern.

At night when I was out drinking with the boys and wasn't dressed in my uniform, women seemed intrigued when I told them I had a badge. This newfound fascination fed my ego even more, and the temptation to seek sexual conquests grew stronger. I had remained faithful to Ana during our relationship. Having intercourse with her was still out of the question, though. I couldn't take the chance of getting her pregnant again. Meanwhile, my sexual urges were becoming too great to contain.

I moved out of my parents' house and into a beautiful historic brownstone on Jackson Boulevard two blocks away from the academy.

"I need my space," I told Ana when she wanted to know why she couldn't move in with me. "Besides, it's just a studio apartment. You could come over anytime you want."

She understood and respected my need for space. She seemed happy that I extended an open invitation to her, but I knew she didn't have a car, and consequently, she would be unable show up at my apartment unexpectedly.

Graduation from the academy turned into a huge drunken festival. We received our badges in a mid-July ceremony. Ana, my father, and Dale came to support me, but when the ceremony was over, I informed them that I was going to celebrate with ten of my closest colleagues. We went out for a festive meal in Greektown where we drank several bottles of ouzo. Upon leaving the restaurant a few of us decided to extend the celebration.

To make our initiation into the brotherhood official, we went to Dugan's, a cop bar on South Halsted Street near Adams Street. There we proceeded to get even more plastered. After two hours and many beers, my buddy, Harris Wroblewski, and I left the bar and got into his Jeep. The top was off and the summer night rejuvenated us. "Where you going, boy?" I slurred as he whipped a turn westbound on Adams.

"Just wait, we need to properly bid adieu to the academy," he said, mischievously laughing to himself.

Before I knew it, we were in front of the academy. Harris had jumped the curb with his Jeep and was doing doughnuts on the lawn. Chunks of dirt and grass were flying everywhere. "We'll lose our badges if we get busted, boy," I said. I was vaguely concerned but thoroughly enjoying the moment of defiant destruction.

"Relax," Harris instructed. "They ain't gonna catch us if I got anything to do with it." He spun one last doughnut and jumped the curb again, heading west on Adams. We drove around for a while as our adrenaline ebbed and then he dropped me off at my apartment. We high-fived and then parted.

From there I got in my car and began my prowl. I was on a solo mission. I went to Shelter, a nightclub on Fulton near Halsted that had just opened. I waited in line, paid the cover charge, and began scanning the talent in the club. I ordered a drink and turned my head, catching sight of this beautiful black girl who had a luscious body and inviting lips. I approached her and we started talking. I bought her whatever she wanted to drink and I began making overt sexual innuendos. She took the bait.

When we went back to my apartment, she saw a picture of Ana hanging on the wall and asked, "Who's that?"

I looked at the picture and shook my head. "I just broke up with her," I explained.

"You still pining over her?" she asked.

I didn't have to think twice about it. "Nope." I walked over to the wall and took the picture down and slid it under my bed. She came over and sat next to me on the bed, and we started making out. I felt no guilt or remorse as we made love.

It was the beginning of my second life, a life I was determined to keep a secret from everyone. Ana was the love of my life, but she had ceased being my lover. I was confident I could get other girls to fill that role. The rush of adrenaline that came with cheating and not getting caught became my drug.

After I left the academy, my father kept his word and had me assigned to the 14th District. Steve Tyler, a cop my dad deeply admired and respected, became my FTO. I felt as if I had just been given the keys to the kingdom. My opportunities were unlimited.

6

INITIATION

THE 14TH DISTRICT was also known as Disco 14 because of the extravagant, multicolored neon lights and glass blocks in the lobby. Police officers in Disco 14 patrol predominately poor Latino neighborhoods that are composed mostly of Puerto Ricans and a smattering of Mexicans and Cubans. Included within its territory is Humboldt Park, an immense and beautiful park of 210 acres, which was constructed at the turn of the century. The park's buildings and numerous statues exhibit French-inspired architecture designed by William Le Baron Jenney. This park was created as an escape from the bustling city. At one time, legions of the wealthy flocked to its green pastures via manicured, tree-lined boulevards. Today, Humboldt Park serves a new purpose.

Humboldt Boulevard, which dissects the park into east and west halves, runs north to south. The street gang the Latin Disciples claim the east end of the park and the neighborhood spreading to Western Avenue between North and Division. The west end of the park and the immediate area running to Central Park Avenue, also between North and Division, is the known as the Latin King 'hood. Each gang pursues its own version of the American dream. Instead of stocks and bonds, real estate holdings, and 401K plans, they stick with what works for them: drug dealing, weapons trafficking, prostitution, and supporting the stolen goods market.

These two gangs have been battling each other since the mid-1960s to protect their sources of income and the small parcel of the city that they thrive in as their self-appointed kingdoms. Any encroachment into their turf, especially a known and safeguarded drug spot, or any disrespect shown to a gang member in any way can result in a variety of retributions often involving bullets and victims, both gang and otherwise. This picturesque park is now an open war zone. Heaven help the kid caught either by the police or a gang on the wrong side of the park.

The 14th District covered this territory. During my first summer at 14, the men's public bathroom on the northwest end of the park had to be closed because it became a crime scene. It now stands as a testament to the viciousness the gangs practice. Earlier that spring, a Latin King entered enemy territory and shot a Latin Disciple, only wounding him. The Latin Disciples wanted retaliation. A young Latin King was walking the park's perimeter on North Avenue in July when three girls he had never seen before approached him. The Latin King began throwing down his rap, asking the girls if they wanted to party. They said yes. Liquor was obtained and they headed toward the west end of the park where the Latin King felt at home on his turf. They drank and got high, and then the talk turned to sex when one of the girls offered to give him head. He wanted to go to the bathroom first. The girls accompanied him. When he began to piss, one of the girls took out a handgun and shot him in the head, execution style. The girls bolted from the bathroom and headed toward the east end of the park. They were female Latin Disciples.

Detectives caught up to all three of them later that night after getting numerous tips from snitches. The girls couldn't keep their mouths shut and bragged all over the neighborhood about capping the King. The detectives arrested and charged them with first-degree murder. When the girls left their arraignment, they were caught on the local news flashing the Disciples' gang sign and throwing down the crown, the sign of the Latin Kings, signifying the Disciples superiority over the Latin Kings. The Disciples had won this battle. It was a blatant form of disrespect, the worst I had ever seen, and it was an open invitation to escalate a war that has been raging for decades. To me, this event provided a shocking insight into how little human life meant to gangbangers. They were completely willing to perpetuate the violence and hate. But it wasn't always gang against gang.

In the summer of 1966, Chicago, as well as the whole country, was in the midst of civil unrest. Discussions about racism, equal rights, and the realities of Vietnam were common. The nation boiled with tension. Martin Luther King Jr. was living on Chicago's West Side championing the cause of justice and affordable housing for black Americans. On a smaller regional scale, the Puerto Rican community of Humboldt Park was experiencing racial prejudice and hostility from the Chicago Police Department.

Shortly after the annual Puerto Rican Festival in Humboldt Park, two white police officers shot an unarmed Puerto Rican youth allegedly without provocation, setting off the first Puerto Rican riot in America. For three consecutive nights, there was rioting and looting of the stores along West Division Street. Numerous shop windows were broken, thousands of dollars' worth of merchandise was stolen, and police cars were torched and overturned. The police responded rapidly and a hundred Puerto Ricans were arrested. Many in the Puerto Rican community believed the riot was the direct result of the continued hostility from and unjust actions of the police, which had been increasing steadily in the community. The neighborhood was ready to erupt, and the shooting of the kid was the flash point.

The police action was the spark igniting and fueling the frustration of a group of people who demonstrated they would no longer tolerate the subpar living conditions, racial animosity, police brutality and abuse, and blatant social segregation they'd had forced upon them. The police review board, made up of high-ranking police officials who get together in a round-table meeting to decide if the shooting of a citizen was justified, exonerated the two white policemen involved. The officers were merely transferred, without fanfare or press coverage, to another district. This decision verified the community's fear that they would always be treated like second-class citizens. While the Puerto Rican community was outraged, their pleas fell on deaf ears. The cops were getting away with shooting an unarmed youth and the city wasn't going to bend. Some social programs focusing on teen pregnancies and violent youth were formed for the Humboldt Park area because the city, led by Mayor Richard J. Daley, needed to pacify the community, but no real justice was ever offered. The community's rage continued at a slow simmer, and it took eleven years to boil over.

In the summer of 1977, two white cops shot and killed two unarmed Puerto Rican youths. No cops were shot at and no one else died. The official police report stated the cops were attempting to quell the gang activity that flourished during the Puerto Rican Festival. But many eyewitness accounts didn't jibe with that story; they said it was a cold-blooded murder, another case of the police abusing their power.

This time two days of rioting and violence ensued and, once again, a hundred Puerto Rican dissenters were arrested while the two white cops were exonerated. The officers were quickly and quietly transferred to another district as members of the community shook their heads in wonder that American justice could be this blind.

Years later, one of the cops involved in the shooting was made a captain and, still later, a commander of the police academy. It appeared to many Humboldt Park residents that the cops had impunity when it came to killing young Puerto Rican males. This wasn't far from the truth. A supervisor I once worked under told me there was a saying among the ranks during the early 1970s: "If you want to get promoted, shoot a Mexican or Puerto Rican." Minorities had no protection or received no justice from the police and continued to fear most those who were charged with keeping the peace. Is it any wonder that the community's disdain toward the police and authority in general still exists today?

The Humboldt Park community never seemed to heal from the vicious assaults that triggered the riots and the injustices doled out by the police and their review board after investigating both of these cases. In addition, members of this community continued to deal with substandard education, as evidenced by the high illiteracy, dropout, and teenage-pregnancy rates.

Humboldt Park continues to be one of the worst places in Chicago when it comes to rampant gang violence and drug activity, which peaks during the hot and humid summer months. The academy taught me lawful procedures and constitutional laws while the districts indoctrinated me and other newly hired cops into the force by teaching us efficacious street tactics and cover-your-ass-and-put-the-bad-guy-in-jail writing skills. It was in this simmering cauldron that I tried to distinguish between the thug mentality and the survival tactics used by the local residents—all while following proper police conduct. Life teetered on knowing the boundaries: if you respected them, you'd survive; if you didn't, you'd have to face the consequences.

7

PERKS AND PRIVILEGES

STEVE TYLER PREPARED ME WELL to be a cop. Taking me under his wing, he taught me everything I needed to know about basic paperwork and filling out complaints, arrest forms, and traffic and parking citations. He also informed me of protocol: the senior officer drives and the passenger always does the paperwork and handles the radio. Many of his other lessons came to me while we were cruising in the squad.

I thought the wisecracks I'd heard about cops and doughnuts as a kid were in jest, but Steve proved my assumptions wrong. Every day after roll call, he drove east down Fullerton to the Dunkin' Donuts at Elston Avenue.

"Can I have a Boston cream and a large coffee," Steve said to the employee behind the counter. He then looked at me, "You want anything, kid?" I didn't like coffee, so I ordered a chocolate doughnut and milk. Steve then asked the employee, "How're things going? Any trouble lately?"

The employee poured the coffee and got the doughnuts from the shelf, "No, no problems." He put our order on the counter. "Who's your new partner?"

"This is Officer Juarez," Steve answered. "He's a new recruit. If he gives you any trouble, let me know." They both laughed as I nodded to the employee. Steve took the bag and we found a table near the rear of the place and sat down. No money was exchanged. "Lesson one kid, whenever you're in a restaurant, always face the door. You wanna see what's going on and who's coming in. Keep your eyes open and be prepared."

Steve taught his lessons very clearly and answered all my questions, but I was wary of broaching certain topics because of the hint of tension that lingered ever since the night of my first arrest with him. I wanted to know why we hadn't paid for our order, but I decided not to ask.

"Lesson two," he began. "Dunkin' Donuts offers coppers complimentary doughnuts and coffee. Just don't get greedy. The guys on the front desk think they can come here and get a dozen for free. Cops don't know how to treat a good thing sometimes."

"What do you mean?" I asked.

"Once cops get freebies, they think every place'll treat them the same way. There's nothing worse than an arrogant cop who's always expecting to be taken care of. Then they get all full of piss and vinegar when they don't get their way."

After loading up on caffeine and sugar, we left and headed south on Damen Avenue. Before we got to Webster Avenue, Steve pulled the squad over when he saw a Mexican outside a body shop. "What's going on, Steve?" I asked, wondering if I hadn't been paying enough attention to the action on the street. A short, chubby brown-skinned man wearing paint-covered overalls approached the car with a smile that showed a few gold caps.

"Mr. Steve," I heard the man say with both his arms open.

"Come on, Juan," Steve said as he got out of the squad. "I have to introduce you to Nelson. He's a great mechanic."

I got out and stood there as the two began to talk.

"Mr. Steve, it's damn good to see you. How you doing?"

"I'm doing great. The question is how's my baby doing?" Steve asked.

"Come on in and take a look," Nelson said. He motioned us to follow him in. Nelson showed Steve a newly painted 1970 Cutlass. "How does it look to you?"

"Wow, Nelson," Steve whistled. "You did a great job on it." Steve then began to tell the story of how this car, his baby, had an electrical fire when he was driving it to work one day. It burned up the dashboard and ruined the paint on the hood. He nudged me in the ribs. "What do ya think, kid?"

"You do nice work, Nelson," I said.

Steve started to walk out of the garage saying, "This is a new kid on the block. His name's Juan. I'm sure he's gonna need ya sooner or later, so can you take good care of him when he does? He's a friend of the family." Steve winked at me.

"Any friend of Mr. Steve is a friend of mine," Nelson said as his Bondo-smeared hand enveloped mine. "Nice to meet you, Mr. Juan. I have to get back to work, Mr. Steve." To me he added, "Bring me your car when you need some work on it."

I turned around to walk back to the squad, but Steve crossed the street and headed toward a car-wash and -detailing business. There was a line of cars waiting to be serviced. I jogged a bit to catch up with him.

"That guy knows everything there is to know about cars," Steve informed me. "He's a good guy and only charges me cost for parts. Keep it under your hat, willya?"

"Why? Don't other cops know?" I asked.

"Only a few, and I wanna keep it that way," Steve said, as he stopped on the sidewalk in front of the car wash. "You tell one about a good connection, and before you know it, the whole damn District is lining up, wanting the same treatment."

"Where are we going now?" I asked as we entered the office of the car wash. Two cars were being washed inside and one was being waxed in a separate room.

"I gotta introduce you to someone else," he said as a young blonde woman came to greet us. "Hi Linda," he said, and then he turned to me. "She's the floor manager here. This is Juarez, he's new in 14." She smiled and said she was pleased to meet me. After they had shared a bit of small talk, we left. "They charge coppers half-boat on detailing and car washes. There's no reason to be driving around in a dirty car."

"Cop cars?" I asked as he opened my side of the squad.

He was taken aback by my question, "Your personal vehicle, kid. You take the squads to the place on Fullerton." He went around the squad, got in, and started the engine. As we drove off, he continued his lesson. "Ain't no reason why you should pay full-boat for anything in this district. Stick with me kid, and I'll show you a thing or two."

On my first day with him, he'd shown me something I'd never forget, and now he was teaching me things that would benefit me. We drove around the District and Steve showed me restaurants and stores that gave cops half-boat discounts. This is sweet, I thought. My father never shared stories like this with me, but my cousin Paco had given me a few insights about the treatment cops get. I never imagined it was so widespread. I was amazed at how many people and businesses wanted cops as friends. I knew there had to be a catch.

"What do these people want from us?" I asked him.

"They want to be able to get personal service when they call the police," he said. "If something happens to their business, they'll expect you to show up and help 'em out."

That's nothing, I mused. It seemed like that was our job, but Steve continued lighting my path toward understanding. "Or if they get a parking ticket, if a family member gets arrested, or if anything else happens involving the police, they might ask you a favor and see what you can do for 'em. We can do a lot of things that the regular citizen can't, so they value our relationship. It's always nice to have friends who are cops. I'm sure you can understand that since your old man's one."

"I can understand that, but what happens if you can't do anything for them?"

"Just tell 'em, 'I'm sorry. I tried my best but I can't help.' All they want is a little consideration. If you can help 'em, great; if you can't, oh well."

Sweet Jesus! Cops were getting freebies and preferential treatment all for a little consideration. I was already beginning to understand just how little the consideration had to be. Did showing up at their business with an open hand translate to consideration? I wondered. I was ready to start making my own connections. "You know, Steve, someday I won't be working with you. How do you find out if a place takes care of cops?" I asked.

"All you hafta do is ask, 'I'm a cop, is there anything you can do for me?'"

I suddenly felt like a kid in Willie Wonkaland grazing upon the sweets of the earth without a care in the world. It didn't take long before "I'm a cop, is there anything you can do for me?" became my favorite question.

I still loved biking, so I ventured into a bike store in my neighborhood, spotted a sweet Cannondale Killer V mountain bike, asked my favorite question, and got a 20 percent discount. There was no stopping this cascade of gifts as I hit every sports store around and collected my bargain-priced goodies. When I went to movies, I found out I paid half price. Baseball games at Wrigley Field or Comiskey Park were free because cops worked security. "We take care of our own," they told me at the ticket gates. My badge came with a key to the city that kept unlocking more doors and exposing endless privileges. As each day passed, I found more to love about being a cop.

8

GOOD COP, BAD COP

AFTER WORKING SIXTY DAYS with my FTO, I said goodbye to Steve Tyler. His parting advice was: "Keep your nose clean, kid, and don't take shit from no one."

I was amazed how quickly my training period had passed, and now I was nervous about leaving his side. The paperwork I could deal with, but the daily challenge of confronting criminals without a veteran's guidance was something I didn't feel adequately prepared for. Fortunately, I didn't have to do it alone.

I followed district protocol and floated around—the method new cops use to find compatible partners—working with a bunch of different cops. I couldn't connect with any of them on a professional level. "Partners are vital," my father told me, "because you need to be on the same page and, at the same time, you have to balance each other out. If you're not careful, your partner will get you into all kinds of shit."

With this in mind, floating around was difficult because I never knew what to expect from the different partners I was assigned to. I wanted things to flow smoothly, as I was in a car with another cop for eight hours. With the right partner, the shift usually slides instead of grinds. I learned a lesson from my FTO—Dunkin' Donuts after roll call, a little public-relations maintenance, and then work; it was a routine. After two weeks of floating around, I finally found someone who also worked a steady third shift (4 P.M. to midnight), Don Williams, a four-year veteran who agreed to be my partner.

Don was a behemoth, standing nearly six-foot-four and weighing in at 250 pounds. He had biceps the size of my thighs, but he also had an incredibly soft and compassionate side. His muscular build, intimidating height, bald head, and skin as dark as night demanded instant respect, which was why I wanted to be partnered up with him. I figured the best way to keep out of shit was to work with someone whose appearance alone would intimidate people. I was two inches shorter than Don, and I was about ninety pounds lighter. I didn't always feel like I had the strength to back up my words. Don gave me that backup. Whenever we'd go to a call that began to turn ugly, Don would listen to all sides of the dispute, and then he'd look intently at the troublemaker as if to ask, "Do ya really wanna do that?" Nine times out of ten the developing issue would be settled. "But," Don would tell them as we began walking to our squad, "if we gotta come back here, someone's going to jail." That usually did the trick and settled the disturbance. I can't recall ever going back once Don had issued his warning.

Don loved talking sense to people caught up in their own shit. He valued communication and was a true diplomat in every sense of the word. "Hey, Juan," he told me one day as we were cruising near Evergreen and Maplewood, "see that boy on the corner?" I looked and saw a skinny, dark-skinned Puerto Rican kid, around sixteen. He was swinging a stick and kicking some pebbles. "He's slinging some rocks (dealing crack cocaine)."

"How do you know?" I asked. The kid didn't seem to be doing anything suspicious.

"C'mon, boy. I'll show you," he said, throwing the car in park and getting out. We walked over to the kid when Don threw an arm around him and said, "Hello." The kid didn't know what to do in the crook of Don's massive arm, so he said "hello" back and became a bit jittery as Don didn't release his grip.

"Look in that there soda pop can, Juan," he directed. I looked down at a crumpled soda can that was near the kid's foot. I picked it up, turned it over and out came four plastic-knotted baggies, each containing what looked like a little white pebble.

The kid began telling a story about how they weren't his and how he had no idea how they got there.

"Pick up those bags and throw them in the sewer, Juan" he told me as he began telling the kid to simmer down. "I don't wanna hear your shit, boy. You ain't going to jail, so cool your jets. But," Don warned before letting go of the kid, "if I see your ass out here again slinging dope, you're going to jail. Do we understand each other?" Don tightened his arm around the kid's neck to stress his point and then released him.

The kid looked at Don like he had received a gift. "Yes sir, Mr. Officer. I understand," he said, stepping back and rubbing his neck. "Thank you. You won't see me out here anymore." The kid walked away and waved over his shoulder. I thought it was a weird way to handle the situation, but Don must have had a reason for letting the kid skate. I kicked the can away.

Once we were back in the car, Don explained that the stuff in the bags was rock cocaine. "Called crack on the streets." Although a crack arrest was a felony, Don hoped the kid had learned more by being allowed to leave without being arrested. "All he's gonna learn in jail won't help him and he'll probably make a harder, more learned, criminal. Remember this: not everyone needs to be arrested, Juan."

I grew to enjoy his laid-back approach to the job and succinct honesty. I also began to open up to him during conversations in our squad. A partner was entrusted with the other partner's secrets. I told him about my recent past: Northeastern, the ladies, Ana, and my wayward cheating. My willingness to talk allowed him to be open, so he told me of his stint in the army, his son, his marriage to his son's mother that was "more of an obligation than love," and his experiences with cheating. "I always try to keep one on the side. It's just nice to know there's somewhere else I could go instead of home." Don and I got along amazingly well.

Every cop coming out of the academy gets placed on mandatory probation. It's a testing ground for both parties—if a recruit doesn't like the reality of the streets after going through the academy training, he or she can quit; if the Department doesn't believe a recruit demonstrates the skills and strengths to be a productive cop, it can discharge the officer without reason during the probationary period. My probation period was slated to end in July 1991, which was a good ten months away. As we were driving around in the squad one day, I sought Don's advice. I wanted to know what he thought about me risking my year-long probation by going back to school in September.

"Let's eat first," he said. "Where do you wanna go?"

"Some place decent and not too greasy," I replied.

Don cruised to a nice Italian restaurant on Fullerton Avenue and parked in the lot. "Is this good enough?" he asked, ready to get out of the car. I looked at the place doubtfully; it was new to me and seemed like an upscale restaurant. Don noticed my apprehension. "Come on, boy. They take care of us here." That was all I needed to know.

I followed Don in and he shook hands with the host who then led us through a heavily curtained waiting room to our table. It was a high-class joint: rich burgundy tapestries hung from the walls, candlelight replaced electric lights, the table settings had three types of forks and knives, and a pianist was providing music. I was feeling a bit uncomfortable in uniform, more so when everybody in the place looked at us as we entered the dining room and sat down. I guess they thought it strange that cops would eat in a place like this. For a second, I did too, but then I saw the menu and made up my mind to enjoy this luxury. Our waiter came and Don ordered prime rib and I began to wonder why other cops on our watch would eat at any old dive. "I'll have the salmon," I said, looking forward to a good meal. "Should I request lunch now?" I asked Don. I picked up my radio ready to notify the dispatcher of our exact location.

"Fuck 'em," Don said. "Wait till we get our food so we can have a full half hour to eat." Then Don and I began to discuss my dilemma with school.

"What you got to lose?" he asked as our salads came. "All they'll tell you is drop the class." My father had basically told me the same thing, but I wanted a second opinion. With four years on the job, Don had some experience with department bureaucracy. "This job ain't for real. Do what you need to and then get out."

"What do you mean, this job ain't for real?"

"It just ain't, bro'. Look. Crime's always been around and it ain't going nowhere. You put one hood in jail and there's ten more after him. I just wanna make it home every night. I ain't gonna die for this job. It ain't that serious, that's for sure."

We talked all through lunch, and when the bill came the meal was half price. At that moment I made two decisions: the first was that I would eat in good restaurants from that point on. And the second was that I was going to register for school. Starting in September meant I'd have to pay tuition every quarter for my one class, but I didn't care. I couldn't stand not being intellectually challenged, especially now that Ana was in school full time and shared what she was learning with me. I realized school was too important for me to put off, and I wouldn't be satisfied learning vicariously through Ana.

Ana, who had given me her blessing about becoming a cop with the understanding that I would eventually quit, supported me in my decision to quietly break my probationary contract. "You need to go back to school, otherwise you won't be happy, Juan." I had been out of school for two quarters and felt that a huge part of me was missing. Now, I was poised to get that part back.

"Besides going back to school, you should quit that job to keep your sanity. I don't know how you do it," she huffed, after I described the first stiff I saw and the accompanying smells of putrid flesh. My war stories from the streets didn't sit well with her. "I'm worried you're gonna change from being so close to violence and death. I'm scared for you, Juan."

The more stories I told her, the more her concern for me grew. So I started putting a filter on what I revealed. I felt like I was getting away with something by keeping the truth from her and that felt good too.

We had recently celebrated our third anniversary, and our relationship was getting better. Maybe it was because I knew what I needed to do to make her happy, or it might have been because I was happy now that I got my way by becoming a cop. We took weekend trips to Lake Geneva, spent quality time together and with our families, and began biking, horseback riding, and cooking together. But making love to Ana was still out of the question. A year and a half had passed since the abortion, but Ana accepted my guilt-ridden excuses and made no fuss about them. We were just happy being in each other's company doing the things we enjoyed. I couldn't ask for a better reality: my personal life—Ana and resuming school—was comfortable and fulfilling while my professional life—work-

ing in a good district and having a compatible partner—was challenging
and full of lessons.

Whether he knew it or not, Don was teaching me something with every
call we were assigned. With his quiet confidence and well-defined sense
of justice, Don put my mind at ease as we slowly ironed out all the kinks
in our work routine. My first winter in uniform came and went with little
fanfare.

Don called in sick one day in late spring. Even though I could have
worked by myself, the timekeeper took it upon himself to find me a partner. I looked at the timesheets and noticed I was paired up with Officer
Locallo. I had seen him at roll call; he was a short Italian cop who had
thick, wavy hair and only one eyebrow. From the look of him, he pumped
iron every day. He was stout like a pug, highly charged and very aggressive in his walk. He had a pair of leather driving gloves that were tucked
into his pants pocket.

The sight of Locallo's gloves made me recall something Don had previously said: "You gotta watch out for cops who take this job seriously,
boy, they give all of us a bad name."

"How do you know which ones are serious?" I asked.

"They wear these little, sissified leather driving gloves. You know, the
ones with the holes in the knuckles."

I had heard rumors about Officer Locallo. He'd earned a reputation
in the District as a hardworking cop because of all the pinches he had to
his credit. The rumors circulated that he loved to beat people up and that
gangbangers on the street made sure to stay away from him. I was feeling
anxious, wondering if his gloves had holes in the knuckles and hoping the
rumors weren't valid. We finished roll call and headed out to the south end
of the District, around the area of Potomac and Campbell.

In the 1940s and '50s Polish immigrants had called this area home,
but it had slowly transitioned to a Puerto Rican neighborhood. Street
gangs proliferated, violence increased dramatically, and the narcotics flow
surged.

"We need to rid the streets of the garbage," Locallo began earnestly while we waited at a light at North and California. "And I see the police as being sorta like garbage collectors who hafta throw the trash out. And there's lotsa fuckin' trash around here."

I wanted to clean the streets of gangbangers or "trash" as well, but I hadn't yet developed a plan. Locallo seemed to have a plan and his rhetoric had some bite—I was apprehensive, and he was ready for action. He emphasized his point by stretching out his right arm and pulling up his glove tightly with his left hand. His gloves had holes in the knuckles.

Locallo was slowly cruising southbound on Campbell Avenue when he said to me with disdain in his voice, "There's Li'l Mickey, a fuckin' thug lowlife from the Disciples."

"Which one is he?" I asked, seeing a group of Puerto Rican kids standing on the corner.

"He's the shithead in the white T-shirt," Locallo informed me. That description didn't help much either because two kids had on white T-shirts.

One of the kids looked in our direction and frowned. I discerned that one was Li'l Mickey. He was about five-foot-seven, 180 pounds, slightly chubby with a round face, closely cropped hair, and a full goatee. He looked like a regular kid to me. Maybe it was the way Li'l Mickey was dressed that incensed Locallo. He had on a pair of blue jeans that hung down way below his waist, a pair of boxer shorts that came above the waistband of his pants, an untied pair of Air Jordans, and a beeper connected to a key chain.

Locallo stopped the car in the middle of the one-way street, unconcerned with the traffic he blocked, and approached the group, all the while yelling instructions to Li'l Mickey's friends. "Get the fuck out of here if you don't wanna go ta jail!" They all scattered.

"What did I do now?" communicated the look on Li'l Mickey's face as he began to roll his eyes and grimace, cursing the moment he'd rolled out of bed that morning.

Cops have many weapons in their arsenal, and Locallo was using one of them, a street stop. Cops can stop anyone at anytime on the street or in a car, with or without PC (probable cause). The goal of a street stop is to find something illegal or shake someone down for information that will perhaps lead to a bust.

Officer Locallo approached Li'l Mickey and gave him an extra firm slap on the nape of his neck. He then guided Li'l Mickey into a nearby apartment vestibule away from the probing eyes of the neighborhood. I watched closely. I was bewildered by this street cop's uncanny skill at coercion. I wondered if I could ever be a badass like that. I wasn't sure I wanted to be.

"What's up, asshole?" Locallo said, pushing Li'l Mickey against the wall of the urine-tainted vestibule. Suddenly, Locallo grabbed Li'l Mickey's left arm, straightened it out by locking the elbow with his free hand, turned him around, and threw him into the cinder-block wall lined with mail boxes. I heard a dull thud as Li'l Mickey's face and chest hit the wall. A deep, resounding "omph" escaped his lungs. Locallo slowly nodded his head in self-approval. A snide smile of satisfaction creased his mouth as he snickered, "How the fuck ya been, Li'l Mickey?"

"Why ya hafta do dat, Locoman? I ain't got shit on me an' there ain't no need ta sweat me! You ain't right, Locoman! You just ain't right!"

Locoman? *Loco* means crazy in Spanish and I watched, wondering if this would set Locallo off even more. Locallo's behavior was usually reserved for only a selected few street stops. I wondered where Locallo learned his technique because I sure hadn't learned anything like that in the academy.

I later learned that most street stops are illegal and can only be justified by expert writing skills just to prove PC. A cop could come into the District with an arrest and a seizure of a hundred pounds of marijuana or cocaine, but if there's no PC for the arrest, it'll get tossed out before a state's attorney can be called. It only takes one line on an arrest-report narrative— such as "subject was seen urinating on public property," "subject was heard causing a disturbance," or "subject ran when we told them to stop"—to turn this crime into a story meant to ensure PC. There's a fine line between writing up an arrest narrative and writing a story. But this distinction doesn't matter to many cops because many civilians don't even know their basic rights. They are either too intimidated or too fearful of the police to ask questions. Furthermore, woe to the individual who does know his or her rights and questions the authority of a cop. Cops don't like that.

★ ★ ★

"Shut the fuck up, asshole! I'll drop a case on you in a heartbeat, you fuckin' thug," Locallo barked at the kid. "Assume the position, mother-fucker!" he ordered. Li'l Mickey gave in and adopted the stance against the wall to be searched. Face to the wall, arms outstretched over his head, feet a good distance from the wall and spread four to five feet apart, and his torso left vulnerable, he looked like the perfect X. And to fuck around with Li'l Mickey some more, Locallo kicked his feet until they were at least six feet apart, resulting in a painful, groin-splitting position.

This was the first time I worked with Locallo and I kept quiet, fear-ing his hair-trigger rage. I didn't want it turned on me, and I didn't want to make any trouble. I was a rookie, wet behind the ears, and for me it was all a learning process—learning what worked and what didn't.

"What do you want me to do?" I asked Locallo, not certain what I should be doing. I remember thinking that what Locallo was doing was fucked up, but Li'l Mickey was just a gangbanger—an uneducated punk well on his way to becoming just another statistic. Still, in my mind, this didn't give Locallo the right to beat his ass.

"Just stand by the door and cover my back," he directed me. Then he focused on Li'l Mickey again. "Who's holding out here, shithead?" Locallo was determined to find a street dealer or perhaps someone with a gun.

"Man, I don't know shit! Why don't ya do yer own job and find it yo'self?"

This guy's got balls, I thought, and I couldn't help chuckling. Locallo slapped an open palm against the back of Li'l Mickey's head. He would have liked to smack me too, judging by the glare he shot my way.

"Don't get smart with me, asshole!" Locallo yelled. "Keep looking at the fuckin' wall!"

I nervously peered out the window on the door to make sure no one was coming. I was getting concerned now because I had no idea how far Locallo would take this game. Turning my head back to the action in the vestibule, I noticed a glare of certain hatred escape the corner of the gang-banger's seething eyes. Things would be quite different, in my opinion, if Locallo didn't have a gun and a badge backing him up. But he did.

"You sure you don't know who's holding out here, Li'l Mickey?" Locallo asked as he began a cursory search, starting at the ankles, slowly working his way up.

"I don't know shit, Loco," he responded. Then, in a flash, Locallo abruptly swung a right-handed uppercut to Li'l Mickey's testicles. The kid's knees buckled, but he didn't fall.

"What the fuck you do dat for? I already told you once, Locofuck! I don't know shit!" Li'l Mickey exclaimed as he continued looking straight ahead at the wall.

"I know, but maybe you just forgot," Locallo continued, turning his body from his hips and cocking his right arm. "And this," he said, driving a fist into Li'l Mickey's back near his kidneys, "is just in case."

"Holy shit!" I said under my breath.

This punch did the trick. Li'l Mickey's knees wobbled and he began to slide down the wall as Locallo warned, "You'd better pray that I don't see your Puerto Rican ass on the street for the rest of the night, cuz if I do, your ass is going ta jail. Understand?"

Li'l Mickey looked up at Locallo with furious eyes and protested, "What for? What the fuck did I do?"

"'Cuz I said so. But don't you fuckin' worry, I'll think a something." I was really feeling screwed now. First, if this kid complained, I'd have a brutality beef lodged against me just because I was working with Locallo. Second, Locallo was ready to perjure himself on official court documents. I was between a rock and a hard place. But at least I wasn't Li'l Mickey.

"Now get the fuck out of here you piece a shit!" Locallo hollered. "You hear me? Now!" He stuck out his chest in a menacing manner surely meant to intimidate Li'l Mickey.

Li'l Mickey rose from his knees, walked slowly to the door, turned his head, and said, "You just ain't right, Locoman. What goes around comes around, fuckin' pig!" He then bolted out of the door.

Locallo, always needing to have the last word, shouted, "I may not be right, but I'm the police, motherfucker," as the soles of the gangbanger's Air Jordans hurtled northbound and out of sight. "And don't you forget it!"

I was puzzled. What was the exact purpose of this street stop? Did Locallo think Li'l Mickey would roll over on someone or did Locallo need to vent some pent-up shit he was dealing with? Reduced to sitting on pins and needles for the rest of the shift, I didn't pipe up once, afraid to incur some of Locallo's wrath. The tension in the car was so thick that we didn't exchange the frivolous banter of getting to know a partner, if only for one night. I felt like I knew everything I wanted to know about him. In the end, this whole confusing incident left a nasty taste in my mouth.

When Don returned the next night, we went to Quenchers, the local cop bar, to have a nightcap after our shift. Every district has a place or two in its boundaries where cops go and unwind in the comfort of alcohol. We ordered two beers and found a table.

"Yo Don, Locallo's a fuckin' nut!" I told him. "He beat this gang-banger ugly. And he didn't come up with shit!" I scanned the room, making sure none of Locallo's cohorts were present, not really caring if they were. I was indignant and the alcohol was giving me some courage to speak.

Don took a swig of his beer, laughed and said, "Loco must be training for the tac (tactical) team. It ain't nothing new. There are cops out there who take this job seriously."

Maybe to him it wasn't anything new, but to me it was. "Yeah, but it's bullshit!" I insisted. "That kid wasn't doing shit and Locallo just started thumping on him." I took a long swig of my beer and looked around the bar, seeing at least ten cops from the same watch, wondering how many of them stepped over the line and joined the culture of corruption.

"Don't you know, junior, CPD (Chicago Police Department) is the baddest gang in town. You just got initiated," Don stated unequivocally. Initiated into what? A gang? A frat house? A cult? Was swallowing my words and not speaking up part of the code that ran so deep among the ranks? "So, schoolboy? What you gonna do?" asked Don. "Snitch? You gonna rat him out?"

I didn't know what to say.

"Listen," Don continued, "if you got any notions about snitching, drop 'em. Making enemies on this job ain't worth it. You'll be blackballed, you'll never have a partner, and nobody will ever, ever back you up."

I didn't want to become a pariah on the job, and the notion of never having backup didn't sound too enticing either. So I asked the soft-spoken veteran, "What do you suggest I do?"

"Go tell the watch commander you can't work with Locallo because you have 'conflicting personalities,' and you'll never work with him again."

"But what if the watch commander asks me what the conflict is?" I persisted. "What should I do then?"

"He won't ask. If anyone else does, make something up. But never snitch," he warned, wagging his finger. "That's the last thing you wanna do."

9

FIND 'EM AND FUCK 'EM

DON WAS SCHEDULED to go on his furlough during the next period, so I had to find someone else to work with while he was gone. I had been working out in the District gym before my 4:00 shift. I had noticed Xavier Estrada, another cop on the third watch, was always there pumping iron. Other coppers on the same watch told me Estrada preferred to work alone, but I needed a partner. I didn't feel confident navigating the streets alone. A day before Don started his furlough, I caught up with X in the locker room.

"Hey X, you wanna partner up for the next three weeks? Don starts vacation tomorrow and I'm sure a vet like you could teach me some things."

He looked in the mirror in my direction, seemingly annoyed. "Nah, that's OK, you'll cramp my style; I got an image to keep." Around the station X was known as a player, leaving a trail of women's panties and broken hearts in his wake, and I could see why as he maintained a steady gaze in the mirror. He was built like a defensive end—tall and athletic— and he took great pride in his appearance.

"Come on, bro', it's only for three weeks. How much damage could I do to your image in that time?" I pestered. I was afraid of having another day of work with an unknown cop like Locallo.

He said, "I'll think about it, rook."

Arriving the next day at the station to work out before my shift, I looked at the work sheets that listed what car and partner I'd be working with. I had been paired up with X. Without hesitating a moment, I ran down to the front desk and called Don to see what he knew about X. Don said not to worry because X wasn't into brutality tactics; he had a different agenda and really didn't do too much work. I had no idea what to expect, but I was open to just about anything after working with Locallo.

"Don't get your hopes up, Juan. It's a one-day trial; I need to see if you're down," X said in the locker room while he put on his one-size-too-small-police-uniform shirt, making his arms look like massive muscular sausages ready to burst out of their casings. He sauntered over to the mirror. Taking out a comb and pushing back his hair, he blew himself a kiss and then left for roll call. Well, I thought, it was better than leather gloves.

"I'm driving. You take care of the radio," X said. "I got some things I need to do right out of the box, so don't go volunteering us for any shit. Understand?"

First stop was his girlfriend's house on the east side of Humboldt Park. "Stay in the car, bro'. I'll be right back."

"What if we get a call?" I asked as X got out of the car and began walking toward his girlfriend who was standing on the stairs of her house in jean shorts and a flimsy T-shirt.

He turned around, "Don't answer the radio. It's watch change, they'll assign it to another car."

The watch change guaranteed a bit more leeway in answering radio calls, I learned, because some cops took their sweet time cleaning out their cars or getting into them. Dispatchers took that fact into account when they assigned jobs. The slow transition provided X with the free time he needed.

Waiting inside the squad, I took out a book and began reading while I listened to the chatter on the radio. Twenty minutes later, he exited her house, still buttoning up his shirt. He jumped into the car whistling. His mood had changed dramatically. At the station he'd seemed cocky and full of himself, but now he appeared relaxed and subdued.

"Got to do a little hit and run to take the edge off," he chuckled, winking at me. "Did we get any calls?"

"Nope. Nada," I responded as his girlfriend appeared at the front door of her house and blew X a kiss. "Damn, bro'!" I exclaimed as he began driving away. "She's fine."

X laughed. "Lesson number one, rook," he declared, looking at himself in the mirror. "All bitches are the same—they just wanna get fucked."

The dispatcher called out our squad number.

I looked over at X and he gave me the go-ahead nod.

"We got a call of a domestic dispute on Sawyer and Potomac, third floor," the dispatcher said. "Complainant's name is Sanchez, Aracelli Sanchez."

"Ten-four, squad," I replied as X drove westbound through Humboldt Park on Luis Munoz Marin Drive. Once we crossed Humboldt Boulevard, he saw a group of guys who looked like gangbangers on a park bench. They had tattoos and were drinking out of paper bags. X drove up on the grass and stopped. They didn't appear nervous at the sight of our car, and visions of Locallo entered my mind. X got out of the squad and shook their hands in a series of signals that ended in what looked like "I love you" in sign language. It seemed like a gang sign to me, but X was a cop, so I didn't pursue this line of thought. They chatted in Spanish for a few minutes and then we left.

"What was all that about, X?" I asked. The stop had made me wonder about his priorities. A domestic call that went unanswered could prolong a husband's pounding on his wife. I remembered the times I wished the cops had come to stop my dad from beating my mom, and they hadn't. Maybe they were out fucking around, chatting with their friends.

"Nothing. Just some boys I grew up with," he said casually.

"They looked like gangbangers to me," I said.

"That don't make them bad people," he replied. I didn't know whether he really believed that, but I surely didn't. I remembered something in the handbook from the academy forbidding fraternizing with gang members. I decided not to pursue the matter for fear of getting X pissed off.

As we continued on the drive, X pointed out the various food vendors around Humboldt Park and told me which ones were cool to the police and would give up a plate of food for free. Every day I learned more about the perks of being a cop. I felt fortunate and envisioned never spending a dollar while I worked.

We arrived on the scene for our assigned radio call and I pulled out a general offense case report (GOCR) form to begin the process of recording this incident as I had been taught to do in the academy and with my FTO. X tapped me on the shoulder, shaking his head. "First we need to see what she wants us to do, so put that report away." We exited the squad and approached the complainant who was smoking a cigarette and pacing outside the front door of the apartment building. She was about twenty-three, slender yet curvaceous, with straight, shoulder-length brown hair and cocoa-brown skin. She didn't look battered or bruised, but she did appear to have been crying. She threw out one cigarette before it was finished and lit another one. I could see she was definitely agitated. My heart went out to her for having to call the police to protect herself in her own apartment.

"The asshole's upstairs, and I want him outta my place," she lamented, pointing her burning cigarette upward. "What the hell took you guys so long?"

I looked at X and he instantly responded, "We were on another call." I was amazed at how easily the lie slid out of his mouth. Then he went to work, "What floor's he on, baby?"

"I'll take you up. C'mon, follow me," she instructed, stomping out her cigarette before leading the way up the stairs.

There was loud music playing in her apartment when X began pounding on the door. "It's the police! Open up the door!" he hollered. I flashed back to my first day on the job when Steve Tyler had considered a door an expendable obstacle. I felt nervous and a bit hesitant. Anything could be lurking behind that door. No response. X continued banging on the door, which caused a neighbor to open up her door to see what the commotion was about.

"It's OK, ma'am, we're the police," I informed her. "You can go back inside." Still no response at Sanchez's door.

"We're not leaving until you open up the damn door!" X threatened. "If I have ta break this goddamn door down, I will, and then you'll be real sorry!"

Sanchez stood behind X, who was flexing his muscles in preparation of breaking down the door when she dangled the keys in front of him. Just then the door opened.

"Get the fuck outta here!" X forcefully demanded, putting his hand on his holstered gun.

The man, a short and slender light-skinned Puerto Rican with green eyes, was in his late twenties. He looked X up and down and said defiantly, "Why?" from his side of the threshold.

"Because your woman don't want you here, and I'm telling you ta get the fuck outta here, *entiendes*?"

"Listen," the man began as he stepped into the hallway. He looked harmless to me. I wondered what thrills he got from beating his woman.

X grabbed the man's collar with his left hand and pulled him closer as he kept his right hand at his side, clenched in a fist. The man's face was now two inches away from X's. "No! You listen! I'm gonna give you three seconds ta get your shit and get the fuck outta here." X pushed the man back into the apartment. "One!"

The man went inside and came back a minute later with a bag and a jacket, "Bitch!" he said, looking at the complainant. "I'm done with you." He stared at X and gave him the evil eye. It didn't matter.

"Fine! Get the fuck outta my apartment, you piece a shit!" Sanchez demanded, watching him go down the stairs. X chimed in, "And don't come back!" We heard the front door downstairs close, and through a window we saw the man cross the street.

"Listen, girl. I'm Officer Estrada and I'll always be here if you need my help," X promised as he pulled out one of his business cards. "Don't be afraid ta page me if you ever, ever need anything." He handed her the card and nodded. *"Llamame."*

Sanchez graciously took the card, looked at it, and then gazed at X. "That's really nice of you, officer. I'll keep it in mind."

"You do that," X said as we began walking down the stairs. "Gimme a call whenever you want."

When we got inside the car, X gleefully told me, "Today's complainant is tomorrow night's fuck."

I wondered if that's how he had met the girlfriend we'd visited less than an hour earlier. Thinking about Ana, I was glad she didn't live in the District. X was taking unnecessary chances by doing this in his own backyard. Then again, maybe he didn't care if his girlfriend found out about his cheating ways. I knew it was a behavior I didn't want to follow—I had no plans of getting busted.

The rest of the night was spent pulling over cars driven by women X thought were attractive. Whatever police calls we received, we handled with a modicum of responsibility, going to the scene and not doing much more than 19 (other miscellaneous incident)—Paul-ing them. I remember thinking that doing police work was a ludicrously easy way to meet women—if you could call what we were doing police work.

Cops are basically free to be their own bosses when they aren't answering radio calls. They can choose to do police work or just be spectators in their cars. We were being spectators. Loafing like this and getting paid for it was something I could do once in a while. But I wanted to do some—even just a little—police work. Don was right, though: it wasn't going to happen if I worked with X. It didn't take me long to accept that fact.

I put my expectations of doing police work on hold and decided I was going to take a three-week vacation as well. I rationalized that there were many other cops in the District who were doing official police work and making up for our disinterested approach.

I admired the way X handled woman, and I definitely liked the attention the women gave us as we pulled them over and started talking to them. By the end of the shift, he had ten phone numbers in his chest pocket. I had none.

"You passed the test, Juan," X informed me later as we drank some beers at Quenchers after our shift. "You gonna learn the secrets of a player working with me." I thought of the night I got my badge and how easy it was to get laid because I had it. I was excited. Working with X made meeting women on the streets look easy—and doing police work even easier—so I was pleased that he had decided to take me under his wing.

My vow of not making love to Ana was excruciatingly difficult. I loved her—the taste of her skin, the feel of her body next to mine—but I just couldn't do it. My battle to control my sexual urges was at its breaking point. I wanted to find women to take Ana's place in my bed and I imagined this would be simple. If my first night working with X was any indication, I would soon have more women than I could handle.

It was summertime in Humboldt Park, and the Puerto Rican and Mexican women were shedding their cold-weather clothes for the tightest and shortest skirts and shorts and the skimpiest form-fitting camisoles. I wanted to reach out and touch them all. I wanted to taste them—each and every one of them. The Puerto Rican Festival was in full swing, which multiplied the number of Latinas on the streets. Coming from every part of the city and surrounding suburbs, brown women of every size and shape paraded down California Avenue between North and Division. I knew I was there to serve and protect, but I wasn't about to let an opportunity of this magnitude escape. I could allow things to get way out of hand, due to my insatiable sexual appetite if I wasn't careful. The last thing I wanted was to have Ana find out—it would break her heart. I was going to have to be careful because between what X had showed me and the power of the uniform I'd experienced already, I felt that no woman was beyond my reach.

"Take your pick, bro'. They all wanna get fucked, and if you don't do 'em, somebody else will," X assured me, constantly turning his head at every woman who caught his eye.

"14—," the dispatcher interrupted, "we got a call to check the well-being at 21— North Mozart," Basically, this meant we had to go see if the resident was injured, incapacitated, or even deceased because some family member or friend hadn't heard from the person for a while. I hoped we didn't have a stiff on our hands; that would tie us up for hours doing paperwork. I wanted to get back to the park and feast on eye candy.

Apparently X felt the same. "Shit!" he said. "Let's hurry up over there and get our asses back ta where the action is." This was one of the few days X permitted me to drive and I felt like he was finally beginning to trust me after working together for two weeks. On the way to the call I saw a fine Puerto Rican woman driving on Armitage Avenue. Speeding up, I got behind her and activated the flashing mars lights on top of the squad. I decided if it was OK for X to make diversions on the way to a call, it should be fine for me as well. Besides, if there was a stiff at our call, I can guarantee you they weren't going anywhere.

"Oh shit!" X chortled. "Rook's got his nose open."

I slowly approached the car and as the woman rolled down the driver's window, I caught a glimpse of her striking beauty. "Good afternoon, ma'am," I started. "I need to see your license. One of your brake lights is out." This was a line I'd heard X use.

Looking at me quizzically, she gave me her license and asked, "Are you sure?"

"Lisa Lopes, huh? Where are you going, Lisa?" I asked, cocking my head to get a better look at her.

"I'm heading to school. I just got finished practicing for the Puerto Rican Day parade. I'm in the queen's court," she informed me, smiling.

"How come you're not the queen?" I asked. "You're so fine." I looked out of the corner of my eye at X, who was stifling laughter in the squad.

"Excuse me, Officer Juarez," she said, looking at my nameplate. "I need to get going because I'm late for a night class I have at UIC. If you wanna talk, I work at my family's restaurant on Kimball and Palmer."

God, this was so simple! "What class is it?" I asked, more interested now knowing she went to school.

"Biology," she replied as her frustration at being stopped slowly mounted.

"OK, Lisa, I won't give you a ticket this time, but be careful. The next cop might not be as understanding," I politely warned. I gave her back the license and watched as she drove away.

"Smooth move, Ex-Lax," X laughed, bringing me back to reality as I entered the car. "Let's head over and see if there's a stiff at our call."

"She's a damn PR queen!" I boasted, thinking he'd be impressed.

"Whatever, bro'," X said dully, shaking his head. "She's just a bitch. Find 'em, fuck 'em, and throw 'em out. That's my motto." I wondered if X was honorable in any of his relationships.

We proceeded to Mozart Street and found the address of our call. I parked the car and we got out to investigate. X checked the back door; I tried the front and rang the bell.

"Squad, who made the call?" X asked the dispatcher, peering through the windows in the gangway.

"The next-door neighbor. He doesn't know if she's out of town or in the house. Proceed as you wish," the dispatcher responded.

"Ten-four, squad," X answered. He turned to me. "OK, bro', there ain't no one home and from what I see, ain't no one around."

"Should we just 19–Paul it?" I asked.

"Hell no! We were sent to check the well-being and that's what we gotta do," X replied. I was stunned; I had never seen X this committed to any type of police work before, especially knowing what was waiting for us back at the park.

"Over here, rook," X called. "This window's broken, see?" he said, pointing to a small window on the back door. I looked and it was only cracked. He pressed the window with the tip of his nightstick until the glass broke and fell inside the house. "See, bro', it's broken." Now it is,

I thought to myself, and I realized that X had no boundaries whatsoever. Girls were one thing, but breaking and entering is a whole different ball of wax—it could get us fired and thrown in jail. X stuck the nightstick through the new hole and cleared out the remaining glass. Reaching his hand through the pane, he unlocked the door. We went in.

"I don't smell no stiff, X," I said, "and I don't think she's home."

"Keep looking," X directed, as he began rifling through dresser drawers like he was searching for something.

"What ya doing, bro'?" I asked.

X turned his head and looked at me like he thought the question was rhetorical. When he realized it wasn't, he explained how he was looking for valuables, anything small that would fit in his pockets but wouldn't be immediately missed. I wondered if X felt he could answer me honestly now because I had started mimicking his doggish behavior with women.

"Bro', this shit ain't cool," I said, beginning to understand why he liked working alone yet not quite certain if anything had made its way into his pockets.

"Hey, Juan. The door was open and we had to secure the premises— that's the story. Understand?" X gazed at me intently. There was malice in his eyes.

"Sure, bro'. I understand," I lied. The search ended on that note. A feeling of relief enveloped me as we left the house because I had made my point, however meekly.

"Head into the District, will ya?" X flatly requested when we got back into the car. The only time to go into the station was during the start and end of the shift or to fill up with gas. We had half a tank. I did as he asked and didn't question it.

I could feel this aggressive energy in the air as X sat rigidly in his seat, neck erect, with his eyes straight ahead as I drove. His lips remained tightly shut, and he didn't say anything. I began to get nervous and scared; I had no idea what was going to happen to me once we reached the station, and I felt as if I was being silently reprimanded for asking about something I should have just accepted because he was my partner. His whole attitude baffled me.

When we arrived at the station X got out and slammed the door. I exited the car and followed him at a distance. He never once looked back

at me, as he walked with a purpose to the front desk and informed the officer who made the sheets, "I can't work with this kid anymore. He's a pain
in my ass." He walked away to talk to the watch commander and then
turned in a slip to take off the rest of the shift. And that was that. I never
worked with Xavier Estrada again.

I was OK with that. The only thing I had learned from him, I mused
as I drove 99 (alone) the rest of the shift, was that all women are bitches
and want to get fucked. I wasn't concerned about what transpired in the
commander's office either because all he did was ask for time. I was, however, pissed off that he went to the timekeeper with some bullshit story
about me being a pain in the ass because that could influence who my partners would be in the future.

The next day I visited Lisa Lopes before my assigned shift at her family's
restaurant; we hit it off and started dating. This was my first long-term
affair during my relationship with Ana. It would last thirteen months.
Being involved with Lisa made me realize that I needed to get a pager, so
I could give that number out instead of my home phone number to the girls
I met on duty. After I visited Lisa I went to a beeper dealer in the District and got a special cop price. When Ana asked why I needed a pager,
I told her it was for work. "In case I'm needed in court or if my partner
needs to get in touch with me," I explained.

Whenever I was with Ana, I had to remember to keep the beeper on
silent mode. I didn't want her to grow suspicious or ask me any questions
when I was paged. The beeper kept me on my cheating toes and set off a
chain reaction that allowed me to have numerous weeklong flings. I
engaged in wild sex with scores of different women and then left them.
The exhilaration of keeping my cheating life a secret and not getting busted
by Ana, Lisa, or the other girls proved increasingly addictive. It was all a
challenging game to me, a game I wasn't about to lose.

My taste for living on the edge reached its zenith when I had sex with
X's girlfriend. She swore she would never tell anyone what we did. Maybe
she knew X was cheating on her and thought it was the sweetest revenge
or maybe she just wanted me. It didn't matter. She was good in bed, but
the experience rattled me a bit. Every time I saw X in the District after

that I kept my head down and never looked him in the eye. I envisioned him taking out his gun and shooting me in the neon-lighted lobby.

I was getting pretty good at juggling my two lives and making sure to keep them separate. With Ana I was the supportive, nurturing, and chaste boyfriend. At work I was a thrill-seeking, arrogant, skirt chaser. I felt omnipotent and insatiable.

10

A PIECE OF THE ACTION

THE DISPATCHER'S VOICE CRACKLED through my radio: "14—, we got a call of a theft of property with offender making a return visit at 18— North Washtenaw."

I had no partner now that X was gone and Don wasn't slated to come back to work for a few more days, so I responded, "10-99 squad."

"14—, let me know if you need someone to ride with you on this job."

"Will do, squad." Working 99 wasn't all that scary; it just meant I had to keep my skills of observation sharp and constantly assess situations. After a year and a half on the job, I had honed some street skills and that made me confident working 99, but I still had problems finding streets and addresses. My trusty district map, in a state of deterioration from heavy use, guided me to this call. Driving south on Washtenaw Avenue, I saw a young woman in the middle of the street frantically jumping up and down and waving her arms. I pulled up beside her.

"Did you call the police, ma'am?" I asked.

"Yes, I did. That guy riding the bike over there just stole it from my back porch. It's the second one he took today."

I peered through the windshield and observed a guy with a head of dirty blond hair pedaling southbound on Washtenaw. He was only a block away.

"I'll be right back," I told the complainant as I sped off. The guy turned his head as he heard the Caprice pick up speed. Realizing I was after him, he immediately dropped the bike and ran off down a gangway.

I slammed on the brakes, jumped out of the squad, and began an adrenaline-producing foot chase.

He jumped over backyard fences and threw garbage cans in my way, but his efforts didn't prevent me from catching him. I loved this type of chase! Unlike some cops, I didn't find it necessary to pound on people who ran from me. Catching them and throwing them into jail was good enough for me.

"Why did ya run?" I asked. I gripped his jacket and began regaining my breath.

"I dunno," he responded with vacant eyes. I cuffed him, led him back to the squad, and put him in the rear seat. Then I retrieved the bike, threw it in the trunk and headed back to see the complainant; she was still standing in the street.

"Ma'am," I said, pointing to the guy in the backseat, "is this the guy who stole your bike?"

"Yes, it is," she responded. "And he took another one off my back porch earlier today."

"Do you have any receipts for the bicycles?" I inquired, as I took out a GOCR from my briefcase.

"Yes, I do. They're in my house. I'll go get them." She smiled before running up the stairs of her front porch two at a time. She returned a couple of minutes later with a folder in her hand. "I have receipts and police registration in case they were ever stolen. Here's the one for the bike in the trunk," she said, flipping through documents in the folder. "I just bought it for my son at the Zayre on Western. And here's the receipt for the other one he took. God only knows where that crackhead hocked it."

I got out of the car, took the papers, and verified the serial number of the bike in the trunk. "OK, ma'am. The numbers match, so I'll do a report for that one. Now, when did he take the other bike?"

She shook her head and laughed, "About an hour ago."

I gave her the bike and wrote down the serial number of the other one. "I'll be right back," I told her as I got into the car and began questioning the suspect through the Plexiglas partition.

"All right. I am only going to ask you one time," I started, imitating the tough-guy cops I'd worked with. "Where's the bike?"

"I don't know what bike you're talking about."

"The bike you fuckin' stole, dickhead! Where is it?"

"It was in your trunk. You just gave it to her," he said. I looked in the rearview mirror at him. I could feel my patience getting shorter and shorter. My adrenaline had ebbed, but his continuing shenanigans reignited it, turning it into a simmering rage.

"Listen, dumb fuck! You know what bike I'm fuckin' talkin' about! Where is it?"

He continued his game. "I dunno."

My rage reached its boiling point. I gripped my nightstick. I felt like getting in the backseat and giving the kid a good whack. If the woman hadn't been standing there I would have beaten the truth out of that junkie. But she *was* there, and I wasn't going to get the answers I needed in front of her. I calmly got out of the squad and told the complainant that I knew where the bike was and I'd be right back with it. I got in the squad and jammed the gear selector into drive. With my jaw clenched and teeth grinding, I drove one block and turned onto Bloomingdale Avenue, a vacant street surrounded by empty factories and bordered by train tracks. Perfect, I thought, no one around to see me do what I need to do. I was hoping this scare tactic would make him tell me where the bike was. If it didn't, oh well—I was aching to flex my muscles if he kept it up with the attitude. I opened his door, yanked him out of the car by his jacket, and whipped him around to face me. He stood five-foot-nine, about 130 pounds. He had a pockmarked face and wasn't more than twenty-five years old. I could see the fear in his eyes.

"Listen, you piece a shit!" I yelled one inch from his face. "Where's the fuckin' bike? I know and you know you took it, so where the fuck is it?"

"I dunno," he repeated as he backed away from me. Glancing around he noticed that there was no one around to save him.

"How the fuck don't you know?"

His two-word answers made me flip. I swung my right arm back and opened my hand. "Maybe this will help you fuckin' remember!" I screamed as my hand came down solidly on his left ear. I heard his teeth clatter as his head recoiled from the blow and he dropped to one knee. It felt so good to release my anger that I was willing to smack him again and again if necessary.

"You want me to fuckin' hit you again, you fuckin' junkie?" I shouted, standing over him. No response. "Huh? You piece a shit! Tell me! Where's the fuckin' bike?" I drew my right back, ready to strike again.

"I sold it. I sold it," he said. "I'll take you where it is. Just don't hit me again."

That was easy. My rush of adrenaline was justified, I reasoned, because I had extracted the truth and got what I wanted. I grabbed him by his jacket, jerked him off the ground, and threw him in the back of the squad. "Take a right on Homer, and I'll show you the house," the junkie told me, his voice quivering.

He directed me to a ramshackle abode that looked abandoned. Securing the doors of the squad, I approached the house and knocked. A robust woman in a housedress opened the door. I told her the purpose of my visit. She asked me to come in. "If you find it, take it. I don't want no problems with the police up in here," she said, directing my attention to at least twenty bikes piled in the corner. "I swear, officer, I didn't know it was stolen."

I found the bike easily, verified the serial numbers, and thanked the woman for assisting me in this matter. It never dawned on me that this was a house filled with stolen goods, so I left and put the bike in the trunk.

The complainant was sitting on her porch when I pulled up in front with the bike. She jumped up and ran to the car to greet me. Her happiness at getting the bike back further justified my smacking the kid—she was the real victim and I had helped her. I looked in the rearview mirror and for a fleeting moment, I felt a tinge of guilt. The kid was just a junkie feeding his addiction, and from all appearances, he didn't have anything or anyone in this world. I tuned out that little voice of concern as I turned my focus to the complainant's milewide smile.

"You don't know how much this means to me," she said. When I got out of the car she gave me a hug. She signed the complaints and I went to the District to process this bicycle thief. I wrote up the theft case report and in the narrative a portion stated: "R/O (reporting officer), after a brief chase, apprehended the subject and, after skillful interrogation of subject on the street, was able to determine the location of the stolen property, recovered it, and then returned it to the owner who provided proper paperwork."

I was fortunate that the junkie wasn't bleeding from my "skillful inter-rogation" because then I would have had to concoct a story about how he got hurt during the brief chase. It didn't matter to me. I was prepared to do whatever it took to justify the means to the end. This arrest made me feel great because this was the type of police work I wanted to do—help victims while throwing lowlifes in jail.

This was the first time I had ever laid hands on anyone, and I was stunned at how easily I had gotten what I wanted. The bicycle thief con-fessed after one slap to the head, and the case was solved. Later that eve-ning, my guilt about resorting to physical coercion revisited me, but after a few drinks, the guilt subsided and I slept soundly.

11

PRINCE OF THE CITY

DURING MY HIGH SCHOOL YEARS, I had learned the four magic words that got me out of trouble with the police and allowed me to get away with all kinds of mischief: "My dad's a cop!" I'd had a little taste of the power of being connected to a cop. But now I *was* one. "I'm a cop" was a simple enough phrase, and it unlocked many closed doors and provided me with a sense of entitlement that could not be taken away as long as I had a badge.

Late one Saturday night, Edgar, a cop I had been at the academy with who was also assigned to the 14th District, suggested going out for some drinks. He wanted to go to Crobar, a trendy nightclub on Kingston. It was half past midnight as I changed into my street clothes, shut my locker, and walked down the stairs to the station lobby.

"Edgar's waiting in the parking lot, Juarez," the desk sergeant told me, as I hovered around, looking at the next night's work sheets.

"Thanks," I said, heading out to the rear parking lot.

Edgar had displayed such aggressive street savvy during his stint with his FTO that the tactical-unit lieutenant had asked him to join the team. The tactical unit is made up of the most aggressive officers in the districts who are then given certain perks. They drive unmarked cars, wear plain clothes, and work in every sector, responding to any call they want. This freedom gives many of them a feeling that they are one step above a beat

cop in the District pecking order. Edgar basked in his new title after his
first month in tac. He never let me forget his higher status, but I gave him
shit in return.

"What the fuck took you so long?" Edgar complained, downing the
last of a beer and throwing the empty bottle in the garbage.

"I had to change, dickhead. I'm not fortunate like your brown-nosing
ass to work in tac," I joked as I jumped into the passenger seat of his brand
new Mitsubishi 3000 GT. "Nice ride, *puto*. What happened to the Mus-
tang?" I asked, admiring the fine leather seats and sweet sound system
that blew away those of his former car.

"I wrecked it last weekend," he said turning the key in the ignition.
He put the car in drive and laid a patch. We were soon flying down North
Avenue toward the lake, listening to the Bucketheads at ear-shattering volume. We crossed the bridge over the Chicago River and he made a sharp
right onto Kingston.

"Holy shit, bro'! That's a long fuckin' line," I declared, checking out
the number of people waiting to get into the popular nightspot.

"Ain't no thang," he assured me. He pulled into a reserved parking
spot not more than fifteen feet from the front door of the club. The door-
man waved as we got out of the car and then shouted, "Yo, Head, what's
happening?"

Edgar walked over and gave the guy a hug and a hand slap. "Hey,
José," Edgar said, nodding his head toward me. "This is Juarez. He's one
of us. Juan, this is José." I shook the bouncer's hand and checked out all
the females waiting in line to get in. Edgar noticed the women too and let
out a low whistle.

"How's the action tonight, José?" he asked.

"It's going on. It started off as a sword fight, but now all the little
chickies are out to play," José stated emphatically.

"José," I interrupted, "where you work?"

"Twelfth District," was his reply. "You guys gonna step on in?" he
asked. Not waiting for an answer, José caught the eye of the woman at the
ticket window. "Hey hon', these two are OK," he said, nodding at us. He
escorted us to the front door and held it open.

"Thanks, bro'," I offered as Edgar and I stepped into the club.

"I'll catch you later. Enjoy!" José replied as the door shut behind us.

From the outside, the club, once an industrial factory, looked like nothing more than a huge bricked square, but once inside that image vanished. A metal stairway, thronged with people, led to a second-floor dance area and bar that had a soundproof window exposing the main floor. The strobe lights flashed in time with the music that blared out of huge speakers placed strategically on the dance floor. We snaked through the crowd as sweating couples gyrated provocatively on every side. After we made it to the bar, Edgar introduced me to the bartender, who hooked us up with complimentary beers and shots of tequila.

"You da man, Edgar!" I said putting my hand out for him to give me some skin.

"Nah, you da man, you da man!" he replied, slapping my hand and raising his shot glass.

How fucking cool is this, I thought. We get a prime parking spot, bypass the ridiculous line to get in, and enter without paying the cover charge—all because we're cops. Edgar later clued me into the fact that all the clubs—Metro, Elixir, Excalibur, Shelter, and Neo's—hired off-duty cops as bouncers.

"All you gotta do is tell 'em, 'I'm a cop,' show 'em your badge, and you're in," he confided, laughing with me at the bar. "This job's all about making connections, Juan."

It was true; at every club I began visiting, I found cops working the front doors. My nightlife took off once I learned this secret. As part of my boyfriend duties, I started going out clubbing with Ana on the weekends. During the week I went out with friends from work. In no time at all, I knew which clubs had the best ladies' nights; I got to know the bouncers at those clubs. I became a regular face on the tavern circuit. The badge was opening doors.

During my first furlough, I wound up heading south to New Orleans and its fabled drunken orgy known as Mardi Gras. I had been there the year before with Ana, but I vowed never to take her again because there were tons of single, horny women there. I had it all planned out—the manipulation and the excuse.

Ana and I celebrated Valentine's Day weekend at the Hilton. It had been more than a year since her abortion and the last time we had intercourse. I planned to use the weekend to reignite our physical relationship. With dinner reservations at an extremely romantic restaurant on Michigan Avenue followed by tickets to the ballet, the groundwork was complete. Ana looked stunning in a form-fitting dress and high heels; I struggled to keep my hands off her; I took every opportunity to touch her sensuously or warm her neck with my breath. The cab ride back to the hotel was a scene of passionate making out, lasting until we reached the hotel, and if it wasn't for the fact that the elevator stopped at our floor, we would have made love in it. I made a production out of carrying her over the threshold. When we were done making tender and passionate love, I told her, "I'm leaving next week for Mardi Gras." There was no asking; I wasn't giving her any choice but to let me go.

"How come I can't go?" she asked. She was fuming, but I shrugged my shoulders and said, "It's a boys' trip, that's why." The conversation ended and I got my way.

I called Harris, a buddy from my academy days who was working the 24th District near Rogers Park, and he said he was game for the trip. He asked if he could bring his college buddy Sam with us. "The more the merrier," I replied. We made hotel reservations, packed a rental car—a new Lincoln Continental—and set our sights nine hundred miles south.

"Juan, chicks show you their tits for a bunch of fuckin' plastic beads. It's crazy," Harris said, as the miles began adding up on the odometer.

"I know," I agreed. "It's outta control. A bunch of drunken, horny college chicks always get my attention. There ain't no laws on Bourbon Street." I knew Harris and Sam were pumped for the trip; so was I, and going without Ana would open up huge possibilities for getting laid. "Madness is only four hours away, my boys," I said.

Just then I spotted a Mississippi state trooper with his flashers on in my rearview mirror. "Shit, guys. It's a trooper. I think I was speeding." I began to pull over to the shoulder of the highway and the trooper fell in right behind me. I watched in the rearview mirror as he radioed in the stop and got out of his car. I had my badge in my hand as he approached my open window.

"Excuse me, sir," he began. "Can I see your—"

"I'm a cop," I interrupted, showing him my badge. "I'm on my way to Louisiana. Is there any way I could get a play?"

"Where ya a copper from, son?" the trooper asked, lowering his intense eyes into the car and checking out Harris, who also had his badge in his hand, and Sam, who shyly shrunk in the backseat.

"Chicago."

"Well, y'all driving likes bats outta hell," he informed us. "I'm gonna let y'all slide, but I don't wanna see ya fly by me again. My radar clocked ya doing 90."

"At least I know the speedometer is calibrated correctly," I joked.

"Keep the foot light on the gas, son. Y'all wanna make it where ya going."

We drove away and watched the trooper make a U-turn, heading off in the opposite direction. I slowed down to 85.

Bourbon Street hadn't changed much in the year I had been away. We hit the celebration on Sunday and had three days to get obliterated, as Fat Tuesday signaled the end of Mardi Gras. The holiday is a time to lose all inhibitions and revel in excess, and that was our purpose. Bourbon Street was flooded with people from everywhere in the world sharing this same vision. We sidestepped into a liquor store and bought numerous 28-ounce cans of Guinness along with a variety of plastic beaded necklaces. It was time to join the fray.

"C'mon, pussy!" Harris egged me on, standing on the sidewalk out-side the store. "Let's see you guzzle your beer." Sam already had opened his can and tilted his head back, downing his beer before the challenge was finished. Fucking party animals, I thought.

I popped open the tab on the can and brought it up to my lips, tilting my head back to let the heavy dark beer ease down my throat. It was too much; I couldn't finish it.

"See, you're a pussy," Harris proclaimed as I pulled the can from my lips, leaving a trail of foam on my chin. "Pussy!"

Night had slowly descended and the bright streetlights illuminated a solid six blocks of packed balconies above us and heads in front of us.

"Show us yer tits!" Sam yelled from behind me. I looked around to see who he was taunting, and I didn't see anyone. "Show us yer titties!" he yelled again. I glanced up on the balcony above and saw a woman leaning over the railing and teasing the crowd by pulling her shirt up, revealing two huge mounds restrained by her bra. Harris and I looked at each other and shook our heads in disbelief as Sam kept yelling.

"That's bullshit!" he complained, holding a string of gold and green beads. "If you want these beads, those titties need ta come outta yer bra. Show me yer tits!"

The crowd around us began the chant, "Show yer tits, show yer tits." I checked out Harris; his eyes were glued to the balcony. "C'mon baby," Harris crooned, "show my boy your nice, beautiful, big titties."

"Show daddy your titties! Be a good girl, please," Sam begged.

Stepping back from the railing, she jiggled her shoulders, causing her breasts to slowly slip out of the top of her bra, inciting a ripple of shouting below.

"Let those babies out!" Harris demanded.

She kept jiggling her shoulders, as more and more flesh popped out until, with one final, rapid quiver, they were free—free for the world to see.

"That's what I'm talking about, baby! That's what daddy wanted to see!" Sam whooped, as he threw a string of beads at her. His beads weren't the only ones thrown. Every guy in the vicinity of the balcony lobbed beads in her direction. Harris opened his beer and downed it in one gulp.

"That's how you do it, pussy boy!" he chided. He whipped his empty can, slightly above head level, into the crowd.

"That wasn't cool, dude," I told Harris as we watched the aluminum can hit someone in the head. It skimmed off his head, hitting another person, skimmed off someone else's noggin, and then disappeared into the crowd. It was like watching a stone skip across the water's surface. I shook my head as Harris doubled over laughing his ass off. The people who got hit in the head were pissed off, but the pandemonium was such that it was impossible for them to know for certain who had thrown it.

Out of the corner of my eye, I saw two burly uniformed cops coming over, intent on grabbing Harris. They gruffly yanked him by his shirt, leaving Harris speechless and definitely confused. They cuffed him faster than I had ever seen anyone cuffed before.

"Hey!" I yelled, as they began pushing Harris toward a side street. "Hey!" I tried again, walking more quickly, only ten feet behind them. They turned a corner as Harris looked back at me, not sure what was happening.

"Hey guys!" I hollered to the cops who stopped walking and turned around with anger in their eyes.

"Listen, we're cops from Chicago. I know what my friend did was stupid, but he's drunk," I pleaded. "He's stupid drunk."

They eyed Harris up and down and then looked at me, "Where's your badge?" I took out my wallet and showed them my star. Satisfied, they glanced over at Harris, "Where's numb nuts's badge?"

"It's in my back pocket," Harris meekly replied.

They searched his pocket and pulled out his badge. "Y'all silly, man. Don't be doing that stupid shit here! Understand?" one of the cops said as he uncuffed Harris. The cops kept shaking their heads. "Next time, some good ole southern boy is gonna whomp on yer silly ass, and ain't nuttin' we can do to stop 'em!" he continued. "Now I suggest y'all keep yer noses clean and stay outta my face."

We turned around, got back onto Bourbon Street, and found Sam still gazing up at the balcony. "Where you guys been?" Sam asked. We didn't answer but resumed our course, losing ourselves in the crowd. "You saved me from getting an ass beating, Juan. Thanks," Harris said rather shamefacedly.

"No problem, man," I returned, nodding my head. "I sure would've hated to see what they'd do to you around that corner."

"I'm just glad we're cops," Harris declared.

★ ★ ★

Over the next two days, Harris controlled his behavior, although he got wickedly wasted every day. So did Sam. And they kept out of trouble. I, on the other hand, hit the streets solo one evening after we downed a fifth of Southern Comfort. Harris and Sam got sick and went back to the room.

I met a girl named Valerie. She was stunning with long, dark hair cascading down to her shoulders, deep and inviting almond-shaped eyes, light brown skin, and perfect white teeth. Her smile made the world stop on Bourbon Street. I told her I was a cop, which caught her attention immediately. Thirty minutes after meeting her, we were in a cab heading to my hotel room. Luckily, Harris and Sam were in good enough shape to leave when we got there because Valerie and I were attracted like magnets. This is exactly what I wanted. I wanted to abandon my restraint, make love to her like no one before, and then leave her wanting more. I was ecstatic when Valerie expressed interest and wanted to exchange contact information after our little tête-à-tête ended.

"San Diego, California, huh?" I questioned, reading her address. "I have a sister in L.A. and wouldn't mind visiting her. Could we hook up when I'm out there?" I asked, amazed at my luck. I couldn't have planned a better scenario.

"Surely, my handsome man," she purred. I was enchanted. We said our goodbyes. We both found it difficult to separate.

"You lucky motherfucker!" Harris said later that night when they came back to the hotel room. "Did you fuck that chick?"

"Smell your pillow," I teased. "Of course, bro. I find 'em and fuck 'em. Don't matter where I be."

Thoughts of Valerie filled my mind all the way home and when I got to my apartment, Valerie had called and left a frantic message: "Juan, I lied. I don't live in California. I live in Colorado. Here's my real information. Please call. I'd love to see you again."

This was the beginning of a tempestuous five-month long-distance love affair that cost me hundreds of dollars in phone bills and rental-car expenses. I drove to Colorado twice and flew there once, staying with her for five days at a time. I also used up all my sick days and the compensatory time I had earned at work. Each time Ana asked me where I was going, I told her, "On a trip with the boys." She didn't ask any other questions; she was learning not to ask me about how I spent my time as long as I spent time with her when I could.

My relationship with Valerie was perfect for me—tons of raw sex with no commitment, at least not on my part. In June she called and told me she was coming to Chicago. I had learned not to shit in my own backyard and to keep my two lives separate, so I told her I was going out of town.

I remember thinking that Ana was never going to bust me, no fucking way. I thought that I was way too clever for that and I always had an escape plan. I was living a lie with Ana. I was captivated by the intensity of the affair I was having with Valerie. And the more women I conquered, the more I created an impenetrable coat of armor around myself.

"Why are we going to Saint Martin?" Ana asked when I announced the diversion, knowing I had to escape before Valerie arrived.

"So we can be alone in a romantic place, make love on the beach, and enjoy life," I replied. "Besides that," I added with a triumphant tone in my voice, "I want to celebrate not getting busted by the department and finishing my undergrad."

Completing my degree from DePaul earlier that same month gave me the perfect excuse. I felt everything was going my way. My path of higher education had taken me on a six-year-long journey and I was able to persevere and become a college graduate. Ana's face beamed as I crossed the stage to pick up my diploma, but her smile radiated even more on the beaches of Saint Martin as we vowed that nothing was ever going to break us apart.

This vacation gave us time to lose ourselves in each other. With the memory of the abortion finally receding, I felt no restraint in demonstrating my passion for Ana, and she welcomed the sexual intimacy.

When the vacation ended, I returned to my new life as a cop. The lying game was the game I lived by, stretching my web of deceit across state lines. Living a charmed life, I loved that I was able to get everything I wanted and never get caught. The rushes of adrenaline I felt in performing my job became more intense and harder to resist.

I bought a motorcycle—a Ninja 900—and started cruising around with Edgar, who had his own bike. We had no fears, testing our courage by breaking every speed limit in the city and surrounding suburbs. We got stopped by cops plenty of times, but having badges made us kings of the road.

My fascination with speed didn't stop there. I joined a group of coppers who jumped out of planes at 15,000 feet. During our tandem jumps, we reached speeds of 120 miles per hour, plummeting almost 7,000 feet before we pulled the rip cords on our parachutes. What a rush! I stared mortality in the face, challenging it with my every act. Life wasn't going to cheat me out of any thrills. And the thrills kept coming.

"Hey, Juan," Edgar yelled as I was leaving the station one night. "Pearl Jam just announced a private concert tomorrow at the Regal Theater on Seventy-ninth Street. You up to heading over there?"

"Fuck yeah!" I exclaimed. Pearl Jam had just released a new album that was burning up the charts. They had played two sold-out nights in a row at the Chicago Stadium, leaving many fans, like myself, bitter because we couldn't score any tickets. Now they were going to play an exclusive concert at a theater that seated only 1,300 people.

"How'd you score the tickets?" I asked.

"Tickets? We don't need no stinkin' tickets when we got badges." Edgar smiled and told me to meet him at the District's parking lot at 8:00 the next night.

Edgar was exploring all the avenues of connections and taking chances on the road to privilege. Compared to him, I was asleep at the wheel. I told myself that my ignorance had to stop. I had to establish connections for myself and take some chances with entitlement. What the hell, I reasoned, all anyone can do is say no and that wouldn't be the end of the world.

We met the next night in the parking lot and I jumped into his ride while Pearl Jam's "Once" rattled the car's windows. He pulled out two Heinekens from behind the back of his seat.

"Open this, will you, bro'?" he asked, handing me the two bottles. I obliged as he put the pedal to the floor, flying down Fullerton Avenue toward the Kennedy Expressway.

"This is the fuckin' life, bro'!" Edgar proclaimed, getting on the highway and raising his bottle. "*Salúd*," he said as we clinked bottles.

He punched the accelerator and my neck snapped, hitting the headrest as he veered over to the left lane. We were flying. I looked over at the speedometer and the needle was rising—90, 95, 100 miles per hour. All the other cars seemed to be parked as we blew by them. When we hit Thirty-fifth Street, a state trooper chased us down, hit his lights, and pulled us over.

"Gimme your beer, bro," I told Edgar. He passed it to me and I put it on the floor between my feet. The trooper came from the drivers' side as Edgar rolled down his window and began pulling out his badge.

"You boys sure in a hurry to get somewhere," the trooper began. "May I see your license, registration, and proof of insurance?"

"Sorry, office," Edgar began, flipping his wallet open to reveal his badge. "We're Chicago coppers. Could you let us pass with some professional courtesy?"

Professional courtesy? It all came back to me now. Our instructors in the academy told us about this time-honored privilege cops give each other, teachers, doctors, nurses, and other city workers. But it came with a warning, "Use your discretion judiciously," they said. It worked for me on my way to New Orleans, but I was wary of overusing it. I feared Edgar was pushing his luck by brazenly asking for it by name.

"Where do you work at, officer?" the trooper questioned, taken aback by the request. Shit, just what I was afraid of.

"14. Shakespeare," Edgar stated, but he took it one step further and began dropping names. "Do you know Trooper Hugo Sanchez? He always comes into 14 to do his paperwork."

"Sure I do. Just saw him, matter of fact, before the shift started," the trooper replied, seeming to loosen up a bit. "Anyway, slow it down, will ya? I don't wanna be the one writing up a fatality accident, especially yours."

"Sure, will do," Edgar replied, "and tell Hugo, Edgar says, 'What's up?'"

The trooper headed back to his car, shaking his head as Edgar got my attention, "Yo homey, pass me my beer?" The trooper passed us and waved. "Let's roll!" Edgar hollered, flooring the pedal and fishtailing the rear of his car as the tires spat out the roadside gravel. He didn't slow down at all and Pearl Jam's hard-driving "Why Go" blared over the speakers. We got off the highway and headed east toward Stony Island Avenue.

"Damn! Why the hell did P.J. pick this theater?" Edgar wondered aloud. "Ain't nothing but shines 'round here."

"I have no fuckin' idea, just make sure to lock your doors," I suggested, watching Edgar jam his secondary weapon into his waistband. "You bringing that shit inside?"

"Sure as hell not gonna leave it in my ride, tell you that!" he said.

A huge group of people milled about outside the theater as Edgar went into action. He approached a security guard and asked, "Who's running security?"

The guard looked around and pointed to a tall, chubby white guy with a thick brown mustache and receding hairline.

We walked over to him, and Edgar once again took the initiative. "How you doing, office?" he asked. "We're coppers from 14. My name is Barrera," he said, flipping out his badge. "And this is Officer Juarez. We were told you were running security for this event."

"That's a fact, officer. My name is Roger Banderson. How can I help you two tonight?"

"We were wondering if there's a way we can slide in and catch the show," Edgar said.

"It's a packed house," Officer Banderson replied, turning his head and nodding to the growing crowd on the sidewalk. "But I always take care of my own."

The privileges just kept on coming. Having never seen us before in his life, this guy gave us props with no questions asked. "Go inside and— see that redheaded woman sitting down—tell her I said it's OK, and show her your badges." Edgar started to walk in her direction.

"Hey, Roger," I said. "Is this the only gig you run, or do you handle security for other venues, too?"

"I run security at the Aragon and the Riviera. Why?" he asked. "You like concerts?"

"As a matter of fact, I do," I said, nodding.

"Well, if there are any shows you wanna check out at those places, just drop by and see me. I won't be offended if you bring over a bottle of booze once in a while. It's cool. I'll hook you up."

Ah! Finally a connection I made on my own. "Thanks a lot, Roger," I said, shaking his hand. "I will do that, take my word."

"Good," he concluded. "Get inside and enjoy the show."

I was ecstatic. Many of the upcoming concerts I wanted to see were at Banderson's venues, and now I could get myself in for free. I entered the lobby and saw Edgar talking to the redhead who, I found out later, was also a cop. She let us in.

"How fuckin' sweet is that, my brother?" Edgar smiled, walking toward the theater doors while the music of Pearl Jam reverberated through the lobby. We entered and saw a huge legion of screaming fans standing up with their fists in the air.

I led the way down the aisle that security, posted every twenty rows, had kept clear. "I'm a cop," I said, flashing my badge at every security guard we passed. Eventually we made it to the front row. Eddie Vedder was right there, in front of me in a 1976 Cubs jersey, shaking his head like a madman, screaming and spitting out the words to "Jeremy." I was in heaven.

I turned my head and saw a Colombian girl, Maria, who I had met earlier that spring at a bar and had been seeing on the side. She was statuesque and regal and eloquent in her conversation, and to top it off, she was going to UIC to become a CPA. Maria was more than willing to participate in adventurous sex. I couldn't believe it—there she was in the third row. She and her friend were standing up, arms pumping in the air and dancing like the rest of the crowd.

"Edgar," I yelled, "meet me in the lobby after the show." I walked over to Maria. She was glad to see me. We watched the rest of the show together before I left with Edgar. He had two Polish girls lined up and we were going to see them.

After this night, I didn't need any more proof these three little words—*I'm a cop*—could open doors into the world of unlimited privilege. I loved the perks of being a cop!

12

CROSSING THE LINE

I HAD KNOWN OFFICER REYNOLDS in high school and had entered the police academy as he was leaving. When I was assigned to the same district as Reynolds, our paths crossed again, and our past made conversation easy. Reynolds believed Catholic-educated police officers made better cops. He believed we were more compassionate and understanding and, while I agreed in principle, he wasn't the one to convince me.

One night an eighteen-year-old Hispanic male Latin Disciple had the misfortune to be loitering on a street corner during Officer Reynolds's watch. It was before the antigang ordinance was enacted in 1992, which immediately justified cops arresting individuals or whole groups of people congregating on street corners. Up until then the only weapon cops had to combat this crime was a charge of disorderly conduct—a flimsy allegation that many lawyers challenged as a violation of their clients' First Amendment rights.

While hanging out on a corner was legal, a lot of cops couldn't stand the sight of kids sporting low-slung pants and pagers, standing idly on corners.

According to witnesses' testimony and police dispatch tapes, the Latin Disciple was picked up by Officer Reynolds, handcuffed, and then placed in the backseat of his squad. The kid later testified that Reynolds began shaking him down for information, asking questions as to the location of Disciples narcotics and demanding to know who was holding and slinging on the street. It appeared as if Officer Reynolds's intent was a drug pinch.

✯ It's a common practice for a police officer to use street tactics, such as verbal threats of imprisonment to coerce a hype (drug user), prostitute, drunk, or gangbanger to drop the dime (snitch) on someone—anyone— in exchange for not having a case, usually a disorderly conduct charge, thrown on him or her. It's a form of pure intimidation.

✯ When this gangbanger remained quiet and refused to divulge any useful information to Officer Reynolds, he was escorted across Humboldt Boulevard into rival Latin King territory. Since the threats weren't working, it was time to put the fear of God in the kid.

I have to assume it was Officer Reynolds's hope that the fear of being released into the Latin Kings' lair would encourage the reluctant gangbanger to drop the dime that would lead to an arrest and seizure of narcotics and, more importantly, a court date. The gangbanger saw through the ruse, called Officer Reynolds's bluff and remained tight lipped. It was then that Officer Reynolds decided to drive the kid deeper into Latin King territory, pulling over at the corner of St. Louis and LeMoyne, and announced on his loudspeaker, "I've got a present for you all." The sleeping Latin Kings awoke. As the message spread, they appeared in droves, brandishing tire irons, baseball bats, and bottles. Eyewitness accounts say the bloodthirsty mob began rocking the police car, screaming to be given the Latin Disciple.

By this point the kid must have been fearful for his life. He may have given some dubious information to Officer Reynolds, or he may have continued to sit there in silence. It's uncertain. But what is certain is that Officer Reynolds unlocked the Latin Disciple's door. The gangbanger was immediately pulled into the middle of the crowd of Latin Kings and received a vicious beating that left him with numerous broken bones, a fractured skull, and one eye because the other was gouged out of its socket. Eyewitnesses say the police officer left the kid to fend for himself as he drove away. They said it was a miracle the gangbanger wasn't killed.

The victim recovered enough to launch a complaint that resulted in a civil lawsuit against Officer Reynolds and the City of Chicago. Officer Reynolds was charged with violating the code of ethics, abusing his authority, and police brutality. The City of Chicago was charged with improperly training this police officer. This investigation was spearheaded by the

✗ Office of Professional Standards (OPS), an office that is managed by the Chicago Police Department but is staffed by civilian department members in the hope of creating an unbiased disciplinary board. Upon a thorough investigation that included gathering statements from witnesses, OPS found Officer Reynolds guilty of some minor infractions and penalized him with a fifteen-day suspension without pay. Fifteen days for a victim's eye was the punishment. This sent an odd message through the ranks of the police force and caused a more uncomfortable unease across the city. (See "The Dirty Truth by the Numbers" on pp. 286 for more information.)

I ran into Reynolds three weeks later, after he had served his suspension but while the civil lawsuit was still pending. He chuckled about the incident and said, "I'll beat it, just like the Kings beat that fuckin' gangbanger." He appeared to have forgotten what he confided to me about Catholic schoolboys being more compassionate. Instead, it appeared that he had turned into a prime example of a brutal cop and another devotee of OPS.

The civil lawsuit was settled out of court to avoid bad press. I can only assume the parents were after justice, but they didn't seek it through the court system. Or maybe they didn't trust the system in light of the OPS determination and thought it better to run with the money. As usual, the whole matter quietly died down. It was promptly swept under the carpet as just another cop got away with an injustice.

The malicious intent behind this incident bothered me. How could Reynolds have done this? And how the fuck could he have gotten away with it? It was as if human life held no value; even if he thought this kid was a useless member of society, it made no sense to me. What gave him the right? What gave Locallo the right?

I couldn't share my concerns about the abuse of power I was witnessing with my fellow officers, so I started confiding in Ana. She was always willing to lend an ear about the moral issues I faced as a cop. She offered solace and support after hearing my stories, but there was really nothing she could do or say to help.

I was now in my sixteenth month on the force. The CPD's problems were deeply rooted in the system, from police officers on up to members of OPS. It was overwhelming and made me feel that there was no way to

@ 16 MONTHS)

change things, so I would have to conform. Consequently, I ceased talking to anyone about my inner turmoil or my experiences on the job. I bottled it all up inside.

★ ★ ★

Witnessing Locallo's tactics, hearing the story of Reynolds's brutality, and constantly seeing the dark underbelly of life—all of this was slowly affecting me, changing my perception of the entire world. I was trying to keep my professional life from bleeding into my personal one, but I felt powerless to stop it. The negative forces were filling me with apathy and stealing away my compassion. This is not who I was in my heart, and I knew it. But I felt powerless to stop the downward spiral.

One summer night, a group of friends and I were riding our motorcycles down Elston Avenue in a heavily industrial area devoid of traffic. We approached a traffic light on Division Street and stopped. One guy, Comet, loved to open up the throttle and haul ass when the light turned green. He did so at that moment. As we watched his taillight gaining distance from us, though, we could see he wasn't going to be able to make the turn. Comet had to be doing close to ninety miles an hour as he slammed into a chain-link fence, went airborne, flew into a pole, and then fell onto the street. Within seconds, another friend hurried to the firehouse at Chicago and Elston, three blocks away, and summoned an ambulance. When the ambulance got there, the paramedics started working on Comet immediately, but they didn't leave the scene. From my experience as a cop I knew that if the paramedics thought there was a chance of saving a life, they'd leave for a hospital. My three other friends began to cry. I knew Comet was dead, but my eyes were dry. And three hours later when we had to tell his wife that her husband, the father of their three kids, had died, my eyes remained dry.

★ ★ ★

I found it increasingly hard not to stereotype people. The more I saw of the dispossessed and downtrodden, the more I categorized people as either good citizens or worthless pieces of shit. I knew that witnessing the unjust actions of some of my co-workers without saying a word to anyone began to manifest in my behavior. Ana saw these changes clearly and even though the trip to Saint Martin brought us back together in a physical sense, I still kept her at an emotional distance.

After returning from Saint Martin, Ana had moved into an apartment on Grace Street near Broadway. Because she didn't have a car, she often had to depend on me for transportation. Her dependence on me changed the way I treated her. I started caring less about my punctuality for dates, and I often refused to return her pages. It pissed her off, but I never paid attention to her feelings.

One day during that summer, Ana's family was celebrating her niece's graduation with a barbecue. I arrived at Ana's apartment two hours late after having spent the night with Maria.

Ana had left for the party without me. One hour later I arrived at Ana's family's place. Jumping off my motorcycle, I strode into the backyard where the family was gathered. Ana was fuming. She slammed the door of the back porch and went up to the second floor. Her brothers looked at me, "What's wrong with her?"

Throughout my life I always tried to appear as if I had everything under control. "I'm going upstairs to find out," was all I said.

I found Ana crying on her old bed. I went over to her and tried to give her a hug. She pushed my arms away and scolded me with her eyes and followed with some words of rebuke, "Don't try that shit with me! You know you fucked up!"

"So I was an hour late, I'm here now," I said.

"What fuckin' clock have you been looking at?" she hollered, wiping tears away with the sheet. "I was waiting like a dumbass for two hours and then had to take the damn bus! What the fuck's going on with you?"

"With me? What? I'm here. You should be happy," I said. "What's wrong with you?"

"Good answer! You just don't get it, do you?" She sat up in the bed. "Where were you?"

"I was out with some friends."

"Who?" she screamed.

"Just some friends," I said.

"Yeah, right!" She got off the bed in a rage. "Juan, you don't even talk or discuss anything anymore! You're always right, and you get so pissed off when you're questioned!" I was silent. "So where the fuck were you?"

My pager began to go off.

"Who's fucking paging you now?" she demanded.

I stood staring at the floor while she seethed. She tried to grab my pager from my belt, but I managed to keep it away from her. I switched it to the silent mode and put it in my pocket.

"Can't you fucking look me in the eyes and be honest?" she asked.

I raised my head, looked up, and gazed into her eyes momentarily. They were red and the skin around them was swollen from crying as tears began rolling down her cheeks. I had to turn my head. I wanted to say, "I never meant to hurt you. I never meant to make you cry. I love you. I'm sorry for all the pain I'm causing you. I never meant to cheat on you and sully your pure love." But I kept those words locked up inside.

I loved Ana and I truly wanted to be with her forever. Our relationship was much more than our lovemaking. It was dynamic, volatile, and uncontrollable. But I wanted to control everything: my time, my life, my love, my feelings, and Ana. Above anything else, I wanted my independence. And I wanted to be happy every moment of my life, so I ran to someone else whenever Ana got too demanding. I didn't want to answer questions; I wanted peace and acceptance without anyone prying into my motives or actions. I knew that if I couldn't get that with Ana, I'd find comfort elsewhere.

13

LUCKY'S WAY

I APPLIED FOR ADMISSION and was accepted into DePaul's Graduate School of Education. Having anticipated this moment and done the paperwork in advance, I put in my application for the tuition-reimbursement program and sent along a report that explained how my going to school would benefit the department. I wrote that I wanted to be the press liaison for the Chicago Police Department. The watch commander (WC) signed off on it, complimenting me on my desire to go to school, and sent my request downtown for approval. Two weeks later it was accepted. However, I wondered how I was going to fit a night class into my work schedule. When I asked the WC for his advice, he told me the solution was simple. Instead of having rotating days off like the rest of the crew, I'd have the same day off every week to attend my one class. Having resolved that issue, I rejoiced in my fortune, but Ana wasn't as excited.

Working the third watch and maintaining my wayward lifestyle had begun to weaken our relationship. Ana worked nine to five, which made it virtually impossible for us to see each other on the days I worked. That left us with the weekend mornings and my days off. I was more than willing to see her as long as the time we spent together wasn't stressful. Whenever it became stressful, I found solace in Maria's arms. Ana continued to be the one true, steady force in my life, but it was always on my terms.

Then Ana and I agreed that one way we could spend more time together was to start running at the lakefront. We were both in excellent shape and began entering 5k and 10k races in Chicago and the suburbs.

I began to realize that sharing our competitive natures was exactly the thing we needed to rejuvenate our relationship. This realization led me to work harder to spend time with her.

Don and I had worked the third watch for ten straight periods, but when he returned from furlough he wanted to go around the clock with the crew. I opted to stay on straight afternoons because I had customized my schedule so it wouldn't conflict with school. The notion of changing shifts every period didn't appeal to me. I had learned some valuable lessons working with Don, especially the importance of conflict resolution without necessarily arresting anyone, but I knew it was time to move on. I needed to find a new partner. It didn't take long.

On a beautiful mid-September day, I arrived at work, scanned the assignment sheets, and saw I was paired with Rufus Hibera. I didn't know the guy so I asked a couple of coppers in the locker room about him, and they looked at each other knowingly and said, "Oh, Lucky, he'll be good for you if you can keep up with him."

While in the roll call assembly, I saw who Lucky was—a slender light-skinned Puerto Rican with a beak like Robert DeNiro. With his hair combed back he had a prominent widow's peak. He seemed intense, but sometimes he'd break into a silly smirk. I learned he had a quick wit to boot. I liked Lucky immediately and knew it would be an interesting day. After roll call, he went to the radio room, grabbed the keys for the car and said, "You the low man, I'm driving today." I had no problem with that; it was protocol. Besides, I was still learning the streets in the District and Lucky appeared to know exactly what he was doing.

"First things first. I need a cup of *café con leché*." We exited the back door of the district and walked across Palmer Street to a Cuban restaurant. He opened the door and began speaking Spanish so rapidly to the guy behind the counter that I quickly lost the thread after, "*Holá, como estas?*" Not understanding my own native tongue made me feel bad, but I didn't have too much time to stew over my own incompetence. Lucky grabbed his *café con leché* and poured about seven seconds' worth of sugar in it. Now I knew what the guys meant earlier about keeping up with him.

"You like some coffee with your sugar," I wisecracked, envisioning the bottom of the Styrofoam cup disintegrating.

"Yup," he nodded.

We got in the squad and cruised west down Palmer when he spotted a kid near Spaulding Avenue wearing a trench coat. "I bet ya the kid's packing a heater," he said, as I was busy organizing all the GOCR forms, complaints, and tickets in my briefcase. When I looked up we were already on top of the kid. Lucky was out of the car and had the kid assuming the position against the brick wall of an apartment as I lagged behind. The kid started saying, "It ain't mine. I'm just holding it for someone." I wondered what he was talking about, and then I saw Lucky holding a .22-caliber rifle in his hands.

"How the fuck did you know that?" I asked. We weren't even a mile away from the District and only twenty minutes into our shift and he'd already made a collar.

"This ain't a thinking man's game, youngblood. You need to listen to your instincts," he informed me. And with those words he forged an image in my head that placed him on a pedestal. This was the kind of cop I wanted to become. Lucky made me see being a cop in a whole different light. My adrenaline was connected to my instincts, and instead of being passive on the streets and letting my partner control a situation, I had to step up and act. I needed to use my head.

"The trench coat?" I asked, thinking of what was wrong with the picture the kid presented. Lucky looked at me and winked, "Exactly! You gotta keep on your toes, boy."

Whenever Don and I had found cocaine on someone, Don would throw it in the sewer and let the kid go. Lucky was different. He loved working the drug game. He knew all the drug spots, and later in our first shift working together, he introduced me to a notorious street in the District known exclusively for supplying junkies, hypes, johns, and prostitutes with crack and heroin. It was called Francis Place.

Lucky and I spent many nights testing the limits of our supervisors' patience because answering the radio wasn't our top priority while we were watching the drug scene on Francis Place. Lucky reasoned, "You only have to open your eyes to see who's dirty on the streets, and radios don't have eyes."

As September ended and the days grew shorter, the drug trade on Francis Place steadily increased. With two hours left in our shift, Lucky and I would grab a cup of *café con leché* and park the squad a block or two from the main drag on Francis Place. We'd then meander through alleys and gangways to set up a surveillance point on the porch of a residence that gave us an unobstructed view of the dope house in question. We'd turn off our radios, fully aware that it was against department regulations, and watch in silence. Just knowing we were violating policy made me feel like I was doing some clandestine shit like I had seen in movies.

Our purpose for setting up surveillance was to see what cars continually drove down Francis Place, who would enter the known drug spot, and how long they'd spend within the location. If it was a five- to ten-minute stop, they were probably picking up a personal-use package. If they extended their stay, a bigger deal could be taking place. We camped out for two days in a row and noticed a white two-door Cadillac with Wisconsin plates pull up to the curb. The passengers got out, entered the spot, and stayed for a while. Surveillance is like gambling; you roll the dice and see what happens. Eventually we knew we'd hit the jackpot. On the third day, the Caddy reappeared and Lucky told me to get the squad. I ran back to the car and slowly drove down the alley to the back of the house where Lucky was.

"Let's drive around to the front. When they get to Armitage, we'll do a street stop," he instructed as he jumped in the car. I turned on the radio just as the dispatcher called our number.

"14—, meet your supervisor. You've just been redlined." This meant we had missed a radio assignment after the dispatcher tried calling us three times. Meanwhile, the occupants of the white Caddy had returned and were beginning to drive away.

"Shit! Don't answer the radio, rook," Lucky ordered. "They can wait. Fuck 'em if they can't take a joke. Remember, it's a case of mind over matter—I don't mind and they don't matter." That was one of his favorite lines, and it always made me laugh.

We observed the Caddy making a left turn onto California Avenue. It headed westbound on Armitage. I punched the accelerator, got right on their tail, hit the flashing mars lights on top of the squad, and pulled them over.

"What's this all about, officer?" asked the driver of the vehicle as he was getting out of the car.

Lucky automatically responded, "Your turn signal's burned out." I don't recall if it was or not, but it didn't matter. "Can we see your driver's license?"

The driver couldn't produce a valid one, so we arrested him for driving without a license. We cuffed the other passenger and placed him in the rear of the squad while we searched the vehicle. In no time at all we found the stash—more than thirty grams of heroin. What a score!

We informed the dispatcher of our location and the bust we had on our hands. Then our supervisor told us he'd meet us at the station.

"You guys are renegades," he told us later. "Always getting into shit and expecting me to cover your asses. I won't be able to do it much longer."

"But sarge, we didn't hear the radio. I think the squelch button was turned on," Lucky improvised. Our sergeant didn't buy the lie, but he let us slide on the reprimand. We did all the necessary paperwork and earned a few hours of overtime for the pinch. A great day's work—Lucky's way. When we went to see the WC to sign off on the reports, he smiled and said, "Nice job, guys. I'm gonna make sure that radio gets fixed."

It wasn't that Lucky and I wanted to be rabble-rousers, but we just wanted to do our brand of work. If it paid off with arrests and seizures, it was well worth it.

★ ★ ★

One night we were six blocks outside our District boundaries because Lucky liked to make sure everything was all right by his parents' house near Palmer and Pulaski. When we turned into the alley to check the back of their house, we saw a kid running from a car parked in the alley. We drove up on the car and saw that the steering column was peeled—it had been stolen.

"I'm gonna get out and see if he's still around," Lucky told me as he shut the door. I drove around the block and passed Lucky once. There was no sign of the kid. I doubled back around the alley when I saw the lights of the stolen car go on and the car began to move. I had a choice to make and not a lot of time to make it: follow the stolen car or look for Lucky. I chose the car.

The driver turned down another alley when he saw I was behind him. He was going ten miles an hour and had his door open with one foot hanging out. I thought he was going to jump out of the car and put it in reverse. I had one foot out my door and one on the gas pedal and my heart was pounding fast. I was ready to run. Approaching Shakespeare Avenue, he slammed his door shut and punched the accelerator. He turned right and began heading east on a westbound street—he was going the wrong way. I turned on the blue strobe lights and began chasing him. I had no contact with Lucky as of yet; he knew better than to get on the radio and give up his position six blocks out of the District. Especially since he didn't have his partner with him.

The stolen car continued picking up speed on the one-way street. We passed Central Park Avenue doing fifty. I prayed no one would turn onto Shakespeare and become a head-on accident victim. I was gaining on him when we neared Kimball Avenue, and then a car turned onto Shakespeare. Oh shit, I thought. The stolen car's brake lights lit up, and then the whole back end lifted off the ground as it smashed, head-on, into the oncoming car. A cloud of smoke rose from the collision. I was about to call the accident in when the occupant of the stolen car got out and ran.

Oh yeah, here we go. I got out of my car and called in the foot chase, keeping the dispatcher informed of my every move. Cops love joining in on foot chases and every cop near the scene responded as I heard sirens wail through the night. The kid stayed in my field of vision, jumping fences and cutting through gangways. Then he turned a corner and disappeared.

I slowly walked around a Toyota pickup truck when the kid stood up and threw a punch at me. It glanced off my shoulder. I could hear Lucky, who was listening to the chase on his radio, cheer me on. "Get him, Juan. Get him." I threw a punch, and we started grappling and fell into someone's front lawn. We were wrestling in the grass and I had the upper position when a cab appeared on the scene. The driver got out and hit the kid right in the mouth with a stream of pepper spray. The kid started gagging and throwing up. I looked around but the cabdriver had left after he sprayed the kid. Other police cars arrived on the scene as I cuffed the kid. I turned him over to another squad so they could bring him to the District. I wanted to hurry up and pick up Lucky before anyone asked questions.

"Hey, Juarez." I turned and there was the sergeant. "Great job. Where's your partner?"

"We got separated on the chase, he's only two blocks away," I said. "I'll go pick him up."

"No need," the sergeant replied, "I'll go get him. You can head into the District and get the paperwork started."

A lump formed in my throat. "Sarge, he's not two blocks away. He's all the way near Pulaski."

The sergeant looked at me and shook his head. "You guys are too much." He radioed Lucky, found out his position, and picked him up. Lucky laughed his balls off when he got to the station and told the story. Even the WC couldn't help laughing.

I was having fun and learning a lot working with Lucky. Every day was a new adventure. We never got in trouble; instead what we got were awards and honorable mentions for jobs well done. Lucky's energy complimented my taste for adventure and need for an adrenaline rush.

The next period, we requested a change to the first watch (midnight to 8 A.M.), as my classes at DePaul demanded more of my attention. Lucky and I had developed a great relationship and enjoyed working as a team, learning to trust each other's instincts, so there was no need to break up a good thing. Working midnights would be a nice change he reasoned because the only people who'd be out during those hours had to be dirty. Plus there was less radio chatter, giving us plenty of time to do our style of work. But the first watch proved to be grueling, both for my relationship with Ana and my professional life.

Sleeping over at Ana's apartment pretty much ceased because I was working while she slept. And on my nights off I found Maria's bed more inviting.

Getting sleep became a real challenge. I'd go straight home after work, but I could never fall asleep because my body couldn't adjust to sleeping during the day. I asked my father, who had worked midnights for years, what he did during his days. "I work security at a bank," he informed me. It didn't come as a surprise when I remembered that he was always working when I was a kid. Making more money sounded appealing, as I was falling into heavy debt from foolish spending habits associated with acquiring and maintaining my paramours. I asked my father to hook me up with a moonlighting gig. Soon after, I started working one day a week at a bank. When I finished my shift at 8 A.M., I'd go to the bank and work until 2 P.M. Then I'd go to DePaul's library to study. I'd sometimes meet Ana later for an evening run. On the other days, I'd do a solo morning run after my shift, try to take a four- or five-hour nap, and then head to the library to get some studying done before I went to my night class from 5:30 to 9:00. By that time I was exhausted and sleep came easily—too easily. Many nights I slept through the ringing of my alarm clock and never heard my phone. I'd finally awaken to hear Lucky beating on my door at half past midnight. After this happened a couple of times, Lucky pressed me for answers regarding my sudden lackadaisical approach to the job.

"School's more important to me, Lucky," I answered.

"I don't know how you do it, bro'," he replied. "I loved school too and wish I was still taking classes, but I ain't got the time. What you going to school for, Juan? You planning on getting out of this rattrap?"

I thought about it for a moment before I answered. "I don't know, bro'. I can't tell the future. But I do know this: there's got to be something better than this job, but it'll do for now."

Over the next eleven months, we had more than our share of adventures, car chases, gun cases, and verbal reprimands for disobeying protocol, but the consequences were never serious enough to dissuade us from doing what we wanted. We wanted to do police work and we wanted to do it the Lucky way.

The more I worked with Lucky, the more fun I had doing investigatory work and taking chances. Meanwhile, my disdain for answering radio calls and being held accountable for my every movement increased.

If I saw the radio as a ball and chain, the same could be said about my relationship with Ana. My relationship with her, which had been changing for the better when we began training together, took a heavy hit when I made the shift to midnights. Even though I had slowed down the affair with Maria, I was either at work or in class or was too tired to see Ana. I needed to conform to the rigors grad school demanded. More and more, my weekdays were spent at the library. This wore me out and it pissed Ana off, but what could she do? Wasn't I being the man she wanted me to be by committing myself completely to my schooling?

While we were in New York ringing in the New Year with some of her friends, Ana said to me, "Things really aren't working out for us right now, Juan."

"What are you talking about?" I asked.

"I think we should break up." I couldn't believe she said it. It surprised the hell out of me. She was offering me a way out of the relationship. I would be freed from my web of lies and cheating and could see as many women as I wanted. But I was surprised at the conflicting emotions her words stirred in me.

"We can work things out," I begged. "There's no need to do that. I love you and you love me. What else do we need?"

We talked into the early hours. She finally agreed to try to work things out. In my heart and soul, I had been afraid and couldn't stand the idea of yet another person walking out on me—no matter how despicably I treated her. I had been testing Ana with every lie and with every woman I fucked. Having Ana in my life was important to me, but not so much that I was willing to reform my behavior.

Even as Ana and I were working things out after our near breakup, I couldn't subdue my desires for other women. The simmering affair I was having with Maria was becoming a relationship, and the excitement of learning all about her and the challenges of keeping her interested in me provided plenty of stimulation.

Maria was from the suburbs and was different from Ana in many ways. Being with her was like falling in love again. I gave her volumes of poetry that melted her heart. I had recently changed my focus from

education to English, and my creativity was awakened. I loved introducing this suburban girl to cultural events all in the city—modern jazz
troupes, ballet performances, and plays. She loved adventure too; she even
jumped out of a plane with me.

Maria had her own place in Lincolnwood where we could get lost in
carnal pleasures and share stories about our lives. The best thing about
this relationship was that I could come and go as I pleased—she was never
demanding of my time and was satisfied with what I had to give her. She
offered me everything I had with Ana except that it was new and without
baggage.

14

SITTING DUCKS

"HEY, ASSHOLE!" a drunken cop named Bill O'Malley challenged no one in particular. "I bet you can't shoot one of those ducks."

It was two in the morning at a watch party in Humboldt Park.

"Hey! Fucking asshole," Bill's voice continued. "Are you chickenshit or what?"

"You talkin' to me, man?" It was Louie Gomes. "Dey jus sittin' ducks. Dat's easy." He was taking the open challenge of target practice here at the lagoon.

A large congregation, mostly from the third watch, had gathered on the lagoon-side of the boathouse patio. People were lining up along the balustrade, peering into the enveloping darkness of the pond. A flashlight materialized and illuminated a flock of ducks floating lazily on the calm waters. The crowd grew larger and more boisterous around the two officers involved in this display of machismo, bravado, and arrogance.

After having been a cop for close to two years, I had seen my share of irresponsible and reckless professional behavior. Before I'd realized that it wasn't my style, I had even slapped around a kid to get the truth out of him. But I tried to distance myself from officers who sullied my perspective of what being a cop was all about. I had worked with solid partners— Don and then Lucky—and I cast away all negativity and let myself enjoy the challenges of the job.

I also realized that working with the same group of people, day in and day out, period after period, created deep-seated friendships and camaraderie. Cops put their lives on the line every shift; they depend on their partners, trusting they'll be there when the shit goes down. Entrusting my life to someone else wasn't easy, but out of necessity I learned to do it. There was no telling when I'd need another officer's assistance on the street, in court, or on paper. I also learned that cops help each other out and keep each other's secrets—it cements trust and strengthens the Department as a whole.

The parties that were held every twenty-eight days or so when watches changed cemented this camaraderie and trust. I made sure to do my part, even turning a blind eye to behavior I didn't agree with.

On this particular night Lucky and I went our separate ways after the 12:15 sign-off. I went to the watch party to kick back, have a beer, and bond with fellow officers. Lucky went home, advising me, "Too much crazy shit goes down at those parties. Besides, I don't want my *vieja* tripping, thinking I'm neglecting my family." Though Lucky and his live-in girlfriend had been traveling a rocky road of late, he was loyal to her and her two daughters, and he put up with the drama she brought to his life. He knew that there would be cop groupies and alcohol at the party—an often lethal combination—and he didn't need the temptation. But the crazy shit was exactly why I wanted to go to the party.

"Have fun and be careful," he warned as he left.

All city parks close at 10:30 P.M. and all unwanted citizens had already been chased from the park, which left the cops to wallow in our vices. Anyone attending the party was expected to bring a donation, and many cops hit liquor stores on their beats. It was all part of the routine. A rapid response to calls near these businesses was the cops' part of the deal. Such preferential treatment from cops was certainly worth a case of beer or a bottle of liquor. And as watch parties were notorious for bleeding into the morning hours, the call for more liquor was ongoing.

By the time I had finished my shift and made it over to the stately boathouse—a huge open-aired patio supported by massive, Ionic columns and framed by ornate stonework—a raucous crowd had gathered. Lively music filled the air. The boathouse was packed with dozens of off-duty cops—mostly male—and groupies, and people were still showing up in droves. Someone had parked a pickup on the patio and turned the tailgate into a self-service bar. I joined the fray and mixed myself a rum and coke. I noticed there were some squad cars from 13 and 14 in the parking lot at the foot of the boathouse. I also saw a couple of guys in uniform I went to the academy with. Discussing old times and new experiences, I talked with them until they had to leave to answer a call but not before we did a couple of shots in memory of old times. I mixed myself another drink and gave in to the festive mood.

As the hours passed and the liquor flowed, an air of recklessness spread through the party. An off-duty cop jumped into a squad and began doing doughnuts in the parking lot, spewing dust and gravel all over the place until someone fired a few warning shots into the air. The driver made an announcement on the car's PA system, "Man down, man down." He emerged from the car and abruptly fell on his face and remained limp as a roar of laughter filled the boathouse.

It wasn't too long before the party lapsed into the ancient ritual of one officer challenging the size of another officer's balls. That's when Bill O'Malley caught sight of the ducks.

"I'll empty out my clip and shoot three of those fuckin' ducks, my brudder," boasted a tipsy Louie. He was having a bit of difficulty pronouncing each word clearly as he stood at the railing.

"Bet!" responded Billy. "You 'Ricans can't shoot shit," he proclaimed, which only further incited Louie.

"What the fuck you talkin' 'bout, man?" Louie spat back.

"Anyone here wanna get in on the deal? We's takin' bets now," bellowed Billy. A hat appeared, bets were made, and money was collected as Louie practiced taking aim into the dark expanse. "Hey," Billy called out to Lieutenant Marshall, a watch supervisor from 14, who was there supporting the troops, "you gonna get in on this?"

Marshall took out a hundred-dollar bill, snickered, and proclaimed, "Ain't no way he's even gonna hit one." Marshall creased the bill and threw it in the hat. The crowd's laughter rippled through the night air. I threw a twenty into the hat.

The collection soon stopped and Billy made an announcement: "Louie here claims he could shoot three ducks with the nine in his clip. Schneider, you got that?" He directed the question to the state's attorney in the crowd to make it nice and official.

"Sure do," Schneider proclaimed. "That's three ducks in nine bullets. Everyone listening?"

A loud cheer of affirmation came from the crowd as Louie focused on the blackness of the still water, trying to find his balance or perhaps trying to find the courage to go through with this challenge. I was caught up in the momentum of the crowd and I rode the wave. With a drink in my hand, I made sure to stay at the far end of the railing, not wanting to get shot by an errant bullet.

"Let the truth prevail," roared Schneider.

"All right! Awww righteee!! Someone light up the targets. Then, on the count of three, Louie, you can light 'em up. And if we're lucky, you won't shoot anyone, *puñeta*."

Beams of light targeted the sleeping ducks as Louie attempted to calm his breathing. A moment of silence filled the boathouse then Billy sang out, "One . . . two . . ." Louie exhaled and jerkily squeezed the trigger of his automatic. Gunshots erupted—one after another—*puh, puh, puh!* The sound recoiled and echoed through the cavernous boathouse as some spent shell casings bounced off the balustrade, falling harmlessly into the water while others landed on the cement floor of the patio. Wings flapped madly; feathers flew everywhere; and the ducks cried out in alarm.

"Three," finished Billy. He was bent over laughing along with everyone else.

The smoke began to clear as the smell of gunpowder overwhelmed the fragrance of the cooking brats and hamburgers and made me feel sick to my stomach. The flashlight beams were still trained on the now-agitated water, and the bodies of two ducks floated lifeless on the murky surface of the lagoon. I stood there, numbed by what I had just seen. The wave of enthusiasm I had ridden in on drained away. Cheers and laughter ensued, but I couldn't join in. For me, the party was over.

"Shots fired near North and Humboldt Boulevard. Anyone riding on it?" a uniformed cop's radio informed the listening audience. There were always radios at watch parties in case there were calls of a disturbance in or around the scene of the party.

"Anyone for duck *à l'orange*?" Billy chimed in, as Louie received congrats from winners and losers alike.

"Someone check the bushes for the second shooter," Marshall muttered sourly. "There ain't no fuckin' way he coulda been the lone shooter."

"Hey! It's the cops," someone in the crowd yelled as if we were at an underage keg party. Laughter erupted from everyone on the boathouse deck except me. As a squad car pulled up into the parking lot, I was thinking of going over to Maria's place in Lincolnwood.

"Squad, give it a slow down on the shots fired. You got a number of a complainant?" the responding officer inquired.

"Nope," the dispatcher replied.

Billy began telling the responding officer and his partner the story, and they laughed as he mimicked Louie, shooting wildly with his eyes closed. Then the two responding officers joined the party, feeling it was their duty to stay at least for a while and join in the merriment.

"Squad, this is 14—, give it a 5-Adam (disturbance; other—not bona fide incident)," one of them radioed back.

15

THE NEED FOR A CHANGE

IT DIDN'T TAKE LONG for me to notice how cops dealt with death—they laughed at it, using dark, obscene humor to mask their emotions. I witnessed many deaths during my service in the 14th District, but the very first death I saw as a cop on the streets made a profound impact on my perception of reality.

During my rookie training on a scorching July evening on a newly tarred stretch of North Avenue near Central Park Avenue, my FTO and I were called to the scene of a motorcycle accident. The biker, who wasn't wearing a helmet, put his bike down more than fifty yards before the intersection and left a trail of brain matter and fluid on the street. His speedometer cable snapped at impact; it was locked at 120. I will never forget the image of his head split open, still oozing, and his brain seeping out while his eyes remained open. His body was twisted as if devoid of bones. I had to turn my head as my stomach began rising to my throat. I found it hard to believe this grotesque figure had been alive ten minutes earlier. My FTO joked, "At least he was wearing eye protection."

Later that month, after a motorcycle enthusiasts' rally at Humboldt Park, we were called to the scene of another accident on the bridge on Damen Avenue just south of Diversey Avenue. This time a motorcyclist hit his highway peg on the curb and lost control of his bike. He flew over the handlebars and skidded, face-first, over the jagged metal grate. His face was shredded away to his ears, leaving blood, muscle, tissue, and bone exposed. The cops searched his motorcycle for identification and found a trophy in his saddlebags from the rally, "Hey, at least he won best of show," one of them hooted.

Another time, we were called to check on an old woman who had not been heard from in several days. She had been dead for some time before we arrived, and there was a chunk of flesh missing from her thigh and her lower left arm had been chewed off. A low, steady growl came from the pantry. I looked at my partner and stepped back. As we both unholstered our guns, the dog appeared with the woman's arm in his foaming mouth. He dropped the arm, howled, and then lunged at us. My FTO shot him dead with one shot. We later joked about reporting the incident as an armed robbery.

One day in the fall, Lucky and I responded to a call of "shots fired" at 20—North Wolcott Avenue. When we arrived, we met a young man on the sidewalk who was shaking and barely coherent. He told us that he and his friend were watching the Bears and Packers game when his friend said, "You wanna see something cool?" He pulled out a .38-caliber revolver from under the couch, placed it against his temple, and pulled the trigger. We went inside and saw a blood-splattered wall and the victim with an eye hanging out of its socket. The responding sergeant came in, saw that the television was on, and asked, "Who's got an eye on this game?"

These stories made for plenty of gallows humor during roll call.

The holidays were usually reserved for domestic problems.

On Thanksgiving we responded to a call at 32— West LeMoyne and arrived to find a man with a six-inch knife stuck through his left hand. He wanted the turkey breast. She wanted sex. There was no compromise.

On Christmas an angry Puerto Rican woman wrapped a string of Christmas lights around her sleeping, drunken husband, turned them on, and then poured a cauldron of scalding hot water on him. The white plastic melted into his skin.

Witnessing death so frequently I found it best to shut off my emotions. I started questioning the existence of God after seeing all the monstrous things humans do to one another. It also made me question the type of world I was living in when someone gets shot for wearing the wrong colors or innocent children are caught in gang cross fire. A Catholic-school education indoctrinated me to believe that I should accept God without question, but now I needed answers. How could the benevolent God I had learned about as a kid let this shit happen to his creations? It's simple, I told myself as I reflected on my past, remembering the connection my cousin Angel had made with God when he was abusing me: there is no God. If there were, God wouldn't have let that happen to me.

The smell of death got into my leather jacket, my shirt, and my pants. I retired the jacket for three months in an attempt to get rid of the stench. The stench never went away and I never wore the jacket again, discarding it along with my belief in God.

I didn't seem to be able to escape death. It was always just a radio assignment away. I'd seen it before becoming a cop—as my great-grandmother had been lain in a casket surrounded by the warmth of my family. I was five years old or so and didn't understand the complexities of the life cycle, but I knew that her death had come at the end of a full life. Now, in this job, I witnessed death taking on horrible new forms—bullet wounds to the head, charred bodies (affectionately known by cops and medical personnel as "crispy critters"), mangled masses of flesh in auto wrecks—and there was no end to it. One thing was certain: if death wanted you, it took you.

Early one morning my former FTO was responding to a 10–1 (officer needs assistance) and sped to the scene when his squad car went airborne and wrapped itself around a tree. He was ejected from the car and was later found a hundred yards away from it. He was DOA. Here yesterday, gone today—that was the only thought that registered in my mind when I saw his corpse at the wake. The one lesson his death taught me was that death did not discriminate. The more I saw death, the closer it seemed to me. It had taken my FTO and my motorcycle-riding buddy, Comet, so I had to ask myself what protected me from it. As I put on my uniform at the beginning of each shift, I wondered if death would come for me that day.

Death was everywhere. I was tied down to a radio and had little freedom to do real investigations except when I worked with Lucky, but there was a price to be paid for working this way, and after a while, our effort didn't seem worth the trouble. Who exactly was I serving? Who was I protecting?

I knew I needed to escape the ominous presence of death and the mundane routine of listening to a police radio. I made sure I fulfilled all the requirements of my job. I wrote my quota of tickets for each twenty-eight-day period—thirty movers and parkers—making sure the city was getting a good return in revenues for their investment in me as a cop. I also wrote up a slew of other verifiable incidents—curfew violations, dog-bite cards, bus checks—and I remained aggressive on the street working with Lucky. Meanwhile, I was showing more promise with my pen. I was schooled by veterans in the fine art of case-report writing; I could make trifling misdemeanors sound like heinous felonies. Well-written reports equaled trials and convictions, which equaled court time for me, which equaled overtime. I was making good money and throwing a lot of people in jail. Still, after my second anniversary as a cop, my desire to get out of the District intensified.

Every piece of paper with a RD (records division) number proved productivity, and I was being productive. I believed that supervisors would notice my hard work, which would result in my promotion to a unit. When I talked about this to some of my colleagues, it made them laugh. "It's not what you know, but who you know," they told me.

Working with Lucky allowed me to focus on why I wanted to be a cop in the first place. Aside from enjoying the fringe benefits, deep down I still believed I could serve the community as a cop by making streets safer, helping to rid them of guns and drugs. I thought I'd have to be in a special unit that focused specifically on gangs or narcotics to accomplish that desire. I wanted to go for the big criminals—the gun-toting, drug-slinging gang leaders, the Mercedes-driving drug kingpins, and the menaces to society who made it a challenge for kids to go outside and play. I knew what it was like to grow up with the fear of gangs, and I wanted to make things better for kids today. That chance surfaced while I was working with Lucky.

In the summer of 1992, an inner-department memo announced that the Organized Crime Division (OCD), Narcotics Section was seeking new blood. They wanted young, aggressive, streetwise cops. Those who spoke Spanish were preferred. I jumped at the opportunity. Envisioning a chance to make a much greater difference as a cop, I sent in my application and a letter of intent and then waited for a response. When I shared my desires with Ana, she supported me. Recently her brother had been detailed to the OCD Gambling Section. He had told us the benefits of working in a specialized unit. When he spoke of working straight days (8 A.M. to 4 P.M.) and having the weekends off, my interest grew even more.

I also badgered my father, who worked in the 23rd District and had twelve years of seniority under his badge, to pull some strings to help me get into Narcotics. Over his years, I reasoned, he must have made some power connections since he was on the tac team in his district for a brief time. When I asked him what he had to do to get there, he said, "I had to run around, like a chicken without a head, looking for trouble." My father and I rarely talked about what we saw on the job, but when I heard he had been on the tac team I found it hard to believe he was once an aggressive cop. I couldn't imagine him running after anyone.

"So what happened? How come you're back on the beat?" I asked.

"Once I got on the tac team I had to produce, but I wasn't going to compromise myself to stay there," he said flatly. He then told me stories of how other guys on his team inflated their productivity by making tons of disorderly conduct arrests or embellishing crimes with the stroke of a pen. That really didn't surprise me, as I had been guilty of some creative writing myself.

"Do you think working in Narcotics would be the same?" I persisted.

"I don't know. Why you wanna go there? Too many coppers get jammed up (in trouble) in that unit on money beefs," he warned me.

His words didn't sway me from my desire to get into Narcotics and make a greater impact. My growing apathy for the work I was doing in the District was directly connected to my feeling that I was not making a difference. I thought this chance was the opportunity to get out of my rut. I confided my desire to Lucky as well.

"Boy, you dreaming," Lucky informed me one night after we made a pinch for possession of crack cocaine. "Ain't no way in hell you gonna wind up at 3540 (South Normal Street, Narcotics Headquarters) without a Chinaman, and you ain't got no Chinaman."

In the structure and lingo of the Chicago Police Department, a Chinaman is someone in a white shirt (above the rank of beat cop) with heavy political pull—a person who could, with one word, make or break a cop's career. These Chinamen have done nothing illustrious to gain such prestige; their power comes from their connections to people in high places.

I didn't know anyone on the job who had rank, but I maintained my resolve. I was convinced that the Department rewarded diligent cops. The Narcotics Unit had been a clandestine operation during its nearly twenty-year existence. It had only fifty cops, but I had heard the unit was planning on more than doubling its size. I figured there had to be a spot for me. A few months later, I was granted an interview.

Commander Paul Manikowski and some of his top administrators interviewed me, and I thought it went well. But while visiting their headquarters I didn't see one cop even close to my age. All the cops were veterans and many looked like they were days away from retirement. The majority of them were white, and they all seemed too square to work the street-drug scene successfully. Obviously a spot in this Unit was a reward for those with seniority or granted at the behest of a Chinaman. But how effective were Narcotics officers when it came to fighting drugs? Maybe the huge expansion of the Unit was designed to address this issue. Whatever the reason, none of it made sense to me. I just shrugged my shoulders and left it up to fate. Hey, at least I tried.

Two days before the end of the period, I was called into the watch commander's office after processing two car thieves. Captain White told me, "Juan, I don't know who the fuck you know, but you'll never have to shave again, you lucky fuck."

I had no idea what he meant. Was I being dumped to the deuce, the 2nd District and home of the Robert Taylor Homes, or transferred to another district? My face must have given away my confusion.

"Go check the transfer order, Juan," White told me with a smile on his face.

I went to the front desk and saw Lucky, who gave me a shit-eating grin. "You ain't got no Chinaman, huh?" I stared at the transfer order and couldn't believe my eyes—I was going to Narcotics. To this day I don't know who pulled the strings. I was finally going to make a difference by becoming a part of the war on drugs.

16

WELCOME TO PARADISE

I REMEMBER WALKING THROUGH the door marked "City of Chicago Colleges" dressed in the shabbiest clothes I had and a five-day growth of beard on my face. I was ready to take on the drug world. Excited to prove myself and prepared to do whatever it took, I sauntered up the flight of stairs to the Narcotics Unit like a badass. I was not willing to let anyone know how nervous I was. The unit was sequestered in a rundown, nondescript brick two-story building at 3540 South Normal Street. It didn't look like a police station. It was the end of summer.

I was twenty-five years old and full of attitude. "My name's Juarez. I've just been transferred here. I'm supposed to report to Sergeant Moore," I told the gaunt, bespectacled veteran at the desk at the top of the stairs. "Could you direct me to his office?"

He eyed me conspicuously over his plastic bifocals, "How many years you got on the job, office?"

I didn't think it mattered, but I answered anyway, "Two."

"You must have some pretty heavy clout to be down here, boy," he said.

"I'm an exception. Hard work got me down here," I replied half-jokingly. I knew someone had to have pulled some strings to get me here, but I had no clue who it had been.

He rocked back in his chair and laughed so hard I could see his bridgework. "That's a good one," he said, continuing to laugh and shake his head. "Sergeant Moore's downstairs, ready to teach all you newcomers about the dope game. Go down the stairs, open the door on the right. It's the first classroom on your left. You got that?"

I thanked the old man, ignoring his condescension, and headed down the stairs with an extra bounce in my step. I knew I'd like this place. It was undercover, and I was now a part of it.

Whenever I'd seen Narcotics officers come into 14, they'd take over some prisoner-processing rooms, keeping their mission a secret, and get down to business. They had their own supervisors, investigations, undercover cars, and special radios. They were doing super-secret undercover work. The unit had an enigmatic aura because not many of us knew what they were up to.

It was a small unit; as it turned out, I was part of the largest transfer order in the Unit's history. Over a six-month time frame the 50-member staff was bolstered to 120 members as all the SNIP (Street Narcotic Impact Program) teams from every area and some handpicked district officers were to supplement the existing personnel. I was in the last batch of the new cops transferred in. (See "The Dirty Truth by the Numbers" on page 286 for more information.)

Entering the classroom, I was floored by what I saw. First of all, nobody had apparently paid any attention to the regulations about hairstyle. I saw before me an ocean of hair—dreadlocks, long hair, braided hair, Fu Manchu mustaches, goatees, and mutton-chop sideburns. The rest of the coppers in the room had haggard and hard faces, deep creased with experience. They had obviously served their time on the streets. I was, by far, the youngest one in the room, and that fact inflated my already-expanding ego. I wasn't just a cop anymore—I was in Narcotics.

"All right, ladies," a middle-aged black officer with salt and pepper in his thickening stubble announced. "I'm Sergeant Moore. I'm here to instruct y'all on the finer points of this unit." Everyone began taking seats, and I quickly found one near the back of the room and took out a small notepad. I felt apprehensive and a bit out of place. When I looked around I saw not a single familiar face. As I scanned the room again, I noticed that three quarters of the coppers were black. There were a couple of tall and lanky black guys who looked like drug addicts in the corner, some hipper guys who could easily pass for rappers sat up front, and next to me a rough-looking crew of muscle-bound cops were taking their seats. This was a far cry from the day I came to interview when all I saw was white faces everywhere.

The elder statesman stood at the lectern and began the presentation with some basic details that I began writing down: the name of the officer in charge of distributing equipment and money for buys, the name of the boss's secretary, and a catalog of sergeants and lieutenants. Then he listed the timekeepers, the ones who record vacations and comp hours, and all the coppers riding the desks. Lock-up and prisoner-transportation processes were also included in our list of people and things to know. My hand couldn't keep up when he began the procedures to get and register a CI (confidential informant), so I put away my pad and listened. He warned us, "CIs are dirty, drug-using fiends, always scheming up ways to rip anyone off—just make sure it don't happen to you. And never, ever let a CI out of your sight when you work with one or else you might find yourself knee-deep in shit." He was pacing the room but now he stopped at the lectern. "CIs are like your child, they's your responsibility. Keep 'em on a short leash."

I was feeling overwhelmed by the flood of information, so I raised my hand. "I see we got someone here with a question," Sergeant Moore declared, as he walked over to the frosted window. Everyone in the assembly room turned toward me expectantly. "Well, go on, we ain't got all day," he snapped.

"I was wondering how we're supposed to remember all this?" I asked, expecting him to say they had printed handouts or something along that line.

He smiled and nodded his head. "You will remember what is useful, son." He sounded like a Zen master who never answers a question and instead allows the student to find the answers on his own. I looked around the room and saw everyone shaking their heads as if it was the dumbest question ever asked. I still didn't have the answer I needed when Moore offered, "All you hafta do is ask anyone up here. They'll either tell you or direct you to someone who can. Don't worry." Shortly after, the first half of class ended, and we were given two hours for lunch with the admonition, "Don't fuck up on your first day by coming back late."

I got up with the rest of the room to leave, when I felt Sergeant Moore holding me in his gaze. I turned my head and, sure enough, he was looking at me. "Can you remember that?" he asked. The bustling room busted out in laughter.

"Yeah, Sarge, I can remember that," I replied. "You did say three hours, didn't you?" Everyone in the room whooped and hollered.

"Two hours, smartass," he shot back with a grin on his face.

A two-hour lunch? I was used to a measly half hour. Man, I thought to myself, this unit was getting better every minute.

A lot of cops lingered in the room, getting to know each other or renewing friendships. I took the opportunity to make connections as well. I got some shit for my age, but then I met someone from Public Housing North who knew my dad. He was in a group of ten officers who were all present in the orientation and they invited me to join them for lunch. We hit a local Italian fast-food joint on Thirty-first Street and the name-dropping began.

"You know Calabrese, the lieutenant from 17? His whole tac team's down here," the cop at the head of the long, narrow table offered once we were settled into our seats.

"No shit," someone responded. "You know the deputy chief who got shot?"

"Murphy? You talkin' 'bout Joe Murphy?" the cop next to me said as he tried to manage an enormous cheeseburger that was dripping grease.

"Yeah, from the North Side. Got shot in the seventies."

"That's the one."

"His kid's down here. Seems like if you take a bullet, your family gets life privileges on the force."

"How about Suarez and Manriquez?" the cop across from me said as fries disappeared into his mouth. "Looks like their PR (Puerto Rican) connection in city hall pulled some strings."

"They haven't worked a damn day since they got on the job," a black veteran noted, biting into his Italian beef.

"Neither have you," the cop who knew my dad replied laughing. "Looking at your big, black fat ass, I could tell you never got out your car." Everyone laughed, but it was all in good humor.

"Only for food, only for food, my friend," the black cop replied as he passed a napkin across his lips. "And if it weren't for your damn cousin, your white ass would still be pushing a pen."

I listened in amazement as they continued to discuss cop families and power connections, who knew which politicians, and who was whose Chinaman all through lunch. Everyone at the table seemed to be well connected. Then their attention focused on me.

"Hey, Juarez," some guy from the 12th District asked while I was chomping on a slice of pizza, "who's your connect?"

"I don't know," I said. That reply started the second round of ribbing at my expense, but it also made me start thinking. Was it Mark, Ana's brother, who pulled the strings for me? He didn't have any rank and just because he was in a special unit didn't mean he had clout. I couldn't spend too much time pondering that issue because the laughter had died down and I knew I was going to get some real shit now.

"You're twenty-five, in Narcotics, and don't know how the hell you got down here?"

I remembered how hard the cop at the front desk laughed earlier that day, so I repeated, "Hard work got me down here." The table erupted in laughter and cops pounded the table with their fists trying not to spit out their food. The ease with which their laughter came broke down whatever walls separated us.

"It don't matter who you know, you're down here now," my dad's friend told me when the laughter died down. "Enjoy it for what it is." The rest of the meal finished with more namedropping and humor until we had to return for the afternoon portion of the presentation. I returned to my seat in the back of the room, but now I felt more relaxed.

The second half was more interesting than the first because corruption was the topic. Sergeant Moore started off by informing us of the multitude of benefits that came with the job: plentiful overtime, flexible work schedules, departmental covert vehicles, weekends off, and connections to unique side jobs. "Hell, one guy here runs security for Michael Jordan," Moore proclaimed.

I thought back to Edgar and how easy it was for him to make all those connections. Cops are afforded introductions into worlds the regular civilian isn't. I found out that a gun and a badge make it easy to get plugged into the powerful political grid that makes Chicago run. It's up to the individual cop to take those connections as far as possible.

Moore looked around the room, nodding his head in satisfaction. "I see a bunch of y'all already know we ain't got no uniform or hair regulations. That's good; you'll fit in. And if you stay here," he paused, giving a thread of fear time to run through us, "keep using what's workin' for ya. This spot's treated me kindly over my twenty-odd years down here, but I got to warn y'all," a hush fell over the room and everyone lifted their heads to hear this, "IAD (Internal Affairs Division) will pounce on you faster than a rabbit fucks if you tip the till in your pockets or even think 'bout scratching some inventoried seizures."

I had already seen IAD in action. Some copper in 14 was taking ten-dollar bribes on traffic tickets, so they sent in an agent with marked money and caught him three times in one night. He was taken to the station, relieved of his gun and badge, handcuffed, and taken away—in his uniform.

"IAD is watching you," Moore continued. "Don't fuck up and be driving up to work in no fancy, new automobile. That's a red flag, for sure. I suggest takin' a different route every day when you come to work, because IAD are tricky motherfuckers. One thing you don't wanna be up in here is predictable."

What the hell was this shit? I had envisioned this as a permanent assignment and just as I was coming to grips it may not be, he threw this IAD crap at us. Now I knew I was deep undercover, and I definitely didn't want to do anything to jeopardize my new status. I was going to find a different route every day, that's for sure.

"Corruption be a huge problem up here, and I can't say enough against it. So I'm gonna show you a little film called *Prince of the City*, which'll give y'all something to think about." Moore walked over and snapped off the lights.

The movie followed a group of narcotics specialists in New York City during the Knapp Commission corruption investigation in the early 1970s. These princes were a ruthless bunch of thieves, busting down the doors of drug dealers under the pretext of serving search warrants all the while snatching the drugs and money for themselves. They divided the cash equally and sold the drugs to dealers throughout the city. All the specialists were living the high life, driving new cars, living in houses in well-to-do neighborhoods, and keeping their wives in diamonds and furs. But one day, a copper on the team volunteered to rat on his Mafia connections, which, in the long run, put the spotlight on all the princes. They fell, one by one—a few went to jail and some committed suicide, but whichever way they fell, the game was over.

When the movie ended, Moore hit the lights and warned, "I hope this shit don't happen to none of ya. Cops ain't liked in jail. There's 120 of y'all up in here, an' I hope it stays that way."

So ended our first day in the unit.

The ominous warnings about getting booted out of the Unit and Moore's constant references to IAD had a deflating effect on my enthusiasm. If I wanted to stay in the Unit, I had to find out who my Chinaman was and whether his clout was strong enough to make me feel secure in Narcotics. IAD was another story. They were going to do what they wanted when they wanted, and I wasn't about to give them any reason to follow me. As I drove home however, I couldn't help checking my rearview mirror for suspects.

17

OPERATION IRON WEDGE

AFTER MY FIRST COUPLE OF WEEKS in the Unit, I learned that three levels of teams operated out of the bland building at 3540. Each level had its own lieutenant who worked directly under the unit commander. The lieutenants delegated the Unit's agenda down to the sergeants who had teams of six to eight officers.

The street-level teams were the bottom rung in the unit's pecking order. Street-level was where most of the newly transferred members, including myself, wound up. Our objectives were to hit street-corner dealers and crack houses in a blitz against the deadly crack epidemic that was spreading across America and mostly ravaging the inner-city areas. Street gangs had stepped in to supply the needy.

The street-level teams were part of the solution to this problem. These teams, strongly supported by SNIP members, were the cornerstones of Operation Iron Wedge. The desired effect of this operation was to drive a wedge between the sellers and the users, attacking both ends of the supply-and-demand business so that neither would get what it needed. For the past two years, SNIP had been working out the kinks in Iron Wedge's arrest procedures, surveillance methods, and courtroom ambiguities. By the time I was transferred to Narcotics, Iron Wedge was a pretty smooth-running operation.

Most of the street-level sergeants were former supervisors on SNIP teams and were transferred to Narcotics because they knew the intricacies of the operation. Each sergeant had developed the most efficient workday possible. Each had his own reward system for the crew. The extent and depth of unit perks depended solely on who your sergeant was. Some sergeants wanted to get the workday over as soon as possible. They'd hit the streets, get the required number of buys, and leave an hour or two before the shift ended. Other sergeants wanted to impress the administration and go above and beyond the work quota, which meant everyone worked a full eight-hour shift and carried out as many busts as possible.

Mid-level teams, a mixture of the old-school and newly transferred cops, were more covert and focused on illicit and subtle narcotics trafficking. The Postal Team dealt with contraband sent through ground shipping companies such as the U.S. Postal Service, FedEx, and UPS. Members of this team developed a good rapport with the shipping companies and were called when a suspicious package was located. The officers used dogs, X-rays, or whatever technology was available to check the packages. If a package contained drugs, one of the officers would dress up as a delivery person and make the delivery. They made an arrest as soon as the person to whom the package was addressed accepted it. The Airport Team dealt with drug parcels shipped through the airlines and worked closely with U.S. Customs. The Tavern Team focused on narcotics being sold in establishments holding liquor licenses and worked closely with the Liquor License Commission. The rest of the mid-level teams' primary concerns were obtaining and executing search warrants related only to the drug trade.

And then there were the Heavy Hitters—the long-term, high-level investigation teams manned by the vets. They worked exclusively on long-term operations, wire-tapping, inter- and intrastate drug movement, asset forfeiture, nuisance abatement, vehicular tracking, and other highly sensitive covert operations. They were so secretive about their work that the other levels weren't even aware of what they were working on.

Each team on each level was dynamic in and of itself. They had certain missions and their own bylaws, but one thread ran through the whole Unit, keeping it tightly bound. It was absolutely imperative that we maintain our code of silence. The code is something all cops are asked to uphold but it seemed all the more vital here. It was clear to all coppers in

Narcotics that what happened on the second floor of 3540 *stayed* on the second floor. Failure to follow this basic tenet could result in expulsion from the Unit.

Life on the second floor was great: short workdays, undercover vehicles, no uniform or hair regulations, tons of overtime, and flexible work schedules—all in a laid-back environment. I loved it. I didn't want to get sent back to the District. I was part of the elite War-on-Drugs team, and I would do whatever it took to stay there.

I fully supported the Unit's agenda because I knew from watching the news and reading the newspapers that crack had become a deadly epidemic. An inexpensive derivation of powder cocaine in a concentrated form, crack was easy for the home chemist to make. The basic ingredient—powder cocaine—is mixed with ammonia or baking soda and water and then boiled in a pot over a low flame until it thickens. The pot is removed from the flame and allowed to cool, producing a solid mass of crack. At this stage the mass is broken up in increments of tenths of a gram and readied for street distribution. There are many ways to consume crack—from shooting it up to snorting it—but the preferred method is smoking it in a pipe, which is how it got its name. When the rock is placed in a pipe and a flame held to the rock as a person inhales, a little cracking sound can be heard. The most appealing aspect of crack to the user is its price, as one-tenth of a gram in the 1990s could be had for ten bucks.

Crack was destroying lives. It created fierce new addictions and made criminals out of users who had to feed their habits. It was also destroying neighborhoods where kids played. Gangs were fighting each other in gun battles for selling rights and territories in many parts of the country. Hundreds of innocent kids were dying of wounds from errant bullets. This cheap and accessible drug was costing citizens of this country millions of dollars. More and more, cops were needed to fight the raging crack scourge. At least that's what I read in the papers, and I believed it. I was a cop and it was my job to help eradicate the problem.

The student in me wanted to learn about the enemy I was fighting, so I took it upon myself to learn about the history of cocaine in the drug wars. In 1986 the United States Congress passed a powerful tool to aid states in the War on Drugs—the Anti-Drug Abuse Act. The focus of this act was to prosecute the high-level drug dealer. The act began by distinguishing between crack and powder cocaine, which had previously been categorized as the same thing. The act defines a crack-cocaine dealer as someone who has in his possession five to fifty grams. It specified that the high-level dealer of powder cocaine *starts off* holding from five hundred grams on up to five kilos. This law made the distinction between cheap crack cocaine—a common street drug—and the much more expensive powder cocaine—a drug more common among middle-class users. Further, anyone caught selling any amount of crack cocaine (from .01 grams on up) to an undercover cop would be slapped with a felony charge that came with a mandatory prison sentence of one to five years. To get the same sentence for dealing powder cocaine, a person would have to turn five hundred grams over to a cop. This discrepancy was further amplified by the procedures that made up Operation Iron Wedge.

"Good morning, Sergeant Thomas," I said as I knocked on the door of a small cubicle off the main hallway at 3540. A slender black man was hunched over some papers, which he placed in a file cabinet when I entered. "My name's Juan Juarez. I've been assigned to your team and I'm reporting for duty, sir."

"Juarez," he said, smiling at me genially as he stood up to shake my hand. "My name's Billy, you don't hafta call me sir." Bill Thomas, a veteran of twenty years, was five-foot-ten, 150 pounds—thin as a rail. "Welcome to the team. Roll call isn't for another fifteen minutes. Let's go see Officer Marshall and get you a radio and a battery charger."

We left the cubicle and walked toward the back of the building, passing numerous arterial hallways, each housing four cubicles as small as the one I had just left. I imagined that each room within this sea of cubicles contained its own secrets. The hallways were bustling with undercover cops, many of whom I had seen at my orientation. We entered a larger cubicle and Sergeant Thomas introduced me to the commander's secretary and the timekeepers. Crossing the hall, we met the unit's bursar, Officer Marshall, who had me sign out a radio, a battery charger, and a raid jacket that was exactly like the ones FBI or DEA field agents wore on television—a navy blue Windbreaker with bold white lettering on the back that read *CPD Narcotics Section*. My pride swelled as I received these tools of the trade.

"Come on," Sergeant Thomas said, leading me to the rear of the building where the lockers were, "you can put your things in here. We got to get to roll call." As we walked to the front of the building we heard an announcement over the intercom: "Iron Wedge roll call." The main hallway flooded with cops coming out of their cubicles, heading toward the assembly room up front. We joined the stream.

"Good morning, everyone," Lieutenant Pushman, who led the street-level teams, began. "All teams had a productive day yesterday according to the twenty-four-hour sheets. Mackey's team got three guns off the street, and Taylor's seized ten grams of crack. Keep up the good work." I looked around the large assembly room. There were two holding cells in the far corner. I saw some stragglers trying to sneak into roll call.

"Roll call's at ten sharp! That means everyone!" Pushman said as one of the tardy cops started to say something. "No excuses, so keep your lips zipped, Jones." The offender sheepishly smiled and didn't try another word. "We have some new faces in the room. I'd like to welcome you to the Unit. Those are the nicest words you'll hear from me."

A voice in the room agreed with him, "You sure right 'bout that, boss."

Pushman ignored that remark and continued. "Grazer and Green, your team's heading to Area 5 today. Make sure you hit the west end of Division. Twenty-Five keeps getting lots of complaints about that area. Taylor and Holmes, go to Area 3. Thomas and Abernathy, you guys go back to Area 1 and do something about Forty-seventh and St. Laurence, will ya? Mackey and O'Sullivan, get to Area 4 and target the north and west ends." Pushman looked around the room, "Are there any questions?" No one said a word. "All right then, be careful and remember I'm on the radio." Groans came from everyone. Sergeant Thomas tapped me on my shoulder, signaling me to follow him back toward the cubicle.

When we got there, the tiny cubicle was full of people from my new team. Two were sitting on the desks, another two were sitting in the only chairs in the room, and the rest were standing around the doorway. "Who's the young pup?" asked a black woman in her fifties with a muscle-toned body. Thomas began introducing me to my new team. The three officers who were assigned to make undercover purchases of crack were SNIP veterans. They were Colette and T.J., both nearing retirement, and Nica, a college student in her late thirties. The rest of the cops in the room were enforcement officers who were assigned to make the arrests, do paperwork, and handle prisoner transportation. There was Bill, a veteran who was once assigned to the mayor's detail and was now nearing retirement; Javier, a medium-built Mexican officer from the 12th District with a slight paunch in his early forties; and Mickey, an athletic Asian officer a few years my senior.

"Weren't we supposed to get Franco this period?" Javier asked.

"He's still on furlough," Thomas replied.

"Franco Delgado?" I asked.

"Yeah, that's him," Javier said. "Why? You know him?"

"I play hockey with him," I said, happy to have previously met someone on this team of otherwise complete strangers.

Thomas interrupted us, "I got paperwork to do, so let's meet at Area 1 at noon." The room started emptying out. I looked at my watch; it was 10:30. An-hour-and-a-half lunch sounded good to me and would give me time to get acquainted with my teammates. As I turned to leave, Thomas said, "Juan, you're riding with Mickey. You need to learn the paperwork."

Mickey tapped me on the shoulder, "C'mon, we need to get two inventory books and some evidence bags."

I started to walk out of the office with him and hesitated, "Wait one second, Mickey, I have to ask the sergeant something."

"I'll get the stuff. Just meet me here in five minutes. I have to show you what we need to bring with us." Mickey left the cubicle.

"Sarge, I need to ask you a favor."

"First day here and already asking for favors," he said, shaking his head. I didn't know how to respond. "I'm just messin' with ya, Juan. What do ya need?"

"I go to grad school at DePaul and have classes every Tuesday night. They start at five and I know we work until six."

"A schoolboy. Well, I'll be," he said, looking me up and down. "Don't worry 'bout it. We should be long gone by then. But if for some silly reason we're not, just remind me and I'll cut you loose."

"What do I have to do, give you a slip for two hours?" I figured I'd have to give up two hours of compensatory time for this favor.

"Nah, no need do that. I'll cover you on the sheets." He grabbed a file from the desk and then left the office saying, "I'll see you at Area 1."

Mickey returned to the cubicle and pulled out a large plastic box from underneath one of the desks and opened it, taking out some folders. He began replenishing the folder in the box with papers from the file cabinet.

"We need some arrest reports, witness statements, complaints, case reports, and CAR (contact arrest reports) forms." I noticed that many of the forms were preprinted with some blanks in the middle of the narrative. I asked him about that. "Saves us time. Everyone arrested in this operation basically gets the same charge—delivery of a controlled substance. If they're holding, they also get a possession charge. The only thing that varies is the weight and ESV (estimated street value). So we can expedite the process by having preprinted arrest forms and complaints because the narrative stays the same except for that information. Here's a chart for finding the ESV." He gave me a sheet that had various weights of crack cocaine and their respective street values: .01 gram was valued at $13.68, .02 doubled the price, .03 tripled it, and so on.

"What about powder cocaine?" I asked.

"We don't come across that too much up here, but if we do, just call the front desk and they'll give you the information. Same thing for heroin."

"Who does the case reports?" I asked.

"The buy officers. We get cut after they're done, the prisoners are in lockup, and the dope's been logged in and dropped. That's the last step. The first step is to complete one of these." He handed me a CAR form.

"And who fills these out?"

"The enforcement officers. Each prisoner getting escorted into the processing area comes with one."

I picked up a complaint and noticed they were all assigned to Felony Court. "Everyone busted for delivering or possession of crack gets a felony charge?"

"Each and every one," he stated. "It don't matter what amount they sell, it's a felony. That's why it pays to be a case officer. Our names are on every case report, along with the arresting and buy officers. Our appearances are needed in court and overtime keeps adding up, especially on the 9:30 A.M. call."

"So we get nothing if we go to the afternoon court call?"

"Yeah, we get to leave work early to go to court, and when court goes beyond six, which happens a lot, we start making OT." Mickey completed replenishing the folders, threw them in the box, and took a Polaroid camera and film from another drawer.

"What's that for?"

"Every arrestee gets photographed twice and their pictures get attached to the packet so we can remember who they are when we go to court. We arrest tons of people in this operation, so it pays to have something to jar the memory, especially if the case goes to court months after the buy," he said as he closed the plastic box and we began walking toward the front of the building. He stopped at the top of the stairs and pointed to a small iron safe attached to the floor. "This is the safe we put the dope in and here's the log." A clipboard hung over the safe. "You need to make sure the cylinder goes around and drops the dope in the safe. The inventory information goes on the log. It's the case officer's duty to do this, so listen up. If there's a mix-up, IAD'll come looking for you."

I followed Mickey down the stairs, overwhelmed by all the information I was getting. I pictured IAD taking me away in cuffs just because I made a silly mistake. Fucking IAD was quickly becoming my worst nightmare.

Outside as we approached a 1985 Cutlass, I asked, "Is this yours?"

"Nope," he told me throwing the plastic box in the trunk. "It's an undercover car. Since we're partners, we'll have to alternate who takes it home every period. It's mine for the rest of this one. Juan, where do you live?"

"Near Western and Roscoe; why?"

"Because I live by California and Montrose. If you want, I can pick you up every morning so you don't have to drive your personal car down here."

Yet another perk dropped right into my lap.

Mickey and I went to a Chinese restaurant on the outskirts of China-town and enjoyed an hour-long meal. When we got to Area 1, he showed me how to gas up the undercover car using the vehicle's four-digit ID num-ber that identifies it as a city vehicle. "You can get gas at any city pump with this number. Make sure you remember it."

We headed over to the parking lot, and I was introduced to Sergeant Abernathy and his team. Under Abernathy's supervision were Roland and Vicki, two black buy officers and SNIP vets, and Milli, a white female buy officer. Abernathy's five enforcement officers were: the Russian, Sam, Terry, Link, and Moses.

Sergeant Thomas arrived and held a discussion with Abernathy. They then assigned some areas for the buy officers to check out and headed out to the streets. Because Mickey and I were the case officers, we stayed behind and went to the second floor of Area 1 where the investigative ser-vices offices were located. Mickey talked to some violent-crimes detectives and began setting up our processing center in a room they assigned to us.

This is how Operation Iron Wedge worked: the buy officers scouted tips from communities whose residents were sick and tired of the drug traf-ficking in their neighborhoods. These residents called the 1-800 crack hot-line to lodge official complaints. Since these were public complaints, they got first priority. When the tips didn't pan out, the buy officers would cruise the known hot spots. When they saw a dealer, the buy officer notified the sergeant who assigned another buy officer to set up as the "eyeball." The eyeball's job is to give a radio description of the suspect complete with clothing style and colors, hairstyle, shoes, and other identifying factors. The eyeball gives a play-by-play account via the radio of the transaction until the transaction ends and the offender is in custody.

Once the eyeball is in place, the buy officer approaches the spot, engages the suspected dealer in conversation, makes the transaction, and then returns to the covert vehicle. The buy officer drives away, radios for enforcement if it was a positive transaction, describes the denomination of the currency spent in the transaction (complete with serial number), and informs enforcement who to pick up for the deal. Sometimes another person on the street guides the buy officer to the spot, and sometimes the money is passed off; both of those people can be arrested for delivery of a controlled substance even though they didn't actually make the deal but only facilitated it.

The enforcement teams, usually six to eight officers who are situated around the perimeter of the spot, then move in to arrest the suspect(s) and take them into custody. Then the buy officer slowly drives by to positively identify the suspect(s) as the one(s) who made the transaction. As soon as the arrestee is positively identified, two Polaroids are taken and the enforcement teams began a search for the 1505 funds (the marked money used in the transaction) because those funds are essential to the case. (Once they are found, whatever additional money the dealer has commingled with the marked money is confiscated and inventoried. The seized money reveals just how profitable the drug trade is. Once the court case is over, all the money, both marked and unmarked, comes back to the Unit. Laws give Narcotics the power to fuel the war chest, and the Unit has thousands upon thousands in confiscated money at its disposal to use in the War on Drugs.) Possession of 1505 funds guarantees a conviction because if the arrestee has this money, then he or she had to be involved in the transaction.

The handcuffed arrestee remains in an enforcement car until the next drug deal has been completed, which can take up to an hour or so. Then the arrestee is taken in for processing, which usually takes two to three hours. During that time, they are under the supervision of the intake team as the paperwork is being completed. Once it is done, the handcuffs are finally removed, and the arrestee is turned over to lockup keepers. When the last arrestee is in the lockup, all that remains is for the case officer to return to 3540 to drop off and log the dope.

The next morning, there is a probable-cause hearing to gauge whether or not the state has enough evidence to proceed with the case. This is based strictly on the strength of the case report; neither the case officer nor the buy officer has to be present as the state's attorney levies the charges against the suspected crack dealer.

Narcotic Iron Wedge cases are rarely lost because, as any convict who has been tried for one can tell you, a hand-to-hand delivery case to an undercover police officer is nearly impossible to beat. When probable cause has been established, the suspect, depending on his prior record—and it is likely that the arrestee has a prior record—is remanded into custody to await trial in the comfort of a jail cell.

When the case finally goes to trial, if a plea agreement has not been reached, the arrestee is usually found guilty. According to the statutes of the law regarding crack cocaine, these felons are sentenced to a minimum jail sentence of one year behind bars. (See "The Dirty Truth by the Numbers" on page 286 for more information.)

18

OPERATION ALTGELD GARDENS

THE BATTLE FOR CONTROL of the Altgeld Gardens Public Housing Complex on the far Southeast Side of Chicago had raged all summer. Row after row of single-family, two-level town houses, surrounded by immense swaths of barren earth sprinkled sparsely with grass, made up this community. Composed of 1,500 units, the project encompassed more than 157 acres of city land. The Gangster Disciples and the Vice Lords waged a bloody war for drug-selling rights in this community. With sixty people wounded and twelve killed—many of them innocent bystanders—the gangs had virtually taken over the complex.

No one was safe on the streets of Altgeld Gardens as gunfire reports, screeching tires, and ambulance sirens blared through the summer air. Everyone except the drug-dealing gangbangers remained in their houses during the summer. The complex's streets, once filled with energetic and shouting children, had become eerily silent. And with the heat baking residents in their homes, tempers were rising. The residents wanted to know why the police weren't around in greater numbers.

"We need some police presence!" the residents of the community pleaded in August 1992. At the community meeting in Area 2 of the 5th District, department brass heard an earful. "We need to make these streets safe again so our children can go out and play! So that when the school year begins they can walk to school secure and safe! We need opportunities to offer these boys an alternative to joining gangs! We can't keep storing them in prisons and throwing away the keys! We need to offer them a better life than they're living now! We need to educate them that a life spent chasing money through selling drugs is a life full of emptiness! We need jobs in this community—real jobs! We need help from the city! We need help from the police!"

Later, in a private meeting of the brass in Area 2, there was a war cry, which was relayed to us by Pushman at a pep-rally-style roll call to kick off the special operation. "We're going to take these streets back for the community. We're going to rid the streets of these vicious killers, who have absolutely no regard for their own lives or the lives of others. We need to make the community safe, not just for the children, but for all the residents of Altgeld Gardens." The plan was made clear. "We get the gangbangers out of the complex—that removes the drug element. We get the drug element out of the complex—that removes the violence. The goal is simple—remove the gangbangers."

This was exactly what I wanted to get into. It was why I had come to Narcotics in the first place—to make the streets safer for whole communities. I envisioned a massive sweep and roundup of lowlife gangbangers. In my imagination, this sweep would be followed by a heroes' welcome from the residents of the community in question.

As a direct result of this meeting of the minds, Operation Altgeld Gardens was launched in late August. Narcotics sent in two Iron Wedge teams—about eighteen officers—to work the complex and make the buys, laying the groundwork for the cleanup operation. I was crestfallen to learn that my team wasn't chosen for this part of the mission. We would be participating in the roundup of crack-dealing gangbangers. The teams that were picked to lead Operation Altgeld Gardens were expected to wedge relentlessly, making as many buys as they could from as many individuals as possible.

The ruse used was that these individuals wouldn't be arrested on the day they sold drugs to the undercover officers. Instead, the individuals making the transaction would be stopped, questioned, and identified by the enforcement teams shortly after completing the deal. Once the offenders' personal information, verified by a photo ID, was written down on a CAR form and after a Polaroid picture snapped of them on the streets, they were released. During this time, the buy officer would pass by in a covert vehicle and positively identify the dealers via radio. If the crack dealers didn't possess a valid form of ID, they were driven home and a family member, friend, or whoever was there had to vouch for them. If nobody was home, the officers would have to trust that the offenders were giving them truthful information. A warrant for delivery of a controlled substance was typed up for each individual and then signed by a judge before he or she joined the ever-growing crowd of offenders that was to be rounded up on October 13, 1992.

The Bureau of Alcohol, Tobacco, and Firearms (ATF) began a coordinated gun-buying operation in this same housing project. This federal agency's aim was to infiltrate the gang operations by posing as out-of-town gangbangers seeking firearms. I was proud to be working alongside the feds.

Three weeks into the operation, Pushman informed us at roll call that the ATF guys weren't having much luck. He speculated that it was because the presence of so many outsiders in the Altgeld Gardens complex had made the gangbangers wary. Word had spread that some homies were getting stopped, identified, photographed, and then released immediately after turning a deal. They realized that something had to be up.

★ ★ ★

At 4 A.M. on October 13, 1992, the day of reckoning arrived. I stopped at a convenience store to buy a large coffee before picking up Mickey. I didn't know what to expect, but I wanted to be alert in case it turned out to be a long day. When we got to the 5th District, housed in Area 2, the desk and lobby area was buzzing with nervous anticipation. I stood in awe as I scanned the faces of the multiagency task force formed specifically for this predawn raid that I was part of.

There were members of the Chicago Police Department Narcotics Unit, Cook County Sheriff's Office, State of Illinois Police, Public Housing Police, and State's Attorney Enforcement Office as well as DEA (Drug Enforcement Agency) and ATF agents and a host of officers from the surrounding suburbs. Combined, these enforcement agencies brought together 320 officers, 250 vehicles and some paddy wagons, a command center in a Winnebago, a state helicopter, a pack of drug-detection dogs, and a group of local news reporters.

Our little army was assembled to serve thirty-two arrest warrants, the majority related to drug charges connected to the Narcotics operation. Doing some quick math, I figured that there were ten law enforcement officers for every offender. These offenders were wanted for selling a grand total of less than twenty-five grams of crack cocaine or heroin to undercover officers and some guns to ATF agents. Our supervisors were hoping for substantially more weight in drugs and the ATF wasn't happy with their totals either, but the promise of police presence and immediate productivity was part of our goal: to eradicate drugs and violence from the Altgeld Gardens community. This operation was to prove to the whole city and the Altgeld Gardens community that we could win the War on Drugs. We were going to take back Altgeld Gardens from the gangs.

My nerves were jumping as we congregated in the lobby of Area 2. I mingled with members of the various agencies as television cameras scanned the crowd and recorded images of the man power, the vast array of weaponry, and the different levels of preparedness necessary to complete this mission. I caught up with Mickey and Bill and we began joking about all the mini-Rambos in the room who were disguised as ATF and DEA agents. They were, without a doubt, the most heavily armed of the contingency, dressed in black fatigues, bulletproof vests, and a variety of holsters: ankle, over-the-shoulder, hip, and thigh. All were armed to the teeth and looked ready for war. It was overkill, but they were feds so we expected nothing less. Many of the other officers, most from the Sheriff's Office and Narcotics, were dressed in plainclothes and bulletproof vests. Many had only their service weapons.

Our cache of weapons for breaking down the doors consisted of crowbars, battering rams, and sledgehammers. Checking out the room again, I knew we were going to look pretty good on the nightly news and in tomorrow's newspapers.

The supervisors from all the agencies had been in a meeting and came out with team assignments and manila packets containing CAR reports and pictures of the wanted offenders. After a brief speech by the deputy superintendent, we reported to our respective sergeants and received our assignments. Our team, Sergeant Thomas's whole crew, was given one suspect and an alternate one, just in case we nabbed our guy quickly or he wasn't around for his early morning wake-up call. I was a little disappointed that we had only one target.

I was assigned to ride with Mickey, Bill, and Javier. I felt quite comfortable knowing my teammates were there with me. "Who's gonna work the ram?" Bill asked.

"I will," I immediately offered. The coffee was working its magic on me; I had more energy than I knew what to do with.

"Sure you can handle it?" Bill asked. "We don't wanna be waiting at the door with our dicks in our hands, junior."

"You better take some tweezers just in case, you old fuck," I shot back in good humor.

"Don't drop it on your foot, wee lad," he laughed.

We found our vehicle in the packed parking lot, got in with Bill behind the wheel, and fell in line toward the end of the convoy. "Hurry up and wait," Bill complained. "Who the hell orchestrated this snafu?" We moved at a snail's pace toward Altgeld Gardens with the searchlight-equipped helicopter lighting the way. The excitement of this early morning raid and the heavy caffeine intake played games on my nerves and began wreaking havoc on my stomach as we closed in on our target. This was the kind of shit I had only dreamed of. And now I was in the thick of it; I was ready to do some serious damage when we got to our target.

The convoy was extremely lengthy and we even had to stop a few times because the congestion was so thick. We listened keenly to the radio and I was disappointed to hear that as we were leaving the Area 2 parking lot, twenty-eight blocks away from our destination, the first cars were already entering the Altgeld Gardens complex. There wasn't shit we could do about it; we just had to wait in the traffic we had created.

Upon finally entering the complex, I was amazed at the chaos that I saw and heard on the radio. Although order and control had been stressed at the briefing, many teams had to keep asking for address verification as they inadvertently arrived at incorrect residences and forced entry into houses of innocent people. I saw other teams struggling with the steel doors. I had to keep reminding myself that it takes a well-placed hit from the battering ram to the lock cylinder to break the mechanism. If it isn't done correctly, the officer has to keep hitting the door, which rattles the whole house and gives inhabitants plenty of time to flush the dope down the toilets. Confusion even found its way into our car as Bill had taken the wrong turn, taking us farther from the target.

"Come on, crusty," Mickey poked, "I thought you knew where we were going."

"Relax gook boy," Bill shot back, sounding a bit peeved.

The momentary delay let me see the depths of confusion going on. Police officers were running all over the place, media personnel were shining their camera lights everywhere, the helicopter's spotlight was blindingly ineffective, property was getting destroyed, tranquil homes were being invaded, and innocent residents were getting roused out of bed wailing. The barking of dogs filled the air. "Bill," Sergeant Thomas said curtly over the radio, "Where are you guys? We're waiting."

We finally got to our target location. I jumped out of the car with the battering ram, ready to obliterate the lock on the front door as Sergeant Thomas and the rest of the team went to the back door. Mickey, Bill, and Javier were behind me with guns drawn, prepared to rush into the residence as quickly as they could to nab the offender. My heart was pounding in my ears as the first hit struck the cylinder, but the door didn't move a bit. "Fuck!" I yelled, pulling the ram back and hitting the door again and again until my arms became weak. Finally the door gave way and I let go of the ram, letting it sail into the residence with the force of the final swing. Bill, Mickey, and Javier all rushed in. A startled middle-aged woman in a robe, shaking in fear, stood on the stairs in the hallway. "What do you want?" she asked as Bill pushed her to one side and ran up the stairs. Mickey ran to the back of the house with Javier right behind him. I guided the woman to the couch and started questioning her as to the whereabouts of the offender who turned out to be her son. "He hasn't been home all night. Good Lord, look what y'all did to my door. What gives you the right?"

"Shut your yap," yelled Bill coming down the stairs. "Where's he at?" he demanded taking over the interrogation.

"I don't know, damn it! He just got up and left last night. That's all I know," she said, growing flustered by our presence and the noise of things breaking in the kitchen.

"No one's in the back of the house," said Javier as he came through the kitchen door to the front of the house.

"I done told y'all that he ain't here. What you want him for anyway?"

"Ma'am," Sergeant Thomas stepped in. "We're the Chicago Police, and we have a warrant for your son."

"Seems like your boy sold drugs to an undercover cop," Bill informed her, shoving the warrant under her nose.

"That's enough, Bill," Sergeant Thomas said. "I can handle it."

We talked to her for a moment longer and she gave us the address of her son's girlfriend in Indiana. "What about my door?" she asked before we left.

"Tell housing (Chicago Housing Authority) about it," Sergeant Thomas instructed as we left the house and began walking toward the cars. I felt the need to make up for my failed attempt at the door.

"No need to do that," Sergeant Thomas said. "Seems like word circulated last night about the raid, and everyone jumped into the wind. Lets head back to the Area."

Disappointed, I felt the caffeine lose its grip.

As the sun began to rise and we headed out of Altgeld Gardens, I noticed that the chaos had decreased. The law-enforcement groups were less frantic, the battering rams silenced, and the drone of the helicopter faded. The dawn illuminated the effects of the massive police presence: property thrown out of residences, doors hanging on mangled hinges, broken windows, and a few damaged police vehicles from the frenetic pace and confusion of the early morning raid.

Back at the Area we learned that we had captured 62.5 percent or 20 of the 32 targeted offenders. Later in the day, the deputy superintendent along with an official from the U.S. Department of Treasury claimed a victory in this battle for Altgeld Gardens and gave a long speech about how the community was safer now that the gangbangers were locked up. Not surprisingly, there was never any mention of alternatives for the youth nor was there mention of treatment for addicts or education about addiction. There was no mention of bringing in what the community needed because the city, state, and federal law-enforcement agencies had their own ideas. Enforcement and incarceration were the keys; these were law enforcement's only solutions. The authorities were convinced that this solution—with no involvement from any social service—would free the neighborhood from the threat of gangs.

The operation on October 13 provided the police presence the community was seeking, but this was not an indication of any long-term commitment. When a community calls for greater police presence, they are asking for marked squad cars and uniformed cops. This type of presence provides more security for the community and reduces the number of gangbangers and overall crime on the streets. This is what the community wanted. They were used to seeing unmarked squad cars driving around. Whenever a gangbanger saw a narc, they'd yell "Five-O" and everyone would disband, waiting until the unmarked car went around the corner before coming back out to continue their trade. This was the kind of police presence the city offered the community.

Later in my career, my team spearheaded two similar operations: one in the ABLA Homes (including Jane Addams Homes, Robert Brooks Homes, Loomis Courts, and Grace Abbot Apartments) on the Near West Side and the other at the LeClaire Homes on the Far West Side. Neither federal agencies nor the media volunteered their services for either of these operations. The ABLA Homes operation netted thirty-seven arrest warrants with twenty-seven arrests, with officers purchasing more than thirty grams of crack and seizing just over fifty grams on roundup day. We didn't have the expensive fanfare I saw on October 13, nor did we cause as much property damage. It made me wonder how orchestrated the Altgeld Gardens event was and how much it cost the taxpayers.

Something clicked in my head and made me start questioning why the unit was spending such a large portion of its effort in the poverty-stricken and minority neighborhoods of the city while ignoring white urban communities. The fact that we seldom worked the North Side made me realize that perhaps there was a different agenda behind this war on drugs.

19

MISTAKEN IDENTITY: WRONG PLACE, WRONG TIME

I WASN'T THE ONLY NEW GUY on Sergeant Thomas's Iron Wedge team. Also newly transferred was Franco, a guy whose reputation as a walking brutality beef preceded him. Everyone in the unit knew he loved to use a little extra muscle when he arrested people. Franco worked in 14 before I got there and the beatings he inflicted on gangbangers were legendary. He wasn't ashamed of the legacy he'd created. He even boasted about it.

Franco and I played defense together on the police hockey team, so I felt comfortable exchanging war stories about Disco 14 with him. But Mickey had told me he was a pariah in Narcotics and no team wanted him. Mickey surmised we were on the commander's shit list because our team got stuck with Franco.

"Squads, just some information out there for ya all: a heat warning's in effect," the citywide dispatcher informed us. There was no need to tell us; we could feel the sweat dripping from underneath our bulletproof vests. The bank's digital display read 87 degrees, but the heat index was nearly 100. "Is it hot enough out there for ya all?" the voice concluded.

Sergeant Thomas's team was conducting street buys in the area of Roosevelt Avenue and Central Park Boulevard during the early afternoon hours. The streets were teeming with neighborhood residents. I turned on the car's air conditioning and was met by a blast of hot, stale air.

The heat had put me in a foul mood or maybe it was what I saw that bothered me. I was shocked by the conditions of this neighborhood. There was poverty in 14, but it was nothing like this. Earlier in the day before the heat took hold, a foot chase took us through a chain of these rattraps, as the suspect kept ducking in and out of residences, entering open front doors and flying out through the back. The pursuit included questioning residents about the suspect's whereabouts. I'd had a painful glimpse of the reality of this West Side neighborhood.

Many of the apartments were tiny and squalid. Walls were stained with dirt and water damage. Windows with broken panes were stuffed with yellowed newspapers or bundled up plastic that let no light in. The kitchens were nasty. The stoves, sinks, and countertops were cluttered with unwashed dishes and spoiled food that left a putrid odor in the air. Grease was splattered everywhere and garbage was piled up on the back porches.

Then there were the people who lived in these hovels. The occupants were packed in, sleeping anywhere they could, usually on the floors or couches because any available rooms were used to hold piles of clothes, shoes, bicycles, or car engine parts. There was everything in the bedrooms except beds. I witnessed babies crawling on dirty floors that were nothing more than rotting wood. These conditions were common in low-income minority neighborhoods, the places we hit the hardest. I found it hard to believe people could live like this. Add the heat and humidity to the inherent frustration and tension stemming from living in such an oppressive environment, and the result could be deadly, changing an otherwise controlled operation into a lethal situation.

The heat drained me of energy, leaving my body and mind lethargic. Even the air conditioners in the Areas, normally our places of refuge, were ineffective against the stifling heat. As we continued driving around, I noticed people trying anything to keep cool. Women sat on porch stoops with their skirts hiked up fanning themselves; men, wearing tank tops, shorts, and sandals and draping wet washcloths on their heads, sat in folding chairs; and kids ran back and forth or stood in front of the thick ropes of water coming from open fire hydrants.

A controlled buy had taken place on the south side of Roosevelt, just west of Hamlin Avenue. After receiving a positive notification from the buy officer, all the floating enforcement cars converged for the arrest. One car approached from the west, another from the east, and a third from the south. It was a perfectly executed takedown even though one car—Franco's—was late in arriving on the scene.

We surrounded the suspect and quickly arrested him. In the rush of activity, a man who had absolutely nothing to do with the transaction but happened to be wearing the same color clothing as the suspect walked eastbound away from the scene.

There was an uproar from behind us, and we turned our heads toward its source. Franco and Javier had just arrived, and Franco had mistakenly identified the innocent man as the suspect. Javier stopped the car and Franco got out and charged at the man. He must not have had his radio on, or perhaps he flat-out disregarded the information that we had everything under control. Franco grabbed the guy and landed a left-handed slap followed by a right cross to the jaw. But he wasn't done just yet. He executed a leg sweep that brought the man down to the sidewalk. His final blow was a knee to the neck.

I was stunned. Franco's action was an open and blatant abuse of authority that made Locallo's beatings seem tame. And the growing crowd was there to witness every detail.

Sergeant Thomas, muttering obscenities under his breath, shook his head in disbelief. Franco, beaming proudly, escorted the man toward us. The crowd surrounded us and began to hurl insults. With every passing second the crowd got bigger.

"Motha fuckin' police, why the fuck you do dat?" demanded a woman in a voice full of outrage.

"Fuck da police, y'all ain't shit!" yelled an angry male teenager.

"Hey motha fucker, take off your gun and badge! You ain't nothin' but a pussy! Punk ass!" an incensed male voice screamed, which further incited the crowd. He continued. "Chickenshit!" The crowd sent up another wild cheer. "Bitch!" he spat out. A chorus of the same word rang out.

We stood with guns drawn, ready for the worst as the tension reached potentially explosive dimensions. I was scared as shit; the anger was as palpable as the suffocating heat. I could feel a river of sweat streaming down my chest as my breathing became short and labored.

"Listen," Sergeant Thomas said, straining over the din that was all around us, "you all need to go about your business."

"Hey, boss," the self-appointed ringleader began, "you know that shit weren't right. It just weren't right. That motha fucker over there," he hollered, pointing at Franco, "that fucker just whupped on that brotha for no fuckin' reason. That's bullshit!"

"It may be bullshit. But there are ways to see that what's right happens. And you all know the procedure," Sergeant Thomas responded calmly, as Franco continued past us with a smug grin.

"Ain't nothing gonna happen dat way," the ringleader continued. "The police always coming 'round here and beating and robbing whoever they want. An' nuttin' never happens to 'em."

"Fuck it, deys only eight of dem. What they gonna do to us?" yelled someone else from the crowd. The scene was about one second away from mayhem.

I still don't know how it happened, but Thomas somehow mollified the crowd, and we were able to walk away unscathed. Maybe it was because he was a black man in charge of seven enforcement officers. Thinking back, I don't know if we would have come out of there alive if we'd had a white sergeant. The volatility of race relations in the city and across the nation had skyrocketed in 1992, following the riots that came after the acquittal of the officers involved in the beating of Rodney King.

Franco appeared unfazed by the unfolding of events. He turned to the man he had just pummeled and yelled, "Get out of here!"

One of the onlookers yelled, "This is his damn 'hood, *you* get da fuck out!"

We heeded his advice and took the legitimate suspect to Area 4, at Harrison and Kedzie, for processing.

Thomas berated Franco in front of everyone on the second floor of Area 4. But that was the extent of the immediate repercussions. At the end of that work period, Franco was jettisoned from our team, but he somehow managed to stay in Narcotics. I guess Sergeant Thomas's clout wasn't as heavy as Franco's.

Franco never did change his tactics. He repeated the same malicious actions over and over again, but after that day he was careful not to do it in front of Sergeant Thomas. And though everyone viewed his behavior as a violation of the Officers' Code of Ethics, no one—including myself, OPS, or IAD—did anything about it. The pervasive code of silence was in effect. I wondered if my city's way of waging the War on Drugs was to create a crusade against blacks and poor people.

After spending one of my first few days in Narcotics and witnessing another senseless beating, I realized I needed an outlet to alleviate my on-the-job tension and confusion. I spent many of my nights after work in Ana's company before leaving for booty calls with Maria in Lincolnwood. Ana and I continued running together, but I could feel a distance growing between us. My relationship with Maria, who was satisfying my sexual needs, was growing stronger and stronger.

When Ana noticed my lack of attention, I blamed it on the demands of working in the ghetto. I made it sound as if the job was draining me physically. She suggested that we should both start competing in triathlons. She thought it would be one way I could exorcise the anxiety of work and increase my stamina. Ana knew what drove me—adrenaline in the heat of competition.

I visited the same store where I bought my mountain bike. Tim, the salesman, had become my friend. This time he hooked me up with a triathlon bike at cost. Tim, who went to UIC and studied archaeology, was an avid biker, heavy into single-track mountain biking. This is a sport in which a biker must dodge trees and navigate exposed roots, ruts, and stream crossings while descending down precipitous terrain. It requires tremendous agility and endurance. I asked Tim about it and he gladly offered to take me to Palos Hills Forest near Ninety-seventh and Archer. I fell in love with the sport almost immediately.

Ana's and my training regimen became more intense as we added biking and swimming to our running. I began biking in the morning, getting in an hour or two before Mickey picked me up. After work, I'd meet Ana at the lakefront for five- and six-mile runs, alternating that with swimming laps at a public pool near my house. I was pumped and primed; my body was becoming more toned and sleek. I focused on working out and succeeding in school. Working in Narcotics gave me the time to do it all.

★ ★ ★

One morning in early 1993, I had my own face-to-face encounter with the CPD's racial profiling. One of my noncop friends had started listening to gangsta rap. I had bought a copy of NWA's *Straight Outta Compton*. It featured one song in particular that I couldn't get out of my head. It was called "Fuck tha Police." It's an attack on the practices of inner-city police. It puts a cop on mock trial for harassing blacks and minorities for no other reason than the color of their skin. It was apropos in the wake of the Rodney King incident. I enjoyed the heavy bass and the lyrics, and soon I was listening to it every day on my way to work. It made me examine my role as a cop. I came to new insights about the hatred directed toward the police in the areas where I worked.

I had also bought a 1988 Mercedes 190E for $3,000. It came equipped with a badass sound system, silver and gold rims, and Perreli low-profile tires. But it also had heavy front-end damage from an accident. I took it to Nelson in 14 and got it repaired. He took care of me just as he'd promised he would the day I met him with Steve Tyler. When he finished his work, the car looked brand new and caught everyone's eye.

On the morning in question, with "Fuck tha Police" cranking and the sunroof open, I headed eastbound down Irving Park Road toward Lake Shore Drive on my way to work. I drove through the intersection on Ashland Avenue and was picking up speed when I passed two detectives in an unmarked squad. I caught their eyes and gave them a "what's up" nod. I knew they'd pull a U-turn and come after me because I'd had the nerve to look at them. I was sporting a shaved head and a goatee, not to mention that I was a minority in a Mercedes.

Sure enough, as I checked my rearview mirror, they sped up, got behind me, and threw on their flashing headlights. I pulled over immediately. I could feel their aggression as they got out of the car. The driver marched up to my door. His partner, with gun drawn, took his position along the passenger side of my car. I lowered the volume.

"License and registration," the cop to my left demanded. I had my badge in my hand, but I had a question for him before I showed it.

"What did I do wrong, officer?" I queried with a little cockiness in my tone. I had a badge and knew nothing was going to happen.

"Just gimme your damn license if you got one!"

I held up my badge and said the magic words that made him eat shit, "I'm a cop." He was crestfallen. Relishing the moment, I asked again, "What did I do?"

"Where do you work?" he replied. His partner came around the car for a closer look at my badge. He screwed up his face as he looked at it.

"Where's your ID?" he demanded.

"Right here," I said as I flipped my badge over and showed them my ID. "Can you tell me what I did?"

He looked quizzically at me, "Where do you work?"

"Narcotics."

"Damn! You sure fooled me," the cop confessed. "I, ah, well . . . you . . ." It was no use dancing around it, so he spit out the truth. "It was the car. It looks like a dope dealer's car."

"Nah, I'm just a cop," I said turning the volume back up. "Can I go to work now?"

He seemed a little disturbed by what was playing on the sound system, but he said, "Sure, sorry to stop you."

I sped away, thinking about how many minority drivers in nice cars are pulled over for no reason each day. Luckily, I had my badge and my ID. Without them I might have suffered the same fate as the man Franco beat senseless for the crime of wearing the wrong clothes.

20

IT'S JUST A NUMBERS GAME

ONCE THE DAILY ROUTINE of imprisoning young black men from the ghetto became overwhelmingly obvious, I had to take inventory of what I was actually a part of. Our team spent just about every day on the South and West Sides of the city, arresting four to ten people a day, five days a week. We put twenty to fifty young men in jail each week. I began to feel as if I was doing someone else's dirty work by fucking over minorities. I recalled how infuriated I was at age ten when I saw the realities depicted in the miniseries *Roots* and how indignant I was at sixteen when I read *Bury My Heart at Wounded Knee*. In college, I realized that the history I had been fed since grade school had been whitewashed. But now seeing the depths of poverty in the ghetto, I felt I had to ask Sergeant Thomas, "Why do we hit these depressed areas so hard?"

"Well," he responded dryly as we drove around Seventy-sixth and Phillips, "this department, including this here unit, runs on efficiency. The only way to measure that is by the number of arrests. Each unit needs to qualify its existence and prove to the communities that it's doing its job."

"Like the Altgeld Gardens operation?" I asked sarcastically.

"Something like that," he said. I understood this departmental answer, but I dug deeper because he didn't sound like he bought any of it.

"What about serving and protecting?" I asked. "To me, it's all about serving the fears of the North Side and protecting their property while providing the service of putting all the brothers on the South Side in jail. What happened to so-called desegregation? I mean, how come we never go to the North Side and spread the wealth of arrests?"

He looked at me, pursed his lips, and then shrugged his shoulders. "We do. Shit, we arrest your brothers (Latinos) when we work around Humboldt Park and Twenty-sixth Street. They get the shaft, too."

He knew damn well that I meant white folks. I already knew that Latinos and blacks made up the largest population in the prison industry throughout the country. "The question is: why do we keep shitting on people who've been shit on for the last four hundred years or so? They got nothing, absolutely nothing besides their ghetto living conditions, minimum-wage-if-they-get-one-at-all jobs, discrimination, and racist attitudes to deal with. And now we give them even more shit to deal with? What the fuck!"

He looked at me and waited. So I went on: "I mean, why can't the city or the Police Department offer educational services discussing the downfalls of drugs, some community outreach services for the kids, and some real fucking opportunities in the field of employment and education instead of little bullshit jobs and substandard education? Why is there a kind of hushed 'hands off' when it comes to the nice and neat North Side? Why the fuck are we always locking up minorities?"

"I see your education is making you think," he said wistfully.

"Courtesy of the damn department. Ain't that ironic?" I snapped at him.

"Juan, relax," he instructed. "I've worked for this department over twenty-nine years. When I first got down here in the 1980s we were told to work the districts populated mostly by blacks. Those are the same districts we work today. I once ventured out to 25 (a mostly Caucasian-populated district back then) for a change of pace and arrested fifteen white boys in one day. The next day I got called on the carpet and told, 'Don't be pulling that shit. You weren't assigned there. Go back and work the districts you're assigned to or you'll find yourself out of Narcotics!' So that put an end to that. Shit don't change; that's the way it's always been, the way it is now, and the way it'll always be. Don't lose any sleep over the injustices, you'll get used to them; it's all just a numbers game." (See "The Dirty Truth by the Numbers" on page 286 for more information.)

Here was a black man telling me, without emotion, about injustices being done to his people; that pissed me off even more! Did his quarter

of a century on the job kill whatever feelings he had toward his own race?
I was confused on so many points.

The appearance of a swarm of unmarked police cars on an unsuspecting
target sometimes resulted in a fight-or-flight response. The awesome power
of putting the fear of God into someone thrilled me immensely; often members of my team and I could accomplish this with just our presence. If there
was a foot chase (which I had loved participating in since my Disco 14
days) and the suspect was caught, the routine practice nearly every time
was to give him a beating—minor or major, depending on the mood of the
other enforcement officers. I didn't engage in physically tormenting suspects, but I reveled in the psychological aspect. Seeing the fear in the eyes
of the hunted was good enough for me. Other officers used the rationale
that after getting a beating, a suspect would think twice before running the
next time. And if the suspect wanted to fight instead, he'd always lose.
Man power was always in the cops' favor. I once tried to join in on a group
beating, but when I got punched in the head with some cop's brass knuckles, I decided to stay out of the fray from then on. Justifying this overly
aggressive use of force was simple—the suspect was either fleeing or resist-
ing arrest. It all depended on how the incident got written up on the arrest
report, but either way, the police made sure they were always in the right.

After either running or fighting, a suspect would find his wrists in
exceedingly tight handcuffs or shackled in thick, plastic ties with a strip of
wire in the middle. By pulling on the strap, these ties would magically
tighten, but then they'd have to be cut off the arrestee hours later and—
for some odd reason—it was always difficult to find wire cutters when they
were needed. I saw many arrestees with deep-to-the-bone indentations or
numbed extremities from the plastic handcuffs. My favorite trick, learned
in the unit and reserved for truly troublesome arrestees, was to apply the
handcuffs exactly where the hand met the wrist and then push the back of
the hand toward the wrist. It was amazing how cooperative the arrestee
became at that point.

Once they arrived at the processing center, their treatment didn't
improve. They'd be thrown into a dark, dank holding cell with the cuffs

still on and left there. If they had to use the bathroom, sometimes they were escorted to the john; other times they weren't. All these arcane procedures reminded me of torture tactics used in medieval times. This power was exhilarating but it often resulted in cruel and unusual punishment. Sergeant Thomas never spoke a damn word of protest and rarely put up boundaries. I liked my job, but seeing both the abusive behavior and my sergeant's apathy about it began to make me feel confused. I found myself wondering if there might be an ulterior motive behind Operation Iron Wedge.

21

OPERATION "RISKY BUSINESS"

ONE FALL DAY IN 1993 while working a large-scale Iron Wedge operation, our team was paired off with a mid-level team supervised by Sergeant
Henry Moore. Having had my orientation into the unit with Moore, I
wanted to learn a little more about his career in the unit. I spent the whole
day riding with him. All cops are full of stories and experiences—some
humorous, others insightful—and I made sure I listened to them all.

"Sergeant Moore," I said as I strapped on my bulletproof vest in the
front seat of our car, "while I was in orientation I heard you say you've
been in this unit for a few years, so how long has it really been?"

"Well, Juarez," he began in his light Southern drawl as we left the
parking lot of Area 4, "I first got down here in the late 1970s. I was
aggressive, you know, making drug pinches for marijuana an' cocaine,
when a boss (lieutenant) in my district approached me 'bout joining a citywide narco unit. He thought I'd make a good supervisor."

"So you'd already made sergeant by then?" I asked as we started
heading north on Kedzie from Harrison.

"Yeah, I made sergeant after three years on the job. I knew the paperwork an' had me a pretty good damn crew over in 3. But opportunities
rarely come twice, if they ever come at all in this department, so I jumped
at it. The unit was so tiny when I first got down here, Juarez, it would
make you laugh. Mind you, there weren't many, if any, blacks down here
when I came, so it was a little interesting working with all the white cops."

"There weren't any minorities down here? No Mexicans, no Puerto
Ricans?"

"Hell no!" He laughed and then exhaled through his nose.

"How'n the hell did you manage, sarge?" I heard from other coppers how it wasn't easy being a black cop at that time. They told me about fights between black and white cops in roll call that turned into dirty messes, sometimes with blood being spilt.

"I worked hard to get my props," he admitted. "I studied every department regulation, an' knew my shit. No one was gonna fuck with me. The only thing that beats ignorance is good learning, an' that's what I did," he said, nodding his head. "I learned good about narcotics. I got my hands on every bit of information there was on wire-tapping, surveillance methods, working with damn CIs, an' read it all." He looked at me seriously and continued, "Don't ever trust a CI, Juarez. They worse than whores, tell you that much. Well, my team started to kick some behind. Before I knew it, the commander had me running classes for incoming personnel. It became my job to teach the goings-on in the unit."

The radio interrupted us with news of a prospective corner for a buy. We headed over toward Kostner and Monroe to be near the action. "What did you do for productivity?"

"Juarez, all we did was long-term investigations. Big weight, big money kinds of things. Wasn't much pressure to produce. We didn't have to meet any numbers like we do now. An' we didn't fool around with no little street shit, either. It was fun, but I got burnt out after a while, so I went to the academy (in the eighties) to teach."

"What'd ya teach, traffic enforcement?" I said, chuckling as he looked at me without turning his head.

We drove by the target location and saw the two black kids that were the targeted dealers. We continued driving as Nica, the eyeball for this transaction, moved into position. "I taught all them recruits 'bout search an' seizure, warrant-writing skills an' some basic crime scene investigation. Lots of play-acting finding drugs. You know, so many of these dumb-ass recruits fuck up a crime scene when they get to one. It just amazes me. They stomp all over the place, not even knowing what they doing. I used to ask, 'How can you identify cocaine or heroin?' They'd say, 'Oh, that's easy, sarge. You just taste it, right?' Makes me laugh, so many cops on the streets wouldn't know cocaine if it was stuck up they noses. I got tired of that shit an' came back to the Unit."

"You came back, just like that?" I asked, knowing that getting into the Unit wasn't easy.

"My clout runs deep, an' people like me, Juarez."

"You must've noticed a lot of changes in personnel when you got back," I said as the radio marked a successful buy, and the enforcement teams were being called on for a takedown. Sergeant Moore informed me we'd be staying on the perimeter and would assist only if we were needed. So we continued talking.

"Not really. The only things that changed were the commanders, an' I've seen many come and go, but I'm still here," he asserted. He started telling me about some of the operations he'd worked on. I asked him which one was the most interesting.

"That's easy," he began as the radio informed us of the apprehension of the two wanted street dealers and the 1505 funds. "Happened couple years ago. SNIP was running something called Risky Business. The boss (commander in Narcotics) asked me to go with them to check procedure."

"What was so risky about it?" I asked.

"Can't say I rightly know. SNIP was formed strictly for street dope like we do down here. But Risky Business was something a little different. They went after the buyers—the whores an' junkies—not the dealers."

"I'd think it'd be harder to arrest the buyers. What'd they do, watch the spot, follow the buyer after they copped, then pull 'em over on a street stop?" I asked, envisioning how many problems could surface when it came time to justify the stop. "I mean just about everyone on the West Side is slinging bags, what could be easier than cracking on the dealers like we do now?"

"Actually, Juarez, it was easier an' safer than the shit we do now," he began to explain as the radio broke in again, notifying us of a potential spot on Springfield, between Lake and Randolph. "They'd start their days like we do, send out feelers for locations then radio when they found a spot generating action. Enforcement was sent to the rear of the target an' told to hold their location."

"Was enforcement on foot or did they stay in their cars?"

"Oh, they were on foot. They'd stand at the end of the gangway of the target an' wait until the buy officers were escorting the dealer—"

149

"Wait up, sarge. How'n the hell did the buy officers end up escorting the dealer down the gangway? Ain't no dealer gonna follow a junkie anywhere."

"Well now, that's where it got a little tricky. Two buy officers converged on the dealer at the same time, pretending they'd want some dope. Without causing too much a commotion, they'd use the come-along hold an' take him down the gangway. Enforcement was waiting to cuff 'em an' throw 'em in an unmarked. Less hands touching the arrestees, the fewer the beefs. One of the buy officers then headed back out in front an' start directing buyers down the gangway to the other buy officer who's now a dealer."

"Where'd enforcement hide?" I asked. "Didn't the customers notice a group of people with guns around the dealer?"

"They couldn't see 'em. They hid in the nooks in the rear of the building an' waited for the customers. As soon as they approached asking for rocks, enforcement'd grab an' cuff 'em before anyone was the wiser."

"You're telling me the customers couldn't recognize a different dealer or didn't even suspect anything was up?"

"Shit! You know there's always different dealers on the street every day. Besides, junkies just wanna buy their dope an' get high."

"What were the junkies buying? Did SNIP take the baggies off the dealers and sell them?" I asked.

"I don't think that would hold up in court," Sergeant Moore laughed. "They had to do it legal like. They'd get a CI to get 'em a good amount of rocks, take 'em to the lab for verification, then repackage 'em for this operation." My blank look must have clued him into the fact that I didn't quite understand the process, so he continued. "One of these dealers on the streets gets cracked (arrested) an' knows he's in deep shit. He starts asking if enforcement can do something to reduce his sentence. They'd get together with a state's attorney and throw around some numbers. If all sides agreed to the terms, they'd sign a contract. Whatever narcotics or information the CI gets or provides, he gets paid for an' the weight (amount of drugs) goes toward working off his case (sentence reduction). The key is that the CI must be working (buying drugs from) someone we aren't tied into. If you paid any attention when I was teaching you this shit, you wouldn't be asking silly questions, Juarez."

"I was paying attention," I said, as I thought back to the spiral notepad full of notes from my orientation that hadn't been opened since that day. "I just have to review my notes."

Sergeant Moore informed me that the unit and state's attorneys have a schedule they follow when paying off a CI. The more dope they bring in, the more money they get. If the CI cooperates fully, the cops could kill two birds with one stone in Operation Risky Business—arrest the buyers from the streets and secure a warrant for the dealer the CI was working. I understood now.

"So," I started again, after the refresher course, "the cops are now dealers?"

"Only to catch the buyers, Juarez," Sergeant Moore clarified when the radio announced another successful buy. It was nice to be able to sit in the car while everyone else on my team was working, arresting crack dealers.

"OK, so the customer's at the end of the gangway with cuffs on, now what?"

"They'd throw 'em in the car an' continue the game. Oh man, in an hour or so they had like eight to ten arrestees."

A frantic voice came over the radio; it sounded like Mickey, "The suspect's running, he ducked into a gangway, heading northbound." Sergeant Moore immediately sped in that direction. A few seconds later Mickey's voice returned to the airwaves, "We've got him. Slow it down, slow it down." He was informing enforcement not to break their necks or wreck their cars trying to catch the runner. Sergeant Thomas, who was spearheading this operation, got on the radio and called everyone in to Area 4 for a break.

"See, Juarez," Sergeant Moore said as he turned our vehicle around and headed to the Area, "there was none of that shit in Risky Business. The customers came to us. Enforcement didn't have to do shit."

"If it was so easy, then why'n the hell aren't we doing it now instead of wedging?" I asked.

"Juarez, you wouldn't believe this shit," Moore began, shaking his head. "I looked at the group of arrestees an' saw mostly whiteys."

"Yeah, right. You tellin' me there weren't any brothers?" I said skeptically as we pulled into the parking lot behind Area 4.

"There was one or two, but that's not my point," Moore said as he put the car in park and shut off the engine. "A few of them whiteys looked like they were professionals, an' the rest were blue-collared working stiffs. We got CARs (contact arrest reports) on 'em an' found out some were suburbanites, others lived in the city, but they all had one thing in common—the need to score." He stopped for a moment to think. "Make that two things, they were embarrassed. An' so were the other supervisors around me." He stayed in the car looking out the windshield as Mickey and Javier walked by us with their three prisoners—all young black men.

"So, who cares? White people are included in this War on Drugs, too, you know," I said.

"That's what I said," Moore mused, "But the brass musta thought something was wrong because Risky Business was over an' done with by the week's end after a closed-door meeting downtown."

"Get the fuck outta here! You got to be joking!" I exclaimed, as I turned to face him. "Are you telling me that even though it was safer and more productive and, not to mention, would cut down on beefs, they scrapped the operation?"

"Not entirely. They still had the search warrant from the CI buys. But when it came time to serve the warrant, it couldn't be done. Seems like someone dropped the ball on protocol an' never followed the CI to his buy spot. There was no dealer. *He* was the dealer. He was getting paid twice; the city paid 'em to buy the dope an' then he got paid for delivering the shit. It don't get any better than this, Juarez. The city lost over eighty grand."

"I can't believe this shit."

"Nothing surprises me nowadays," Moore answered. "It didn't bother me until I heard one of the white supervisors say, 'These are all honest, hardworking people. Why should we screw up their lives over twenty-five bucks' worth of crack cocaine?' Of course he was talking about the white people, so do you think he wants us to end Iron Wedge?"

"Yeah, right." I thought about the line of blacks that went through our hands every day. "At least those whiteys arrested in Risky Business went to jail."

Moore gripped the steering wheel and wrung his fingers around it like he was choking someone. "Hardly. When the lab reports went to court with the offenders, they all came back negative. Not a damn one of 'em came back with the presence of cocaine. The court had to drop all charges."

"Everyone went free?"

"Even the token brothers," sighed Sergeant Moore. "Even the token brothers."

"How could they get away with that? You said the dope tested positive before it was sold."

"It did, but I didn't ask any questions. Sometimes it's better not to know the truth," he said sadly.

"What did SNIP do after that?" I asked.

"They started the shit we're doing today," Moore told me. "Operation Iron Wedge."

22

BIG MONEY, BIG DOPE, BIG MISTAKE

RUNNING INTO FRIENDS I had before I became a cop was always very interesting, especially when I told them I worked in Narcotics. All of a sudden, their mouths opened, revealing a pipeline of information about people and places involved in drug trafficking. Their information could never be taken at face value and, of course, I'd have to do a little investigating. Some tips were valid, and others were far-fetched stories for purposes of revenge or another ulterior motive, but when I kept hearing rumors about the Board of Trade, my interest was piqued.

Marcos Sanchez, a kid I'd gone to high school and played hockey with when I was younger, kept up his passion for the sport. Our teams faced off against each other in Skokie one winter night in 1993. It had been nine years since we'd roamed the halls of Gordon Tech together, where I played ice hockey, but I could recognize his skating style anywhere. It was a hilarious moment when we recognized each other, and we made plans to go to a bar after the game to catch up.

Over beers we talked for a while about family, kids we went to school with, and girlfriends. Then I asked where he worked. He told me he was a runner on the floor at the Board of Trade and asked me about my job.

"I'm a cop," I said.

"No shit, Juan. You're only on the police hockey team. What district do you work in?" he asked.

"None," I boasted. "I work in Narcotics." It gave me a thrill to tell people that, even though I risked blowing my cover. What did I have to worry about? I was stuck all day working in the ghetto.

"Like doing what? Some big-time kilo deals and shit like that?" he said, gaining interest.

I would have loved to believe that was what I was doing, but I told him the truth. "Nah, I'm just doing street dope and some small-time investigations."

His eyes brightened. "You want a tip?"

"Sure," I said. I never turned down information from anyone because it was free. Who knows? It could lead me to something big.

"Hey man," he said, glancing uneasily around the bar. "You can't tell anyone where you got this information, but there's some heavy shit going down at the board."

"That's what I've been told," I replied. But all those stories had come from people who heard them secondhand. Marcos was right in the middle of the action. "Tell me more."

"It's crazy, man. It's snowing all over the place."

"What do you mean?" I asked.

"Coke, man. It's everywhere. I can get anything I want at anytime. But, I don't do that shit, too rich for my blood. I just stick to weed." He hesitated for a second, forgetting all the times we got high together in school. "You ain't gonna bust me, are you?"

I had started smoking pot in high school to escape the internal pain I had endured from my parents' divorce and Angel's abuse. I also did it to be accepted by the people I thought were cool—people like Marcos. When I realized the detrimental effect it had on my grades, which happened when I applied for colleges, I stopped cold turkey and never looked back.

"Come on, Marcos. Gimme a break. You haven't changed a bit, still getting high and still paranoid. Listen, weed's small time. I'm looking for coke and heroin." I decided to take a risk since he was the one who brought the subject up. "Can you get me some introductions on the floor?"

He sat up straight on the bar stool. "Hell fuckin' yeah! Those rich, snotty suburban kids get me sick. Driving to work in Porsches their daddies bought them. Getting all the fine pussy. Fuck 'em!"

He sounded like he had an ulterior motive. But then I started to think about the rich and privileged set. Wherever there's wealth and privilege, there's bound to be excess, I reasoned. I thought of Hollywood's actors and directors, the music industry and all the rock stars, how they glamorized drug use and addictions because they know they can check into some trendy detox center and come out on top of the world with their image and wealth intact. I thought of some of the trust-fund babies I knew who were dabbling in all sorts of illegal drugs; they tried to make me believe they were living a tough life. Yeah, right! It amazed me how money insulated and protected privileged people from the shit real people have to go through.

I said, "I'll run it by my sergeant and see what he thinks."

Marcos and I continued talking and exchanging stories. It was refreshing to run into an old friend. It gave me perspective on how much time had actually passed and how much I had changed. The last time we had seen each other was at our graduation as we smoked a joint after the ceremony. It was ironic and pretty hilarious that I was now a cop in Narcotics. We traded phone numbers, promising to keep in touch, and then went on our separate ways. The next morning, full of enthusiasm, I approached Sergeant Thomas about wanting to infiltrate the drug trade at the board. He seemed amused and told me to talk to Sergeant Moore about my desire. I walked down the hall to his office.

"Hey Sarge," I said, entering his team's cubicle, "I'd like to run an idea for an operation past you."

He looked up from a stack of paperwork, "Hey, Juarez. What's going on? What you got?"

"I've been hearing things about some heavy action at the Board of Trade. I got someone who'd sponsor an introduction, and I'm up to working my way in. Sergeant Thomas told me to run it by you, so here I am."

He smiled and slowly nodded his head. "Have a seat, Juarez. Let me give you a rundown on an operation SOS (Special Operations Section) conducted 'bout five years ago."

I sat down as I was instructed. I knew Sergeant Moore knew the ins and outs of the unit and had been key to the planning and execution of numerous operations. This warehouse of knowledge sat back in his chair and began.

"During the late eighties, the unit was flooded with information that powder was flowing at the board. It was out of control, going on like there was no tomorrow. According to a CI, a proper bust was out there for anyone who could get in the mix. SOS assigned a sergeant an' his team to work the information. As they were rolling on the project, they hit a bump in the road—clout. It was so heavy they had to bury the whole operation."

Moore told me that the names of the suspects gathered in the early phases of this investigation were linked to some of the most powerful movers in this city. The majority of those names were children of wealthy and very influential people. The DEA caught wind of the operation, stepped in, and asked for all the information regarding the investigation. The DEA requested a halt to this burgeoning operation without giving a reason. It seemed they used their federal affiliation to get what they wanted.

The operation was consequently suspended, and all of its compiled information was immediately turned over to the DEA; nobody ever heard anything of the investigation again. It vanished without a trace.

My head inched forward and my mouth involuntarily opened.

"Close your mouth before you catch a fly, Juarez," he directed with a straight face. "Shit, you know Chicago runs on clout."

Along with money come power and influence, which equal clout, the system of choice ever since the beginning of Richard J. Daley's first term as mayor. Clout made the city work by greasing the system. Friends and family members of "The Boss"—Daley's nickname—got no-bid contracts and filled top positions in city government. And because of their connections to Daley, they had unparalleled clout. Clout was as powerful as money, if not more so. It could offer privileges that aren't afforded or accessible to the multitude. It could protect one from minor and major brushes with the law. It's a big no-no to mess with someone who has clout. Cops have been transferred or demoted for issuing tickets to or arresting those connected to clout, while some cops have climbed the ranks by gaining and maintaining clout.

I left Sergeant Moore's office with a nasty taste in my mouth. I kept wondering what exactly was the purpose of our mission?

Later that day, we resumed what I was now considering our senseless role in the War on Drugs. Operation Iron Wedge continued putting piss-poor people in jail while the rich and privileged luxuriated under a blanket of clout.

23

HEY, WHERE'S THE MONEY?

OUR TEAM WAS ASKED TO ASSIST in serving a search warrant near Fifty-first and Wood with one of the mid-level teams. Supposedly, the target location was holding some big-weight crack destined for the streets. I was being given the opportunity to observe the working style of a team that specialized in gathering information and executing search warrants. It was an area I wanted to get into because wedging was tedious and lacked challenges, not to mention the fact that the daily doses of injustice were starting to make me sick to my stomach.

This search warrant was executed in the middle of a spring day in 1994. The reason for this timing was simple: we wanted to reduce the possibility of having a lot of bodies at the house. It was a schoolday, and most of the gangbangers, believe it or not, were at school.

Our teams met at 3540 to go over the strategy and instructions. We were assigned perimeter duty and weren't going to be invited to search the target location. That was new to me, and I thought it was strange.

"Hey, Mickey," I said on the way to the spot. "Perimeter. What's up with that shit?"

"They're probably afraid of us seeing them work or afraid we'll stick something in our pockets," he responded mildly. "What else could it be?"

"I guess you could be right," I told Mickey as we pulled up behind the target location and took our positions.

I had heard stories about drugs and money that had been confiscated but never reported on the inventory logs or placed in the evidence safe. I thought back to X in 14 and it made me a bit leery.

One of the feds had once told me about the magical and mysterious disappearance of two pounds of marijuana. Another officer told me of a collection of comic books valued at more than $25,000 that disappeared from a warrant residence. Coin collections vanished. Cell phones and beepers turned up missing. Stories of quickly gained riches while serving search warrants in Narcotics were commonplace throughout the Police Department. Whenever I ran into buddies in 14, the jokes focused on the wealthy guys in Narcotics—some owned numerous buildings, others owned construction firms or travel agencies—and I was always asked if I had hit a big one yet.

Mickey and I were assigned to cover the back door in case anyone decided to run out when they heard the front door being smashed by the ram. Mickey and I took our position and awaited radio directions notifying us when the location was secure. That call came five minutes later: "Hold your positions outside. We got one in here we're interrogating. We'll call ya in a second."

The radio transmission had a tone of disappointment as if the seizure had amounted to less than expected. Mickey and I looked at each other and shrugged. My enthusiasm returned momentarily when they radioed us to come in.

"Hey man, where's the fuckin' dope?" I heard as we entered the house through the back door. The kitchen was in shambles—dishes broken and cabinet drawers spilled on the floor. I wondered how in the hell they were expecting to find contraband in this mess.

"Huh, motherfucker! I asked you a question," shot through the house as we made our way to the front room. It looked like a tornado had hit the kitchen and then blasted its way through the house. "Where's the damn dope?"

The questions were being aimed at an agitated black teenager. He was around seventeen, a bit overweight with a medium Afro and a pick stuck in it. At the end of the pick was a curled fist—the symbol of black power. I wondered what was going on in this kid's head as he sat with his hands cuffed in front of him surrounded by cops. It was strangely quiet until a loud crash, like glass shattering, came from the back of the house.

"Yo, man! What the fuck y'all doin' to my auntie's crib?" the kid hollered, trying to get up. Detective Malfitano, the short Italian-Irish cop who had procured this warrant, put a foot on his chest and pushed him back down onto the sofa. "I done told y'all there ain't shit here!" the kid wailed.

A cop came from the back of the house, approached Malfitano, handed him an object, and then glared at the kid.

"Oh, yeah?" Malfitano said jeeringly. "Then what the hell is this?"

The kid's eyes lit up like he had been hit by lightning as Malfitano held up a small plastic bag with some rocks of crack in it.

"Nah, you motherfuckers. You ain't putting no case on me," the kid protested, shaking his head back and forth.

"Shut the fuck up, mookie," Malfitano ordered. "Or else you'll be eating bologna for dinner." (*Bologna* is copper shorthand for jail food.)

The seizure was less than a gram of crack—far below the expectations of the mid-level team. It wasn't due to a lack of effort though. I looked around the place, shocked by all the destruction.

"Hey, Malfi," Mickey called, "there's a garage out back."

Malfitano turned his head, eyed Mickey, and then nodded toward the kid on the couch, "What you hiding in the garage?" He then answered his own question when the kid remained silent. "You hiding dope in there. Ain't you, mookie?"

"Ain't nuttin' in there but a car," the boy answered without concern. "And I ain't got no keys."

Detective Malfitano knew the garage wasn't listed on the warrant; therefore, it couldn't be legally searched and if any contraband were found in it, it would be thrown out in court. Or so the law says. But, if there were a seizure from the garage, some creative writing would make it legal before it got to court. All Malfitano had to do was type up the case report and claim the dope was found in the house and that was that. It didn't take a mastermind to come up with that change of scenario. The districts taught creative writing 101, but being in a specialized unit was like going to grad school. If it's on paper, it's as good as gold in the court system. As luck would have it, we found the keys.

No one volunteered to go to the garage. Malfitano scanned the room, and his eyes stopped on me. "Hey, Juan," he said, "you wanna do some mid-level work?"

I shrugged. "Why not?"

He threw me the keys. "Make sure to call me on the radio if you find anything."

Mickey and I headed out to the garage. When we opened the door to the two-car garage, we found a pristine light blue 1967 Mercury Cougar in the middle of a clean working area.

"You can take the car, hound dog," I offered. He let out a howl and began a systematic search of the car. I was pissed that we hadn't been included in the search of the residence, so I wasn't about to exert any undue energy searching for another team's dope. I knew we wouldn't even get the props if we did come across something. Besides, the garage was immaculate and there weren't many hiding places. I began opening drawers and cabinets, but I didn't find any paraphernalia or anything remotely connected to dope.

"Fuck it," Mickey uttered as he got out of the car. "It's clean. I'm gonna check the trunk."

I went around to the rear of the car as he popped open the trunk. For a moment, I expected well-packaged kilos of cocaine to blind me, but that wasn't the case. The trunk was spotless, except for the necessary accoutrements for roadside emergencies and a plastic bag containing a box labeled powdered bleach that had already been opened. Purely on a whim, Mickey checked the contents. "Holy shit! Check this out!"

I peered over his shoulder as he flipped back the top of the box. It was filled with greenbacks, two neatly stacked rows of twenties and fifties.

"Is it full?" I inquired.

"Only one way to find out," he replied, sliding his hand down the inside of the box. "It's fuckin' full," Mickey flipped through the first five or six inches of bills. "Shit! This could be one endless vacation in the Bahamas," he mused.

"Or a fucking life in jail!" I countered. I had heard stories about IAD planting money to nail dirty cops.

Mickey pulled out about an inch of the cash and began fanning his face with it. "What the fuck are you doing?" I asked, checking the corners of the garage for hidden cameras.

"I just wanna see how much it is." We counted out $1,000 in that inch or so. "How much you think's in the box?" he inquired solemnly.

"Twenty-five grand," I said.

He got on the radio and transmitted ambiguously, "Hey Malfi, you might want to come out to the garage." We learned early in our careers never to offer a warrant finding over the radio because if it hit the airwaves it could be recorded and the tapes could be retrieved in case there was some discrepancy later. I thought the lesson added to the secretiveness of the unit, so I followed along.

Detective Malfitano rushed out through the back door of the house and asked, "What ya got?"

Mickey made a production of showing him the closed box and, like Vanna White, stepped to the side and let him see for himself. When Malfitano saw the box full of currency, he couldn't have been happier. A shitty warrant had turned around.

We reminded him about the questionable legality of the seizure, and he replied, "Lesson number one: recover (for case-report writing) all property in the residence of the warrant. Maybe that's why you shits are still wedging." Mickey and I looked at each other and rolled our eyes as Malfitano grabbed the box of cash without one word of thanks and left the garage.

We glanced at each other and I jokingly asked, "How much do you think'll make it into the safe?"

"Whose safe?" Mickey replied. "Malfitano's or the unit's?"

After a few minutes, the members of Malfitano's team decided enough energy had been exerted, and they headed back to Thirty-fifth Street to do the paperwork while our team resumed wedging.

The next day Mickey and I checked the twenty-four-hour activity sheets from the prior day. We immediately flipped to the information regarding the warrant we'd assisted in. We noted that only $3,500 had been inventoried.

Our eyes met. "You gotta be fuckin' joking!" I said. "Thirty-five hundred dollars?"

Mickey didn't say a word and we never talked about it again. But after that incident, I began to see recovered property in a whole different light. I knew that if I ever saw another laundry box full of cash, I'd make sure some of it wound up in my pocket. That said, I didn't think I'd ever have that opportunity again. Though the fear of IAD lurking in the shadows was real, I could see myself giving in to the temptation of finally hitting the big one.

Our team was serving a search warrant on the third floor of 64—South Indiana Avenue, and I was riding with Sergeant Abernathy. He volunteered us to guard the back of the residence to ensure that no one ran out as the front door was being knocked in. Driving through the alley, I checked the numbers on the garbage cans, stopping at the target address, and sat in the car while they hit the place.

"Hey, Sarge," Javier called on the radio, "we're in and there're a few people in the place, so it's gonna take a while. We'll call you if we need you. Ten-four?"

"Ten-four," Sergeant Abernathy sighed as I put the car in park and shut off the engine. We were going to sit tight and wait for the call. There were no fences or garages, just garbage cans, dumpsters, and open fields around us, with the back of apartment buildings to our side. I turned my head and looked up at the rear windows of the apartment building just in time to see a black male furtively drop something from the third floor. The object landed in some tall grass. I checked to see if there was any reaction from Sergeant Abernathy. He remained as still and silent as usual, so I assumed he hadn't seen what I saw. I got out of the squad and shut the door.

"Sarge, I'm gonna check out the back and see if I find any tips and clues."

"All right, Juarez. I ain't going nowhere."

I walked away from the car and began picking up discarded items in the yard, inspecting them, and then throwing them back into the grass. After each time I did this, I slowly turned my head toward the car. Sergeant Abernathy never looked in my direction. He just stared off through the windshield.

I slowly walked in the direction of the dropped object; I didn't want to seem too obvious. Smoothing over the high grass with my foot, I saw a roll of U.S. currency. I had the image of the laundry box firmly etched in my mind as I picked up the one-inch roll and held it in my closed hand, visualizing that I just hit the big one. There was no way IAD threw this out the window—and the guy who dropped it would be pissed as all hell that he couldn't find it, but what was he going to do? Call the police and report that someone stole the money he dropped out the window while a search warrant for drugs was being executed at his residence? I didn't think so. Confident I wasn't seen and feeling like I could get away with snagging it, I put the roll in my pocket. The cackle of the radio made me jump, but it was only Javier saying they were done with the search. I went back to the car, and we headed to 3540 to process the paperwork.

I was scared shitless that day and constantly looked over my shoulder for any unusual faces when we got back to the unit. The roll in my pocket was a constant reminder of the theft I was in the process of committing. I wasn't home free yet. Waiting until the right moment, I headed to the men's bathroom and paranoia overcame me. My heart was beating in my ears as I searched every recessed corner for a camera and checked the mirrors to ensure they weren't two-way. I was too nervous to take the bundle out and count it, so it remained in my pocket like a rock.

On the ride home, I thought every car behind me was IAD, waiting for the right moment to pull me over and search my pockets. I imagined the roll had a homing device on it and gave me away. Even when I got home the uneasiness continued, but with palms sweating and a quickened heart rate, I removed the bundle from my pocket. A one-hundred-dollar bill was rolled around the other bills, and I removed the rubber band. With my ears pricked for the sound of feet running up the stairs or the ram smashing my door, I smoothed out the roll and began counting. There were ten hundred-dollar bills. It wasn't even close to being a big one, but it would come in handy when it came time to pay my tuition for the fall semester.

Over the next three or four weeks, I remained uneasy whenever I saw a new face come up the stairs to the second floor of 3540. No one ever came looking for the money and no one ever knew about it except me. However, this action weighed heavily on my conscience. I never did it again.

24

A WORLD APART

DRIVING IN A CAR FOUR HOURS every weekday in the ghetto is both a learning experience and an adventure. We concentrated our daily efforts primarily in the poverty-stricken, gang-heavy, drug-infested areas of the city such as Forty-seventh and St. Laurence, Fifty-fifth and Indiana, Fifty-first and Halsted, the far east end of Seventy-second Street, and Ninety-fifth Street, just to name a few. Areas in or near public housing communities such as Ida B. Wells, Henry Horner, and the ABLA Homes were always targeted, allowing the unit to conduct massive sweeps and arrests while maintaining extraordinarily high levels of productivity. The days I spent wedging forced me to open my eyes to the deplorable living conditions in this other Chicago—a world apart from my own experience.

While I had to deal with outlying gangs and some neighborhood bullies as a kid, my youth was relatively easy and carefree in comparison to what I saw during Iron Wedge. I remember that I envied kids who grew up in the nicer parts of the city, thinking they were privileged and lived a better life than I did, but it never occurred to me that anyone had a much harder existence than I did.

I felt guilty now as I drove daily through the barren blocks, seeing dilapidated housing and neighborhoods that lacked thriving businesses. Kids played in rubble-filled vacant lots teeming with rats and dogs. I wondered where the parks were and when I did find them I marveled at their various states of disrepair: skeletons of rusted swing sets, sandboxes filled with garbage—broken bottles, hypodermic needles, fast-food containers, used condoms, and dead dogs—lined the parks. I had only seen this level of destitution on television and never realized it existed in my own city. My ignorance amazed me now. I wondered how children grew up in these conditions. (See "The Dirty Truth by the Numbers" on page 286 for more information.)

The poverty I saw was making the luster on my Narcotics badge fade. I was completely enamored with the title, prestige, and perks of my job. I had the freedom to attend school, an undercover vehicle, copious amounts of overtime that allowed me to line my pockets with extra pay or vacation in exotic places, and the camaraderie of a tight-knit and relatively autonomous unit.

At the same time, I began to question the actual purpose of our mission. I wanted to put away drug dealers—the people who, in my mind, were responsible for poisoning society while getting wealthy at society's expense. But Iron Wedge presented a conflict.

Here I was working day in and day out in the neglected parts of the city fighting this impossible War on Drugs. I detested crack, powder cocaine, and heroin and knew many families that had been ripped apart by addictions. One of my sisters once had a nasty cocaine habit. Even Ana's sister had a heroin addiction and almost overdosed when I was at Ana's house one day. I firmly understand that overcoming an addiction requires personal fortitude. To be effective, the War on Drugs would have to kill the demand for drugs first. But the escape that drugs provide to those in blighted existences is extraordinarily difficult to resist.

I had been party to the execution of dozens of search warrants that never yielded more than five to ten grams of crack and never more than a couple hundred dollars. Maybe my expectations were too high, or maybe I was caught in the fantasy world of *Miami Vice* or *Blow*, but I had to question: were we making headway and winning this war with busts that yielded such paltry sums of drugs and money? These corner dealers and runners of crack houses were small fries—could it be we were neglecting the obvious locations where big money and extravagant consumption of drugs thrived? It only made sense to me—where there was big money there had to be big dope!

I knew that the big hitters in the unit were focusing on the larger operations, and once in a while I heard about massive cocaine seizures dealing with kilos and marijuana busts measured in hundreds of pounds. I wanted to be part of that. I wanted to go deep undercover, infiltrate some exclusive drug circles, and score big-time seizures, but I couldn't find a way to make that happen.

I never talked to anyone about my growing sense of disillusionment. Since childhood I had kept everything inside because there was no one there who asked, "What's wrong?" And even if there had been, I felt that my feelings weren't really worth sharing and that nobody really cared about what I was experiencing. Ana had been there for me early in our relationship, but ever since her abortion and the day I became I cop, I had kept so much from her. I wasn't about to start weighing her mind down with my problems now. Instead, I found release in physical exertion.

The intensity of my workouts had increased when Ana and I began competing in triathlons throughout the Chicago metropolitan area. I knew I wasn't ever going to stand on the podium as a top finisher, but I trained as if I might. Running three days a week, swimming four days, and biking just about every day made me forget about work and put my mind at ease. Training with Ana was grueling because she had become an incredible athlete; she was constantly finishing in the top of her age group in triathlons. I totally supported her athletic pursuits; I even sent her to a topnotch swimming camp and was thrilled when she blew her competition away. I spent the weekends traveling to compete or to go mountain biking.

Tim and I would go to Palos Hills or Kettle Moraine in Wisconsin for some single-track thrills. I was becoming more adept at the sport, but I couldn't come close to Tim's level of expertise. I loved the adrenaline rush of hurtling down rocky ravines and gnarly, heavily rooted trails. The physical pounding I absorbed from those rides seemed to beat whatever inner turmoil I was experiencing right out of me. With every ride, Tim and I became closer. A couple of times I wanted to unburden myself of my guilt about cheating on Ana, but I just couldn't do it. Instead we talked about our shared passions for biking and academics.

I was halfway done with my graduate degree in English. I figured I'd graduate in two more years. Taking one class every fall and winter quarter suited me just fine and I managed to keep on top of classes, maintaining a 3.0 GPA in the process. I was conquering all the challenges I had set myself in my school and sports activities. Now I needed some new challenges at work.

25

SUMMER MOBILE UNIT

IT WAS THE SPRING OF 1994 when I learned I was going to be detailed to the Summer Mobile Unit (SMU) for four periods starting just before Memorial Day and ending a week after Labor Day. Summer Mobile is a public relations–driven unit providing the public with an image of safety and security along the twenty miles of beaches and lakefront along the city of Chicago. This goal was accomplished through the deployment of about two hundred highly visible uniformed officers.

To man the SMU, the department required two volunteers from every district and unit throughout the city. District cops battled for this assignment because it gave them the chance to enjoy the summer along the lake. Cops in special units dreaded this detail, however, because of its requirements: the donning of the uniform, radio assignments, public contact on a daily basis, eight-hour workdays, and rotating days off. For those reasons, there were few volunteers from Narcotics. Instead the unit implemented a reverse-seniority draft—those with the least amount of time in the department were shipped off to the detail with no guarantee of coming back. I was mortified; I was the last person on the seniority list.

Going to SMU was what I feared most. Ever since I'd arrived in Narcotics, there was grumbling about how a kid with two years on the force could land in such a sweet spot. The brass had since instituted a new requirement for entry into the Unit—an officer now needed to have five years on the force before he or she would even be considered for a transfer to 3540. That was bad news for me because it meant I was going to be the low man on the seniority list for quite some time. I was and would continue to be a relative newcomer and my presence in the unit, I thought, was somewhat tenuous and could be short-lived. Everyone on my team saw through me, noticing the insecurity, so when I was given this assignment, they all joined in to give me shit about it.

"You might as well empty out your locker, rook, you ain't coming back," joked Javier, while Franco assured me, "Hey, I know the commander in 12, maybe I could get you on midnights if you're nice."

As the day of my departure drew closer, the constant ribbing drove its way into my brain. I needed to hear something from someone I could trust to ease my concerns. I went to see Sergeant Thomas.

"Don't worry about a thing, Juan," he told me. "I'll see you back here in September." His assurance allayed my fears somewhat, but I was still uneasy about the new assignment. And while I wasn't thrilled with wedging, I didn't want to leave Narcotics because it offered me perks I wasn't going to get as a beat cop. My fears weren't going to be alleviated until I was back at 3540 in September.

I went to the posted seniority board and noticed that another officer, Gina Velez, had volunteered for the second opening, so I went and tracked her down. We knew each other in passing and had a friendly rapport, but I had never worked with her. She was a feisty Puerto Rican, just under five feet tall, with long, wavy dark hair and a robust, muscular body. Gina had served on this detail the year before, so she gave me the rundown on the expectations of the SMU command. She also agreed to be my partner, which meant that I wasn't going to have to work with someone from another district or unit.

"Juan, it's a sweet spot. Believe me, you'll like it. We don't have to do much 'cept write a few citations for possession of alcohol on park property, arrest a few people for disorderly, and chill the rest of the eight hours checking out the scenery."

I felt better already. In a way, I had been living in seclusion while I worked the last two years in Narcotics. We were always working in fucked-up neighborhoods, and I never got to socialize with the public or flirt with women as I had while working in 14. Working in Narcotics was good for my relationships with Ana and Maria because I wasn't out chasing skirts.

But the prospect of being by the lake during the summer and seeing a lot of women in skimpy swimsuits got me excited.

When the spring finally comes to Chicago, it's not unusual to see people wearing shorts when the temperatures barely hit the sixties, but I guess that's what a little sunshine does for people who've been in hibernation for five months. When summer hits and the beaches open on Memorial Day, Chicagoans flock to the lakefront to play volleyball, rollerblade, run, and bike. The life of the city returns as the sun beats away cabin fever. Nearly every summer weekend features a celebration of some kind; there are plenty of neighborhood festivals, outdoor concerts, and food orgies.

Summer in Chicago is also the height of the tourist season. The lakefront had once been home to a lot of criminal activity, but now it was constantly patrolled to maintain tourism.

In the summer of 1994, the lakefront was going to be in even more vacation pictures because Chicago was one of the American cities chosen to host the World Cup. With soccer fans from all over the world descending on Chicago in droves, the Taste of Chicago, and a litany of other sure-hit street parties, it was going to be an interesting summer to say the least.

Gina suggested we work the late car that started at 1:00 P.M. and ended at 9:00 P.M. Working the later shift was cool with me because it meant that I could have my mornings free for my triathlon training. I was addicted to the intensity of the workouts and wanted to get them in before the workday started, so I'd arrive at work fresh and fit, ready to impress the legions of women flocking to the beaches. Working so close to the lakefront allowed me to do just that. I rode my bike fifteen miles along the lake, swam a mile at Ohio Street Beach, and got in a five-mile run on my way to work at Meigs Field where the SMU was headquartered. I was a lean 170 pounds and easily managed to slip into my old rookie uniform.

Working with Gina was good for many reasons. She was the first woman I worked with consistently in close quarters and I grew to respect her work ethic. Many male officers thought that being a cop was a man's job and women had no place in the department except behind a desk, but Gina didn't buy that shit. She was a no-nonsense cop. A truly devoted mother and police officer, she was totally honest and focused, and she played by the book. She was built like a brick—short and thick—without one ounce of flab. She could be unbelievably aggressive and defend herself better than many male cops I'd worked with. An alternate on the 1992 Olympic Judo team, she trained hard and didn't take shit from anyone on or off the job. If you had a beef with her or gave her some lip, you'd better be ready to go toe to toe because she didn't play. She also had her compassionate and caring side. She'd relax when the day was done by letting her hair down and having a beer with some of the men she met on the beaches, but she wasn't a player and didn't engage in licentious relationships for the hell of it like so many cops I knew.

I had been a player since I started the force. I cheated on Ana and lied to her when it served my interests from the first day I got my badge. One day, early in the detail when we parked the squad at the North Avenue beach house, Gina met Ana. I told Ana to come by and visit me if she had time during her run, so I was expecting her. I introduced her to Gina and we talked for a while. Then Ana brought up the subject of salsa dancing. I didn't have an interest in the topic, so I excused myself and went to the men's room. When I came back they were still talking and laughing as if they had known each other for years. I have to admit I was a bit peeved by the ease with which they bonded, and I was relieved when we got a radio assignment. Ana gave me a hug and a kiss and then continued on her way. Later that day when I started checking out other women along the lakefront, Gina erupted, "Juan!" She playfully slapped me in the head, "Why are you doing that?"

"Because I like checking out other women, that's why."

"You got a lady," she hollered. I felt like she was putting her nose somewhere it didn't belong, but I had only myself to blame for introducing her to Ana.

"So?"

"Don't you know you're disrespecting her by doing that?" My blank expression and silence must have told her I didn't care. Her questioning was like a grating noise in my ears, and her prying annoyed me. "Can't you see you're disrespecting yourself more than anything else with your actions?"

"If I'm disrespecting myself, how come it feels so good?" I was in no mood to explain myself.

"Just because you got a wee-wee don't mean you got to use it. Think with the head on your shoulders, not the one in your pants."

No one ever questioned me but Ana, and she had stopped when she learned that badgering me created even more of a stone wall. Now I was being told how to live and how to act by my partner; I didn't have the patience or the time for it, so I changed the subject. Gina looked at me with frustration and disappointment.

"You're just a silly little boy. Grow up! Obviously Ana loves you and you must feel something for her because you two are together."

She made sense. I heard what she was saying even though I didn't want to. She had no idea what we had been through and what I felt for Ana, I told myself. How could she call me a little boy! I could feel my anger rising as she kept pressing me to be honest and truthful. Finally I just wanted to walk away. I could have kicked myself for allowing them to meet.

"You're gonna throw away six years with Ana for some stanky little piece of pussy? Now that's silly!"

During this lecture I began to think about Maria. I was glad I had never told Gina about her. I couldn't imagine the shit she'd give me about that. The rest of the summer, I chose, under the watchful eyes of Gina, to respect my relationship with Ana and stop checking out other women. But I also chose to keep Maria a secret.

Away from work and Gina and Ana, I had a good thing going with Maria. We loved doing things together. Around her, I never had to answer probing questions about how I was spending my time. I knew our relationship was safe and I never worried about getting busted by Ana or being seen by her friends because Maria and I hardly left the suburbs. And when we did, I made sure to stay on the Far North Side, not willing to take any unnecessary chances. Maria didn't have a clue about Ana. She always assumed I was aloof because of my free-spirited nature.

I had deep feelings for Maria, but I wasn't about to drop Ana for her. Gina helped me realize that much by reminding me, however painful it was, about how fortunate I was to have Ana in my life. And when Gina wasn't busy trying to make me see the error of my ways, she amazed me with her skill for cutting down other men.

I remember one day when we were working Montrose Harbor shagging (disbursing) some drunken Puerto Rican revelers who mistakenly took Gina for a weak female cop. They gave her too much lip, and she quickly got fed up. She turned on the biggest one in the group, got in his face, and said, "Do you have a problem?"

The guy looked around at his three friends, smirked and said, "Yeah, what you gonna do 'bout it?"

Gina executed a lightning fast wrist hold and had the kid on his tip-toes trying to escape the excruciating pain. "This," she said, "is what I'm gonna do. What are you gonna do about it?" She dazzled me with her rapid response.

"Nothing . . . nothing . . ." he whimpered, dancing on his toes as Gina kept up the pressure. "Nothing."

"That's what I thought," she said. "You're all under arrest. You guys can thank your buddy here." We cuffed everyone, inventoried their Budweiser, stuffed them into the squad, and headed into the 23rd District. Putting them in a processing room, we began the paperwork.

"What's your name, son?" she asked the kid who gave her the problem to begin with.

"What's your name, mami?" he responded lasciviously. He began puckering up his lips, ready to blow Gina a kiss. He still hadn't learned his lesson, I thought to myself.

Without looking up and before his lips unpuckered, Gina jabbed her nightstick under the table and sunk it into his belly. That took care of his shenanigans.

"Jose Colón," he whispered sheepishly. Gina kept writing up the arrest report and warned, "I'll scramble your *huevos si tú quieres. Entiendes?*" There were no more problems from that group of arrestees.

The summer developed into a nice vacation from Narcotics. Working with Gina turned out to be a great experience because riding with a woman provided a different perspective. Gina made me see how much Ana meant to me. Gina also had high standards of professionalism and a knockout work ethic. She curbed my wandering eye with just her presence and made me begin to question my actions. I didn't want to mess with her. So I curbed my urges, but not completely.

26

NITWIT POLICE

IN EARLY SEPTEMBER 1994, fall hit hard with bone-chilling arctic blasts coming off Lake Michigan. Gina had taken the last week off, and I had been assigned another partner. My SMU detail was winding down when one day this call came over the radio: "23—, we got a call regarding the homeless making a shelter at Irving and LSD (Lake Shore Drive)."

Although it wasn't our call, we were close by and we had nothing to do now that the beaches were officially closed. We kept the radio off, not wanting to be stuck with a job that wasn't ours; besides, we really had no business going in the first place. Boredom drove us there.

On that day the winds were relentless. My partner and I arrived first on the scene and saw a bicycle lying on the embankment under the viaduct. Attached to its handlebars was a milk crate filled with various items that were secured with a bungee cord. We looked up and saw a man huddled in a ball near the top of the overpass supports. The weather had taken a turn for the worse as a steady drizzle began to fall. Add the driving cold wind, and the rain felt like a constant barrage of tiny pellets hitting my face. It was downright shitty out, but it was tolerable under the overpass. The job was to inform this homeless man that he had to go because there's a law against loitering and making a public structure habitable. That's why there are now see black iron fences making overpass structures inaccessible for anyone who wants to get under them. The 23— officers arrived on the scene and got out of their car: Officers Jimenez, a man, and Sulzer, a woman. We talked briefly, and then Officer Jimenez called out to the homeless man, "Hey, can we have a word with you?"

The homeless man raised his head from the bundle of clothes he had wrapped himself in and wearily agreed to come down and talk. He slid down the embankment, and as he approached I could see he wore a haggard expression. He was Caucasian and appeared to be around sixty or sixty-five. His face was creased with cracks worn deep from living exposed to the elements; his skin was like untreated leather and his hands were callused. This wasn't going to be easy. I wondered how they'd begin the eviction process.

It was ten minutes to four and I knew these officers were finishing a second-watch shift that ended at four. I knew they didn't want to have to tell this homeless man to move on when it was this cold and miserable outside. It's easy for those who have shelters to protect themselves, but when one is homeless there aren't many options available beyond subway stations, public parking lots, doorways, and homeless shelters, which are usually overcrowded. But there's always room for compassion in any situation. I looked over to my partner who was checking out the bicycle and crate full of belongings. Everything this man owned in the world was placed in this little milk crate.

"Good afternoon, officers. I know I can't be here, but it's so cold out and I got nowheres to go. I just wanna wait till it stops raining and then I'll go," he said.

I was relieved that he knew the purpose of our visit, but we couldn't allow him to stay because there was no telling how long it would continue to rain. Some laws are ridiculous and this was one of them. Clearly this man wasn't posing a threat to anyone, not even himself.

Officer Sulzer took the initiative, "You'll have to pack up and go, sir. We'll give you a few minutes to get your things together. If you want, we can load your stuff into our car and take you over to the shelter on Sheffield." I was glad that Sulzer was offering help, but I could see Jimenez wasn't quite as thrilled. "Don't worry," she told her partner, "it's on our way in."

The homeless man trudged back up the embankment to retrieve the bundle of clothes he left there when an unmarked police car pulled up and two officers got out. They were a tactical unit from 23. I knew them from the academy: Officers Dugan and Malloy.

The homeless man sidled down the embankment when Officer Dugan, disregarding our presence, began a string of expletives. "Let's go, old man. Get your shit together and leave. We don't want your stinkin' ass or your Neanderthal types around here." I bet Dugan had been waiting years to use that word. "Are you too lazy to work? I hear Mickey D's are hiring old fucks like you." Dugan looked at Malloy and chuckled at his witticism.

"Hey, Carl, cool out, it's under control," Sulzer interjected. "There's no need for that type of talk here." As she was finishing her sentence, Malloy began to assault the homeless man's bicycle and belongings with his nightstick. He smashed the reflectors with one stroke, a transistor radio with another, and then he jammed his nightstick between the spokes of the back wheel. I looked on in disbelief and could feel my anger welling up as the wheel broke. Before Malloy could do more damage, I wrenched his nightstick away and threw it across the street. I felt a surge of relief, feeling as if I had done something good, once the nightstick clattered near the embankment on the other side of the underpass.

"What the fuck you doin', Malloy?" I yelled.

"Why don't you get back to SMU, Juarez. Let us work our own district."

"Hey, Malloy," Jimenez began, "this is *our* job and we got it under control. I don't remember calling for assistance, so you can just leave!"

The homeless man circled his bike shaking his head. "Why did you ruin my bike, you heartless man? What did I ever do to you?" His eyes were watery and indignation filled his voice.

Dugan had to get in on this, "Shut the fuck up, old man, or else you'll wind up in jail for disorderly."

Sulzer had had enough, "Hey, Nitwit Police, why don't ya get the fuck outta here? Do yourselves a favor and leave."

The 23rd District, located in the heart of Chicago's gay community near Wrigley Field and often referred to as Boys Town, was the home of the Nitwit Police. My father and stepmother, far from being members in this club, both worked there as well and told me that this title was given to a select few by other officers in the District for abuses and behavior beyond comprehension. Members of the Nitwit Police took actions that defied logic, standards, and departmental guidelines. These officers forged stereotypes that stick and undo the work of many damn good cops.

"Oh, that's so nice," Dugan snarled. "Sulzer loves the homeless man. What? Are you some sort of savior pinko liberal or something?"

Finally Dugan and Malloy got in their car, made a U-turn, picked up the nightstick, and drove away.

"I'm sorry about your bike and things," Sulzer shamefacedly offered. "I'll see if anything can be done for you." I could see the embarrassment she felt having been party to this scene. In the five minutes that had passed, the dignity and respect Sulzer and Jimenez had offered this homeless man was shot to shit.

"It's OK. Thanks, but no thanks. I'll manage on my own. I don't trust you police, none of you," he said. I couldn't blame him. "You may not be so bad, but what I know of the police I hate because they hate the homeless people," the man continued. "For what? I didn't ask to be like this, but they have the power to be like they are—assholes."

This incident was one of many that made me consider to what extent law-enforcement agencies in our communities are feared rather than revered. I continued to ask myself this question as I headed back to my team in Narcotics.

All my fears about not returning to the unit were misplaced as I found my spot waiting for me and even returned early my first day back. "Glad to see ya back, Juan," Sergeant Thomas said as I walked into the office. "How was your vacation? Seems like you got a little color." I checked my arms and noticed they were darker from all the sun.

"It was fine and well needed," I replied. I was thinking about the conduct lectures I received from Gina and about all the hot mamas I had seen checking me out in my uniform. My little vacation along the lake revitalized me and made me forget about the problems I had experienced wedging. Now, I was less than thrilled about hitting the streets again in search of small-time dope dealers, but I was happy to be back in the unit.

27

DILL DONALD

SERGEANT THOMAS AND I SAT in our team's cubicle, shooting the breeze about what had gone down in Narcotics during the summer. Slowly other members of the team arrived and, after giving me some shit about working with Gina, Bill, the team's resident goof, asked, "So did you guys do the nasty in the car?"

I looked at him and shook my head. "Is that all you think about, you horny old fuck?"

"What else is there to think about?" he asked.

All of a sudden the lighthearted mood in the room turned serious when Sergeant Thomas mentioned Dill Donald. Nica sat in her chair, let out a low whistle, and shook her head with downcast eyes. I was baffled.

"You didn't hear?" Sergeant Thomas asked.

"No. What happened?" I knew Dill from the day he got into Narcotics. He was the son of an exempt member on the Department. Everyone gave him shit about his old man pulling some strings to get him into Narcotics, but he carried more than his weight in the unit.

A former high school and college football player, Dill was a burly stud, standing five-foot-five with about 250 pounds of pure muscle. He and his partner, Bobby Sands, were two extraordinary black buy officers working Iron Wedge; they were virtually inseparable. I had a chance to work with them one day before I went to SMU. Our meet spot was McKinley Park, and when our team got there I saw these two preparing themselves for the long day ahead. Their prep to impersonate crack fiends was similar to actors priming themselves to go on stage. They came to work in torn, grease-laden overalls and ripped shirts that hadn't seen the wash cycle in three or four months. To make their appearances more disturbing, they rolled around in the grass, picking up loose piles of dirt, and rubbed it on their clothes, hands, and faces. I thought they were overdoing it, but they did even more to get into character.

"Hey Dill," Bobby hollered as he pulled the tab on a can of malt liquor, "You want any of this?" I looked up, thinking he was intent on drinking it, when he took out a rag and poured some beer on it. Bobby then began rubbing the beer-drenched rag over his clothes and neck. These guys were consummate pros and they loved their jobs, fooling everyone they came across on the street. I had deep respect for them.

"It was fucked up, Juan," Nica told me as she continued shaking her head. "I ain't never heard anything more fucked up."

Sergeant Thomas who was shaking his head as well. "You guys gonna tell me or am I gonna have to beat it out of you?" I said finally.

Sergeant Thomas's face changed immediately, "That shit ain't funny, Juan. They were out one day, working over in 15," he began. "You know how Dill and Bobby work, they were on a roll. Dill spotted some players on the corner near Lavergne and Madison, watched 'em make some deals, and wanted to give them a try."

"What he didn't know," interrupted Nica, "was that some lame-ass, white motherfuckin', thick-necked tac boys from 15 were sitting on (conducting surveillance on) the corner." I'd never hear Nica swear before and immediately got the feeling that this was a race issue. She looked over at Bill, the one guy in the room who was white. "Sorry Bill, no offense meant."

"No offense taken," he replied. "You called them out for what they are. Sort of shames me."

"Anyway," Sergeant Thomas continued, "Bobby sets up to eyeball and sees Dill coming up on the players, about to make a deal, when out of nowhere, he gets bum-rushed by all these white dudes. Bobby starts freakin' out, starts yelling on the radio for assistance. All the while Dill's getting his ass beat."

"Next thing ya know," Nica interjects, "Dill's getting the life choked out of him then gets slammed on the stoop of the building as the white boys commence to kick the living shit outta him."

"Where's the fucking backup?" I asked, thinking how the hell could this shit be happening to Dill and then recollecting just how fast things on the street really do happen.

"Bobby jumped out of the car in a hurry," Sergeant Thomas informed me. "And he ran up to Dill with his badge in his hand as Henry (Sergeant Holmes) and enforcement got there. These tac knuckle draggers think Holmes and enforcement are riffraff on the street, rushing them, so they get all defensive like they under attack. Henry, in the meanwhile, is telling them he's a sergeant and that Dill's a cop."

"So what the hell did they do?" I asked.

"They must've thought Henry was lying and that all the enforcement weren't for real because they just kept whupping on Dill while Henry's yelling for them to stop."

"You gotta be kidding me."

"I kid you not, Juan," Sergeant Thomas said. "Finally, enforcement had to pull Dill out of there. It wasn't a pretty sight and even continued into the 15th District."

"Would you believe the watch commander in 15 didn't wanna do shit about it?" Nica said. "Those motherfuckers just kicked the shit out of a cop and he just plays stupid, 'My boys didn't do anything wrong.'"

"How's Dill?" I wondered.

Sergeant Thomas told me that Dill had sustained severe trauma to his stomach and neck and that his injuries needed immediate medical attention. "Dill's been out since then," he said, "and he isn't due back for a couple of months."

"You ask me, he should take off the rest of the damn year. I hope he sues the fuck out of the Department," Nica offered, still seething.

Later on, I learned that this incident was described as an exercise in stupidity and mob brutality by Dill's sergeant, who was a close friend of Sergeant Thomas. Dill did sue the Police Department and eventually won a huge monetary settlement. Not surprisingly, none of the cops involved in the beating got suspended or fired, or even had the balls to apologize to Dill.

After hearing the story, I realized that while it was horrific, it made a weird kind of sense. Dill was, after all, black and all the cops were white.

And a black man getting his ass kicked by cops was something I saw all the time—the difference was that Dill was a cop who'd been beaten by other cops. What baffled me was that they continued to beat Dill even when commanded to stop by a black supervisor. This made me realize that racism ran much deeper in the Department than I had wanted to believe. The War on Drugs was really a war on blacks.

28

WHO REALLY KNOWS?

IT WAS OCTOBER and our team was working Area 2 on Chicago's Far South Side. We were experiencing high productivity around the area of Ninety-sixth and Cole and surpassing with ease our daily quota of four purchases. It was like the dealers were jumping into our cars, wanting to get arrested, but the period was coming to an end and I found myself without any warrants. Narcotics required at least one search warrant a period from every member. I had been relatively successful in this field, making the best of all the tips and clues I accumulated. Along with the daily crack hotline complaints we received on street dealing, we also received tips on crack houses from the communities and from arrestees wanting to snitch on someone in hopes of reducing their sentences. The flow of information was never-ending, and Sergeant Thomas expected us to use the time at the end of the day to check out all the tips we could, hoping we'd unearth warrant locations. That was his justification for cutting us early, but he never pressed us to see if we were doing it. He expected warrants as a payback for his generosity.

I grew to enjoy this time because it allowed us some autonomy in setting up surveillance, sitting on houses, and watching for any signs of dope dealing. It reminded me of the days I worked with Lucky, except that I didn't have to worry about getting redlined. This was my first period back from SMU and it wasn't easy to transition. I was still in vacation mode and wasn't eager to jump right back into the swing of things. I had to pay the price for my lethargy, and I was a little concerned; I had to find a warrant location fast. I confided my situation to Nica, who told me, "Don't sweat it youngblood, there's a crack house on Ninety-sixth serving all day, every day. We hit it about two periods ago while you were chillin' on the beaches. The hit was light, but we got a number (positive raid number). Use the 411 (information) if you want."

"Thanks, Nica."

Nica and I had a good relationship and she was always willing to share information she got from the streets with me. Because we were both in school pursuing degrees, we respected each other even more. She was getting burned out from working as a buy officer for the last five years and she was planning to head west to work with the national park system in an ecological capacity after she did her time—another twelve years—on the job. Nica was using the department the same way I was, as a springboard to bigger and better possibilities, but for now, she was a committed buy officer.

"No problem, Juan," she told me. "You know I got your back."

I accepted the gift and researched the raid number. Two periods prior the house was served a warrant yielding a meager amount of crack, 1.4 grams, and some small currency, about $150. Nevertheless, it was a positive, which was something I could use at the moment.

I was on a bad streak with my warrants as a string of negatives welcomed me back from SMU, but my six were nothing close to Javier's running record of thirteen. Negative search warrants were just that—negative: warrants that turned up no traces of a controlled substance or drug trafficking. There was a vicious competition regarding warrants in the unit, especially on the Iron Wedge teams because it was rumored that the more positives an officer had, the better his or her chance was to move to a mid- or high-level team.

Positives stroked the ego, but these negatives were making me increasingly fearful about the stability of my position in Narcotics. I had heard rumors that if someone didn't produce, he or she would be out of the unit, but then again, I never heard of anyone getting launched for it. I wondered if the rumor was true, but I didn't want to find out the hard way. With that in mind, I focused my attention on testing the target location.

As luck would have it, the crack house had recently drawn the ire of neighborhood activists. There had been numerous crack hotline complaints. The complaints were based on the unusually high foot and vehicular traffic to and from the house—sure signs of drug activity.

Two days of independent surveillance verified the complaints and Nica's information as I witnessed a sporadic flow of foot traffic and hand-to-hand exchanges out of the single-story frame bungalow. That was enough proof for me. My next step was to enlist a buy officer's cooperation in the investigation—T.J. was my choice. I informed Sergeant Thomas of the developing investigation. He approved it and added, "You two watch yourselves. Don't step in no shit out there and stay on the radio."

Making buys for warrants didn't require the presence of the whole team and since we didn't have the man power with us, we had to take extra measures such as making the buy during daylight hours and having an extremely close eyeball position to ensure our safety. It only takes a second for everything to go bad on the streets, but it was a nice change of pace from the daily monotony of Iron Wedge.

I arrived at the target location five minutes before T.J. was to come through so we wouldn't raise any suspicion. Setting up in a parking spot almost directly across the street from the target, I was going to act as an eyeball. I observed one person, a young black female around sixteen, exiting the residence and informed T.J. because I wanted to help him keep track of all movement in front of the house. It's always a good idea to keep buy officers posted just so they'll know what they're heading into.

T.J. radioed back, "Yo Juan, I'm fixin' to roll through now. I'm coming from the east."

"Good luck and be careful, bro'," I responded as his car pulled up to the curb three homes away from the target.

"Will do. I'm shutting down." He clicked off his radio and the door of his covert vehicle opened.

He casually approached the front of the house and knocked on the door. A couple of seconds later a young black man opened the door, chatted with T.J., and then made a hand-to-hand transaction with him. "That's a positive, Juan," he said once he got back in his car. I breathed a sigh of relief—so far so good. We headed back to the unit to do the necessary paperwork, obtain the appropriate signatures, and deposit the evidence into the safe.

Armed with the perfunctory paperwork—including a case report, inventory slips, and search warrant—I headed over to Twenty-sixth and California to see a state's attorney. After reading all the reports, the state's attorney would either sign the search warrant—granting probable cause— or suggest ways to get it.

The state's attorney approved probable cause and happily signed my paperwork. Once that signature was secured, I went to see a judge who had the final say on whether or not I had a serviceable warrant. As Narcotics officers, we knew which judges were more willing to sign without intense scrutiny, so I made sure to visit one of them to expedite the process. Entering the judge's full courtroom, I waited for a break in the court call before I approached his clerk, showed her my badge, and told her my business.

"Wait one moment, officer," she told me. She got up and approached the bench, informing the judge the reason for my visit.

The judge stood up, banged his gavel, and announced, "Court will take a five-minute recess." He got up and walked through a door behind the bench. His clerk then instructed me to go into his chambers.

"Good afternoon, your honor," I began and handed him my file.

"Officer Juarez, do you swear all the facts on this report are true and valid?" he asked after he scanned the reports and saw the state's attorney's signature.

"I do, your honor," was my solemn response. I was confident every word on my request was true.

"Seems pretty cut and dried," he said as he signed the warrant and wished me luck; I had twenty-four hours to execute it. I radioed Sergeant Thomas from the hall of the court building and told him the good news.

"A few brothers get another day of freedom," he said lightheartedly. "Good job, Juan. See ya at ten at Area 2."

Before serving a warrant, our team usually sent a buy officer to the target location to ensure the operation was up and running, guaranteeing a positive raid number with that purchase. Even if the bag that was bought was the last one in the house, we'd still get credit for a positive search warrant and could make the arrest just as we would with an Iron Wedge buy. But that morning we didn't make a buy because it was too early and just went on with plans to execute the warrant.

Sleep deprived and grumbling because we had to meet on the Far South Side at 10:00 A.M., our team, along with Sergeant Abernathy's, assembled at 727 East 111th Street to formulate a plan of attack. I was going to be the front man and hit the door with the ram. Javier and Franco were covering the back, and the rest of the team was going to swarm through the door once I smashed it. T.J. was going to eyeball the scene because he was the buy officer and we didn't want to expose him. I jumped in the car with Javier, Franco, and Mickey and we headed over to the target location to execute the warrant. They began joking about the streak of negatives I had amassed. "Another negative and you're closer to the launching pad; the countdown begins," teased Javier, who was driving. I was sitting right behind him with the ram resting upright on the floor. He made sure to make eye contact with me through the rearview mirror.

"Look whose fuckin' talking," I shot back. "You and your baker's dozen of big-ass zeroes ain't nothin' to be proud of. I'll tell you what, Javi. If this is a positive, you can have the number, how's that? Will that make you feel better, zero-for-thirteen boy?"

Mickey jumped in to break the rising tension, "Oh, oh, oh, can I have it? Can I?" he begged.

I was on edge because I hadn't had any coffee that morning, but I wasn't as panicked as my teammates thought I was. Sergeant Thomas had told me earlier at the Area that he was happy with my overall performance, so that put me at ease.

We didn't see any foot traffic as we approached the location. Nice and safe, I thought to myself, and we continued on. Sergeant Thomas and I were standing at the front door, ready to break it down and simultaneously announce, "Chicago Police," when we heard a female voice yelling from behind it.

"Hey! Hey! Hey, now!" the voice pleaded in a high pitch. "There ain't no need to go busting down my door like y'all did a couple of months ago." Sarge and I exchanged curious looks. I shrugged my shoulders, "She must've seen us coming or something," I offered in a dejected tone, knowing I wasn't going to be able to smash the door down. I wondered if the woman had been tipped off.

The chain on the door rattled and the knob began to turn. "I'm opening the door now, so none of y'all get crazy and shoot a nigga, alright?" she announced as everyone on the team stepped back and drew their guns. Better to be safe than dead in this line of work.

A middle-aged black woman, with a head full of wispy gray hair and slender as a shoestring, opened the door. "Can I help y'all?" she questioned as she stood there with her hands on her hips.

She was pushed to the side as easily as a piece of paper, and the team flooded the house looking for other people. "Ain't no one else here 'cept me!" she hollered. She was right—no one else was there. After securing our safety, I announced my office and what we were doing, "Here's the search warrant signed by the judge giving us permission to search your house."

We began a systematic search of her residence for contraband, emptying out dresser drawers, closets, and cabinets and throwing personal effects on the floor while Mickey interrogated her.

"Y'all ain't gonna find shit!" she hollered. "But y'all go on and waste your time."

We had no luck whatsoever in detecting any contraband in the house. The detainee yelled over her shoulder as if no one had heard her the first time, "Y'all ain't gonna find shit!"

When Mickey pressed her about narcotics being sold out of the house by the man identified in the warrant, she laughed, "My son's in jail; he's the troublemaker 'round my crib. They (5th District officers) done come and picked him up last night on a warrant. I hope they keep 'em locked up because I want my house back. Even after y'all fuck it up," she stated emphatically. It looked as if I had stumbled upon another negative. I shook my head in disbelief. I really thought I would get a positive this time.

"Hey, Juan," Javier called when he saw me shaking my head. "I was just fuckin' with ya in the car. Sorry."

"Don't sweat it, bro', it's not a big thing." The negative bothered me for a moment, but the disappointment passed after I told myself that I had given the investigation a thorough effort. It was really a case of dumb luck. "Hey, Javi, if you still want the number you can have it," I joked, knowing my name was going in the negative ledger once again.

As we were ready to vacate the premises, a fellow officer we called the Russian, asked me to come to the back of the house. A hint of excitement passed through me, thinking he found something. When I got to him, he said, "Do you wanna make this a positive?" His eyes directed me to his right palm, which was holding a tiny, clear ziplock bag containing one white rock. I estimated that this amount of crack had a street value of $27.36.

"Where the fuck did you get that?" I asked.

"It's my insurance policy," he said, winking. "So, do you wanna?"

"Nah, that's all right," I said, wondering if he was trying to set me up or if he was really serious about sandbagging (planting drugs) this woman. "Thanks, but it's not that serious," I said, turning away from him and marching toward the front of the house. "Sorry, ma'am," I offered to the woman before I walked out. She was sitting on her couch with her head in her hands and didn't say a word.

As I headed toward the car, my mind raced. Was the Russian part of IAD trying to set a trap? I suddenly recalled that even before I left for SMU the Russian had been highly successful with warrants. Not many of them were noteworthy for their seizures; but at least they were all positive. Or were they? I now had to wonder how many of his positives were legitimate. Then I began thinking of the day I worked with Malfitano and the kid's voice rang in my head. "Nah, man, you ain't gonna put a case on me!" he'd said. I wondered if Malfitano sandbagged that kid in addition to stealing his money.

I admit I hadn't had any problem picking up that roll of cash when it had flown out of the window last spring, but I never fucked around with anyone's freedom by sandbagging. In my mind, picking up a wad of discarded cash was miles away from framing someone and ruining lives. Shit, the woman of the house had enough problems; she didn't need any more. She had a son in jail and a house in ruins. Despite obstacles she was trying, from the looks of it, to get her life in order. Was the Russian willing to falsely arrest this woman and perjure himself on an official court document for a measly $27.36 worth of crack cocaine? Evidently he was, but I didn't want anything to do with it.

I didn't need to complicate my life any further. My streak of negatives had to end if I wanted to feel secure in Narcotics. Hell, I still had six more to go to catch up to Javier and he was still in the unit, but I wasn't about to accept the kind of help that the Russian had to offer—even if it meant leaving the unit. I never liked the guy to begin with. Now I had no respect for him whatsoever. One day he'd have to answer for his actions—and so would Malfitano—but that was one road I wasn't willing to go down.

29

TIME TO PAY THE PIPER

MARIA CALLED ME ONE FALL DAY and I tried to make plans to see her later. "I don't think that's a good idea, Juan," she said despondently. This was the first time I could remember her rejecting me, and the sadness in her voice was new. "I have to go see a doctor."

I tuned out my inner voice and the sadness in her voice and pursued my own selfish desires. "All right," I said, "Maybe we could hook up tomorrow night?" envisioning wild sexual escapades with her. Silence. My first thought was that she was pregnant and my second thought was that she had decided to have an abortion. "Maria, are you OK?" This was as close as I was going to get to ask her if she was pregnant. No matter how hard I tried to drown it out, my instincts told me that she was, but I wasn't going to ask her to verify my fears. The line remained quiet. "Maria . . . Maria . . . are you there?"

Finally she answered, "Yeah, I'm here. I'm all right. I'll see you," she said before hanging up the phone. Holding the receiver in my hand, I knew the truth—I had gotten another woman pregnant. I couldn't put the phone down, but instead rolled over on my bed, clutching it to my heart.

It hurt knowing I had impregnated another woman and that an unborn fetus was going to be destroyed because of my irresponsibility and lust. What was I so afraid of that kept me away from taking responsibility for my actions? Why hadn't I learned my lesson the first time and used a condom?

The memory of Ana's operation, the thought of desecrating her body, scarring her for life, and forever changing our relationship slapped me—*punched* me—no, stabbed at me repeatedly. And now I had done the same thing to Maria. I buried my head in my pillow, but no tears came. What the fuck was wrong with me? Was I that coldhearted? Had I severed my emotions so thoroughly that I couldn't cry, not for myself, for someone with whom I had been intimately connected?

Once I got over the initial bout of guilt, I decided that finding out whether Maria was pregnant was the last thing I needed. She had never told me she was pregnant. I convinced myself that I was making it all up and that my intuition had deceived me. I distanced myself from my guilt; I stuffed it inside and ignored it. It was her life and her body. She could do whatever she wanted with them.

My heart felt heavy, but I eased my conscience by telling myself that Maria's predicament was no big deal. I still had Ana. I didn't have the integrity to let Maria know how I felt about her, and I didn't have the strength to try and repair the relationship. It would take too much effort on my part and I wasn't willing to make that sacrifice for her. All I knew was that I was never going to see Maria again.

When I went to Ana's later that evening, she was surprised that I wanted to sleep over. I was usually at Maria's, but Ana allowed me into her bed without question. All summer long we had been participating in triathlons, and sleeping next to her well-defined body rekindled my desire to be with her. We made love all night as I put the memory of Maria's call as far away as possible.

And just like that I was back in Ana's life full-time, back in the warmth and security of her arms and her gentle kisses. Her love was motherly in essence—unconditional and soothing—and I felt relieved to be in her good graces once again.

Maybe it was because I knew I would never call Maria again or maybe it was because the things Gina had told me over the summer had finally sunk in, but I wanted my relationship with Ana to be the way it was when we first met. I wanted to feel my heart sing when I saw her, and I wanted to see her every day. I wanted to be there for her because she had always been there for me.

I had been a cop for more than four years, and I had managed to stay focused on school the whole time I was wedging. Sergeant Thomas made my academic pursuit smooth by consistently signing my tuition reimbursement forms without a hassle. He made sure I had ample time to get to my classes or hit the library for finals week. All the while he encouraged me to excel and demanded I get good grades. I didn't disappoint him. I maintained a 3.0.

I was getting closer to finishing my MA in English when Ana said, "Why stop there? You know you always wanted to be a teacher. Why don't you get a master's in education? The department will pay for it, won't they?"

I thought about it for a second, "Hell yeah, they'll pay." And then I realized in my heart that I'd probably never want to stop taking classes, always needing to be a student—challenging myself and strengthening my intellect. I wanted to be a lifelong learner. That was going to be quite an expensive proposition, but as long as I had the city footing the bill I could continue my academic pursuits. So I submitted my application to DePaul's School of Education, knowing that as I was already enrolled in one graduate program, getting accepted into another was just a formality.

During Christmas Ana and I went to Cancún, Mexico. There we rekindled our passions, and I was able to focus on Ana and her place in my life. We took a detour on the way back and went to visit my grandparents in Puebla, my father's hometown, and stayed with them for a week. They immediately took to Ana and welcomed her into the family as if she was their own daughter. It gave me a look into the future with Ana by my side. Our vacation together made me feel like I had weathered the rocky storm of my demanding libido. Our relationship was finally heading onto the right track.

I never heard from Maria after our phone conversation four months earlier and I made no attempt to contact her because my life was going well and I didn't want to revisit old wounds. What good would revisiting the past do me? I was living in the moment and with Maria now gone, I was able to appreciate Ana more fully.

Just after New Year's Ana came by my apartment with a sad look on her face. "I'm four months pregnant, Juan," she told me.

My stomach took the express elevator ride right up to my throat, and I thought I was going to throw up. I closed my eyes, tight, hoping I could escape by doing so, but there was a voice screaming inside my head, getting louder and louder. I had to open my eyes. That's not what we needed right now or maybe it was and I didn't know it.

"What? How did this happen?" I said, confused.

"You know how it happened, Juan. When I didn't have my period, I went to have a test done and the doctor told me I was four months pregnant."

"Why did you wait so long? Why didn't you get tested sooner?"

She looked at me and I could see tears welling up in her eyes. "Ever since we've been together I haven't had a regular cycle, you know that. I didn't think anything of it." I wanted to reach out and hug her, but my body just wouldn't do it. When I imagined a baby in our lives, all I saw were restrictions everywhere—restrictions on what I wanted to do and where I wanted to go.

We talked for hours about our situation, going back and forth over our options. I tried to appear upbeat and elated, talking of marriage and a happy life together. Who was I fooling? I was doing a shitty job of convincing myself, and I definitely wasn't convincing her. She saw right through me. "I'm gonna abort it," she said.

"We can make this work," I said, trying to make her believe me. I couldn't stand the thought of her having a second abortion because of what I did, especially with Maria's situation still fresh in my mind. But in my heart I also couldn't bear the idea of being tied down to the responsibility of having a child.

When she ran out of tears, she made up her mind. "I'm gonna make the appointment tomorrow." I held her as I silently rejoiced. But I also knew that I'd never be able to leave her. There was no way I'd be able to live with the guilt of getting her pregnant twice and then walking away from her. I accepted this as I rocked her in my arms and told her everything was going to be all right.

Ana made her appointment and it was scheduled for one week later. I drove her to the clinic at Foster and Elston. People were demonstrating in front of the place, so we parked in the rear of the clinic. There was dark, plastic sheeting over the fence that protected Ana from seeing the protestors, but she could still hear them and so could I. Beginning to regret our decision or at least our choice of clinics, I felt an intense anger welling up in me. I looked at Ana and she was crying, so I picked up speed and entered the clinic with her clinging to my arm. I signed her in and waited.

As I waited, terrible thoughts came to me about the pain she was going through in the operating room all alone, with no one there to hold her and console her. Such a sweet spirit, I thought, and now she's destroyed. How the fuck had I let this happen to her again? What kind of man was I to let this happen to someone I loved—not once, but twice? When I saw her emerge from the operating room an hour or two later, I ran to her and held her.

We didn't talk the whole ride back to my apartment, and I laid her down to rest in my bed.

The next day I thought long and hard about our relationship and decided it was now or never. Or maybe it was guilt that drove me to it, but I asked Ana to move in with me. "Juan," she said. "That's not necessary."

"It is," I urged. "We've been going out for seven years and I need to prove to you how serious I am about our relationship."

"Maybe you should convince yourself first," she replied.

"I have and this is how I'm gonna prove it to you. I'm serious. Will you move in with me?"

"Can we talk about this later? I want a chance to think about it."

"Think about what, Ana? Don't you love me?"

"You got some nerve asking me that question. Leave me alone!"

"Ana," I begged, "I'm just trying to do what's right."

"You should've thought about that before I had the abortion!" she hollered. Her words burned, but I shrugged them off, turning off my feelings and once again coming up with a perfect excuse.

"I've got to get to work. Would you please think about it?"

When I got home from work, she said she had thought about it and had some reservations. We sat down and talked until the morning when I finally convinced her to move in. I was thrilled to have gotten my way once again and elated that I was going to have a chance to win Ana back.

It was a beautiful spring day when Ana moved in. I was eating lunch with Mickey and Franco when I got a page from her at our apartment. We had moved her stuff in earlier that week and she had taken a day off of work to organize her things. I looked forward to hearing her joy-filled voice when I returned her call from a nearby pay phone. "What the fuck is this shit?" were the angry words that greeted my voice. "Who the fuck is Valerie?"

"What are you talking about?" I asked. My mind raced. How the hell had she found out about my fling from Mardi Gras three years ago? I hadn't heard from Valerie since I left her high and dry in Chicago and jetted off to Saint Martin with Ana. My mind frantically searched for a lie.

"I can't believe this shit! I can't fuckin' believe this!" she sobbed hysterically and then slammed the phone down, cutting me off. I put another thirty cents in the pay phone. As soon as she answered, she yelled, "I'm moving out!" She slammed the phone down again.

I was in deep shit now. I didn't want to lose Ana. She had been my support for the past seven and a half years and I couldn't imagine my life without her. I had done her wrong, but that didn't mean I didn't love her.

"I'm taking the squad home, you guys," I told Mickey and Franco. "Emergency at home." I flew from Thirty-first and Wentworth and arrived home to a red-eyed and distraught Ana.

"What the fuck is this shit? I was looking for some paper to write you a note, and I found this!" she said, throwing a notebook at me. "Who the fuck is this bitch?" She was holding up a letter and poem I had written Valerie but never sent to her.

"It's nothing, Ana. I met her at Mardi Gras and we talked for a while. I was attracted to her, but nothing happened."

"The letter says you'll fucking see her in Colorado. Are you lying to me?"

What was I going to do—tell her the truth? "The letter wasn't sent and I never saw her again after I left New Orleans."

Ana was livid and grew even more distraught as she read the letter out loud, "The sweetness of your kiss, a body Venus made . . ." Her eyes were full of fire as she charged me with her arms flailing, striking out at me with both her fists. I tried to grab her arms and settle her down when my radio started going off.

"Juarez, where you at? We were supposed to meet at noon. You're late," Sergeant Thomas said. What an inopportune time for this, I thought as I was trying to keep Ana's punches from landing.

"It's only a letter, Ana, a letter. Nothing else happened," I said as we continued to struggle. She landed a sharp, right-handed slap to my face. Immediately she stopped her flailing and covered her mouth with her hands.

"Oh, shit! I'm sorry," she cried.

I was transported to my youth, when witnessing my parents fight numbed me, causing me to run for shelter, physical or emotional. I was hurt and resigned myself to accept the slap and another one if she had it in her. My shock overwhelmed me, I couldn't have fought back even if I'd wanted to. I didn't want to perpetuate the physical abuse that tore my parents apart, so I dropped my arms by my side and gazed at her with sadness.

"Juarez," the radio interrupted again. "Where are you?"

I walked into the kitchen. "Sarge," I responded, choosing what was more important—my cop life. "I'm on my way. Gimme me 'bout fifteen minutes."

"Call me when you're at Area 2," he replied.

I walked back to the living room where Ana was sitting on the couch. "Ana, I have to get all the way to 111th Street. Can we talk about this when I get back?"

She got up, walked to the bedroom, and started crying. I left for work and felt like the whole world we shared had just imploded in my living room. When I got home that night, surprised and thankful that she was still there, I continued the damage control as I convinced her that nothing had happened with Valerie.

By the end of our first week living together it seemed as if Ana had forgotten about everything. That's how she was—she was able to forgive and forget. Her love was evident again and I felt secure in her embrace. Still, in my heart I knew things between us would never be the same again.

I enjoyed going to sleep and waking up with Ana next to me. I was spending every day with her and having fun, but it was a different type of fun—it was more like a deep-seated friendship. I loved her, but I wasn't in love with her. I finished the winter quarter at school and began hanging out at bars and drinking with fellow students, losing myself in alcohol and burying my pain in self-pity.

Ana and I had lived together three short months, but in that compressed vacuum of time, we lived a lifetime of experiences and suffered in each other's pain. Soon I wasn't coming home until late at night. When I did come home, I was met by Ana's persistent questions and accusations. Then she started doing something I despised—she'd cry herself to sleep. I couldn't deal with that, so I started drinking more and staying out later. I never answered her pages. Every time I heard her voice, I felt her pain and anger.

I'd jump on my motorcycle, run away to a bar, and find some girl I could stay the night with. I needed to find the warmth of human connection, no matter how empty and pointless it was.

One morning after I stayed out all night, Ana was waiting for me at the apartment. "I'm moving out," she said in a voice utterly lacking in emotion.

"What?" I said. I started to protest, but then it dawned on me that she was offering me exactly what I wanted.

"Don't try to talk me out of it," she said. "My mind is set."

I accepted her wishes and didn't even try to change her mind. This time I knew better. I borrowed my friend's van again and moved her to a place near Barry and Broadway.

When we were done moving her things, I asked, "Does this mean we're breaking up?"

I wanted her to be the one to terminate the relationship, but she said, "Let's take a break from each other for a while."

I really didn't know what that meant, but I didn't ask any questions. I just assumed we were breaking up because that's what I wanted, but I couldn't speak the actual words. And while I kept my eyes shut to my situation with Ana, the realities of working in the ghetto kept pressing me to open them up and take a good hard look at the people I was arresting.

30

THE YOUTH SHALL PAY

"SARGE, LOOKS LIKE THERE'S a possibility at Fifty-fourth and Indiana. Some hype seems to be directing traffic," Colette, who had already secured three of the team's daily quota-required four purchases of crack cocaine, keyed in.

It was one month since Ana had moved out of my apartment. But regardless of my personal turmoil, this was just another day on the job; we were on the streets waging the never-ending battle against narcotics. I was riding with Sergeant Thomas because Mickey was at the Area waiting for Javier, who was out checking warrant locations. "Nica, if that's something you'd like to try, be my guest," Sergeant Thomas said into the radio.

"Cool, I'm coming that way. Thanks for the info, 'lette," Nica keyed back.

"Enforcement," Sergeant Thomas opened the key and inquired, "you nearby?" He wanted to make sure that there were enough officers for the takedown. Ten-fours simultaneously scratched in. "All right Nica, go on," he instructed as he punched the accelerator and our new Caprice sucked up the asphalt on King Drive.

"I'm settin' up at 54— South Indiana," Colette informed all listeners. No more than ten seconds later, she keyed in, "All right, Sarge. I see Nica coming down the block. She's parking on the east side of the street, approaching a hype that has on black-with-dirty-old-stripes-on-the-side sweatpants and a Bulls Three-peat Champs T-shirt."

Colette relayed the best play-by-play by far. As a result, we never lost a suspect when she was eyeballing.

"He's five-nine or -ten, salt and pepper—close to the head—and sorta thick for a hype, around a hundred and thirty pounds. Nica's conversating and the hype pointed her to the gangway at 54—. Uh-oh, some shorty's going to the gangway too. Can't be all of eleven. Man, they keep gettin' younger and younger," she sighed. "He's got a Bulls number twenty-three jersey, stands about four-two and seventy pounds if he's lucky. He just made the exchange with Nica and she's headin' back to her car. She flashed a positive." Nica would indicate a drug purchase by tipping her hat toward the eyeball as she turned to her car.

"I suggest that you all be slick cuz I bet five-to-one that shorty's got some rabbit in him," Colette resumed. It was a fair warning we could have a runner on our hands. The most important thing I had learned from street-buying experiences was to be prepared for anything. I also learned to never second-guess a suspect's flight-or-fight reaction in an arrest situation. The kid's way too young to want to box, I thought. Chances are he'll run. "Nica's back in her car; stand by."

"Sarge, that's a positive and you want the shorty that turned me. You got him in your sights, 'lette?" inquired Nica.

"Sho' nuff. He ain't in no hurry to go nowhere."

"OK, enforcement, move in. I want two from the north and I got the alley," was all Sergeant Thomas said as he began moving our car toward the rear of the target location. The alleys and the gangways were a popular first choice for an escape route. In front is Indiana Avenue; it's an immense street: five lanes wide, all heading north, and it's littered on both sides with vacant lots where houses once stood. We were cutting off the main arteries of escape.

Sergeant Thomas eased the car down Fifty-fourth, turned southbound into the alley, continued to the rear of 54—, and waited as the other cars arrived in front of the location. My adrenaline pumped. I was prepared to jet out of the car if this kid took flight. To me, chasing someone down was just a game; the runner was my prey. I took in a deep breath preparing myself.

Just then Javier's voice on the radio interrupted, "Sarge, we got him. Hey Nica, what's the numbers and denomination?" It turned out that this was one of those rare days when he actually returned to work after checking out warrant locations. Usually he took the whole day scrounging for warrant locations after receiving tips from junky informants that resulted, most of the time, in fruitless endeavors. He was constantly envisioning the big bust. The rest of the team was pretty sure that wedging was way down on his priority list, and since he held a running record of thirteen straight negatives, no one on the team knew exactly what he was actually doing on the streets. We all assumed he was out wasting time. It was a mystery why Sergeant Thomas allowed him free rein, but then again, Sergeant Thomas gave all of us special privileges at times.

"Hey, Javi, you done meeting with your informant?" wisecracked Bill, the valued vet of the team who had seen his share of loafers during his twenty-odd years on the job. Obviously the rumors about getting bounced out of the unit for lack of producing were just that—rumors.

"That's 243D as in David, and that would be on a twenty," Nica answered without hesitation. "Is that you, baby?" she crooned.

"Ten-four. We got it. What's happening, girl?" replied Javier, dancing around the taunt. "You want us to grab the hype for turning the deal?"

"No, you can cut him," Sergeant Thomas directed succinctly. "I think we have enough work with the juve. I'll take him off your hands for notification (of his guardians). You guys can head in and start the paperwork. Mickey, make sure you do a CAR (contact arrest report) on him before we pick him up."

"No need to tell me, Sarge. I got one going now," Mickey responded in his super-efficient tone. Mickey wasn't much of a buy officer, but he knew his way around the intricacies of the time-consuming paper routine. Without a doubt, he was the best paper man on the second floor.

Sergeant Thomas slowly pulled out of the alley. He took a right on Fifty-fifth and another right on Indiana. Mickey and Javier were parked in front of 54—. When we pulled up next to their car, I saw one of the most hardened faces I had ever seen.

He was just a child. His eyes were vacant, glazed over as if unfazed by this episode. His childish form hunched over as he gazed past Mickey and Javier and out the windshield. This was just a regular day in his life.

Mickey got out, opened the rear door of their car, and held onto the cuffed kid. He was a lightly caramelized shade of brown and thin as a thread. The thickest parts of his body were the knots disguised as kneecaps and elbows. I was amazed. Why didn't this kid slip out of the handcuffs? His arms were about two inches in circumference and hung lifelessly. His hands, shackled and twisted so that the backs touched, dangled in front of his body. His arms looked like they were about to snap under their own weight. He moved with the awkwardness of a preadolescent kid.

"C'mon, shorty," Mickey said. "He's living with his grandma down the street at 56— South Indiana, first floor. She's home as we speak, or so he says. By the way, one year off. He's only ten."

"Put him in the car," Sergeant Thomas replied, shaking his head. This was a street reality that was wearing me down. I wondered what it felt like for a twenty-five-year veteran like Thomas. Every day we worked we were throwing young black men—usually between the ages of fourteen and nineteen—into jail. It was a depressing routine to work in these impoverished neighborhoods, under these conditions, and see so many lives wasted. The War on Drugs was an unjust solution to problems of poverty and addiction.

Mickey gave us the prisoner and seat belted him in.

"OK, shorty, what's the story?" Sergeant Thomas began the informal questioning by turning around and looking the kid straight in the eyes. He wanted to know exactly why this kid was working the streets as a crack dealer instead of playing on them like most ten-year-olds.

"Ain't nothin' goin' on here 'cept me going to Fifty-first Street (Area 1). Just another day in the 'hood, what's new?" I could hear in his voice the resignation that had long ago transformed his innocence into cynicism.

"Who's at the house now?" Sergeant Thomas asked.

"My grandma and she don't care one way or another. Might as well not even go by the house cuz she don't want me no way," he answered. He sank deeper into the back seat of the unmarked squad.

I turned and asked, "How do you know that?" A grim face registering disbelief and indignation stared back at me.

"Cuz I do," he replied. "If you's want, go to the house, but I tellin' you straight up, it don't matter." He uttered this last sentence with the conviction of one who has seen more than his share of misery, suffering, and bullshit.

"What about your ma or your dad? What about the schools? Can't they help?" I asked as Sergeant Thomas shook his head sympathetically in response to the kid's answers while nudging me as if to say not to go there. Sergeant Thomas put the car in drive and started over to the kid's grandmother's house.

"Look at this neighborhood, man! I tells you I ain't got no fuckin' chance, simple as that! School's a fuckin' joke. Nobody don't learn, don't wanna learn, and the teachers don't wanna teach, so I ain't got no chance." His torrent continued, "My grandma, she just got stuck with me. My mother dropped me off a month ago and told her she'd be back, and she ain't come back yet. I think she run off and ain't never coming back for me." His chest was heaving as if he had been running hard. He appeared thoroughly exhausted after that tirade.

As we pulled up in front of the house, Sergeant Thomas said, "Hey, shorty, what's your name?"

"David. David Thomson," he responded. I felt sort of stupid for not asking him earlier and even more so for not looking on the CAR Mickey had completed.

"David," I said, turning around to face the kid, trying to gain eye contact. "I'm going to see your grandmother, and notify her where you'll be, and when she'll be able to pick you up. Is there anything you want me to tell her?" He wouldn't look at me. I was hoping to make some type of connection with him because it seemed to me that he was giving up on himself, the neighborhood, and the world around him.

I tried to infuse my voice with a little more hope and assurance than usual. I don't really know if I was reassuring him or myself. I was confused as to my role in society. If I was a part of the solution to combat drugs and improve the living conditions for the people of this city, I certainly didn't feel that way.

I looked at David Thomson's environment—there wasn't much hope for him. And a kid without hope is like a body without a spirit. At such a young age, his life had already been scripted for him. Was I facilitating his demise? I could already see that without guidance, intervention, or education this kid was bound to be a repeat offender. My reflection stopped there; no matter how I felt, I knew what I had to do and where

David Thomson had to go—and where he would likely spend the rest of his life.

"Naw, I ain't got nothin' to say."

I walked to the front door of 56— South Indiana, a shabby and slightly run-down two-story graystone on a ravaged block. There was nothing on the North Side of Chicago that could compare with the deprivation and desolation of this neighborhood. I had no choice but to start believing the kid had a point as I gazed upon the surroundings of his day-to-day reality. To the left was a graystone, boarded-up and crumbling, mirroring the street itself. To the right, thigh-high grass and weeds flourished and the skeleton of a burned-out car was buried among all types of refuse, a testament to the neglect of the community. The back alley was the community dumping grounds. Chicago's motto, "The city that works," had no meaning here. The city's streets and sanitation workers must have taken the last few days or, from the looks of it, months off. There are numerous neighborhoods like this in Chicago and across America. Yet hopeless and neglected as they are, they are home to many.

I rang the bell. In a moment, the door creaked open and a woman's voice knifed through, "Yes! Who is it?" Anger and abruptness tinged the voice while distrust peered out at me.

"Ma'am, my name is Officer Juarez and I'm with the Chicago Police Department. May I have a word with you?"

"If it's 'bout David, I don't wanna hear it. By God! All that child is is trouble and always up to gettin' on my last nerve. Just like his mother." The door closed and she unlatched the security chain. Then she reopened the door allowing us to talk face-to-face. She looked more tired and worn down than her forty-five years or so of life would suggest.

"It is about David, and he's outside in the car. He's just been arrested for selling crack to an undercover police officer, and he's being taken to Fifty-first Street. We'll have to process and turn him over to a juve officer." It was a mechanical delivery, but it seemed to be as much a routine to her as it was to me. I felt like shit about being the messenger of this news, especially when it was so obvious that she was fed up with being a grandmother to a kid she seemingly didn't like or understand.

"He was just there two days ago," she said, throwing her hands in the air wildly. "I swear I don't know what to do with that there boy." She shook her head. "He's a bad seed and his mama's a bad seed too. I haven't seen her for weeks. She just drops the boy with me and tells me that she be back. And me, I'm the fool. I's still waiting. He's my own flesh and blood. I couldn't leave him out on the streets, ya know?"

"What about your husband or the boy's father? Couldn't they be of some assistance?"

"Hmmmph. They both wound up in jail and when they get out, the first thing they wants to do is live the years that been takin' from them and that don't mean raisin' no family. I don't even know where or even *if* my man's still alive. I don't give two shits no way."

I was getting in way over my head. There was nothing I could do to remedy this bleak reality that spanned generations. I had to end this discussion; I just had to get away.

"Sorry to hear that, ma'am. We're going to Fifty-first Street now, and he'll be there for an hour or so. May I have your name for notification purposes?"

"Mayella Hardwell."

What more could I say? "Thanks, I hope you have a nice day" really didn't seem appropriate, so I just said goodbye. Our conversation ended, the door closed, and the chain rattled back into place.

I opened the car door and saw David's swollen eyes and tear-streaked face. He was trying to wipe away the tears with the back of his cuffed hands.

"What happened, Sarge?" I asked.

"We were talking and I asked him what he wanted out of life."

"What'd he say?"

"To have a home and a family."

I looked back at this kid, this ten-year-old kid—and I knew that fulfilling his simple wish was all but impossible in the ghetto.

That mid-April day in 1995 left me with a spiritual heaviness I had never known before. I knew I didn't want to be part of this soul-crushing operation much longer. My perspective on the War on Drugs had changed. While I had once done my perceived duty without question, I was now in need of some justification. I questioned my purpose, the purpose behind Iron Wedge, and the Narcotics Division's purpose in the War on Drugs.

Disillusionment took me down like a landslide. Two years earlier I had begun to wonder if this war had an alternative motive to ensnare and imprison minority youths, charge them as felons, and take away their freedom and their civil liberties. After taking away all their potential, the system seemed happy to return them to mainstream society lacking the very skills they needed to survive. (See "The Dirty Truth by the Numbers" for the statistics.)

The incident with David Thomson convinced me that I could no longer be a foot soldier in this War on Drugs. I had seen enough: racial profiling, blatant brutality, sandbagging, and an overall culture of corruption. I now saw the whole legal process as a race to incarcerate. I felt like a henchman getting paid to destroy lives by throwing people in jail without offering viable opportunities for change. It was a yoke around my neck, and I wanted it removed.

Drinking hard now and finding my solace in alcohol, I was glad that Ana wasn't seeing my downward spiral. We had been on speaking terms, but that stopped. I wanted to be left alone, and Ana granted me my wish. I was irritable and didn't like my job anymore. I needed a change.

There was an opening on the Tavern Team, which was led by Sergeant Mankewicz. I wanted to join this team because it would take me away from wedging. The Tavern Team's goal was to close down bars by making on-site drug purchases. They worked closely with the city's Liquor License Commission (LLC). They worked late hours—8 P.M. until 4 A.M.—so most Narcotics officers were unaware of what they were up to. I had an in, however. My cousin Paco, who had recently transferred to the Unit, was on the Tavern Team.

"It's the best kept secret in the Unit, take my word," Paco told me. I asked him what made it so great. He replied, "Manko's a prince. We do our job and he takes care of us."

"What bones does he throw you guys?" I asked.

Paco told me they worked short hours and got away with it because no one was in the Unit at that time of the night to see what they were doing. Manko's demands were minimal—one takedown a week. The team members chose the bars they worked; the job entailed drinking and trying to score powder cocaine. "We don't do no wedging bullshit," he said, which was the recommendation I needed. "We also make tons of OT," he said with a smile.

I asked what he thought about me joining the team. "Go ask Manko," he replied.

It was early May 1995. I caught up with Sergeant Mankewicz outside his office and asked him if I could join his team. He asked me one question, "Can you buy dope?"

"Can I buy dope?" I repeated, trying to make my words sound rhetorical. Actually his question took me by surprise. I wasn't a buy officer; I had made only three scores on the streets. And trying to score crack wasn't like hitting the bar scene in search of powder.

"Yeah," he said. "Can you buy dope?"

I was willing to try anything once. "Of course I can," I said. As the words left my mouth, the memory of my first attempt at buying a rock of crack cocaine came to mind. It was at the Altgeld Gardens Public Housing Complex in 1992. I walked up to some hustlers who were playing basketball. I asked for a rock. They all looked at me and then at each other. Finally one of them pointed at the pebble-strewn ground and said, "You want a rock? There's one. Pick it up and get the fuck outta here."

"Yeah," I repeated to Manko. "I can buy dope."

"See me when you come back from Summer Mobile and I'll let you know," Manko told me.

I still hadn't moved up the seniority ladder; consequently I'd been drafted for another summer of working the beaches. At least I'd get some immediate relief from working the ghetto.

"I'll take you up on that, Sarge," I said. "Take my word."

31

SUMMER MOBILE UNIT REDUX

THE SUMMER OF 1995, my second in the SMU, was markedly different than the previous summer, during which I had practiced restraint and respect—respect for my job, my partner, Ana, and myself. This summer there were no Ana, no Maria, no Gina, and no boundaries. Entering my second tour of duty along the beaches offered an escape from the day-to-day drudgery of Iron Wedge, and I welcomed the change of scene.

The previous year I had been stymied by Gina's presence, but now working along the beaches aligned with my priorities, which were all about having fun. And having fun meant revisiting the Juan that had worked a beat in 14—the Juan who was an arrogant womanizer. But this time around I was drinking hard. I'd been the cause of three abortions and my relationship with Ana was over. I wanted to escape the pain—the abortions and the no-win wedging war—and I was willing to sacrifice all boundaries in my personal and professional life. I felt I had nothing to lose.

A long-time acquaintance, Mike Roberts, had recently transferred into Narcotics and found himself, along with me, on the bottom of the seniority list. Gina didn't volunteer and I didn't want to work with her anyway as I had a new agenda. Mike worked on Sergeant Abernathy's team, so tracking him down wasn't hard. I talked to him about our impending assignment to SMU and we agreed to be partners. We vowed to make this a summer to remember and I looked forward to my descent into decadence.

He shared his world of connections—both social and departmental—and I was amazed that such a young guy was able to cultivate substantial friendships in every corner of the city and was known by cops virtually everywhere we went.

The commander of SMU that year was Mike's former lieutenant in the Gang Crimes Unit; therefore we had instant privileges. We weren't treated like rookies. We had the freedom to rove the coveted beaches we were assigned to: Ohio and Oak Street, North Avenue—prime bikini turf. Our ten-member team was the only one on the early watch (11 A.M. to 7 P.M.) to be issued ATVs (all-terrain vehicles), making our presence along the lake even more noticeable and enjoyable. But to guarantee a place set apart from the other officers, we affixed bright orange marquees to our ATVs. In the SMU we had to wear uniforms, but we didn't have to adhere to departmental hair regulations because we were from a specialized unit; being different was our strength. We were the fun police, and I intended to make the most of it.

During the first week of cruising on our ATVs, we met several women who wanted to go out partying. After work we found ourselves gallivanting around Lincoln Park. That night I took one of these willing women home with me and totally abandoned myself in the pleasures of the flesh until I felt reborn, confident I still had the magic.

As the days of summer brought crowds to the lakefront, we met more and more women who promised to provide us with as much fun as we wanted. I craved the intoxication of alcohol and sex. I had pretty high expectations: my goal was to have sex-only relationships with seven different women throughout the summer. And then when I'd had my fill of each new woman, I planned to discard her as if she was an empty bottle of tequila.

On Memorial Day weekend, the Chicago Blues Festival in Grant Park was in full swing and our team was posted on its perimeter on Washington Street and Columbus Drive. Two officers drove a paddy wagon to our position and, after parking our ATVs, we went to work. Our duty that day, besides serving and protecting, was to confiscate and remand any and all liquor people brought into the park for the concerts. Our supervisors instructed us to stop anyone who had coolers, backpacks, and picnic baskets—families, men, women, elderly couples, college students. We confiscated their liquor and carefully placed it in the paddy wagon—our mobile liquor store, which would open up after hours when we, the cops, had the lakefront all to ourselves for a huge, blow-out party. Many complained and drew long faces about what bullshit it was, but what could they do? We were the police. In answer to their complaints, we simply pointed to the numerous signs prohibiting liquor in the park.

"Could I bring the booze back to my car and leave it there?" one sorrowful subject asked after we found two bottles of cognac in his picnic basket. He looked pretty miserable as we held the bottles in our hands, and his girlfriend didn't look too happy either.

We were relentless. "We'll have to confiscate it," I said, taking the two bottles and inventorying them in the paddy wagon. By now we had separated the booty into sections along the interior walls of the mobile liquor store. There was a beer section divided into imported and domestic brands, a wine collection, and a hard-liquor area organized by labels, ranging from Smirnoff to Ketel One vodka. As I was taking inventory, the guy's girlfriend appeared at the back door of the wagon, smiled, and said, "Holy shit! You guys must be planning a massive party."

"Not really," I lied, "we're just enforcing the laws of the city."

"Well," she began, lifting her tank top, "is there any way I could have my liquor back?" Two rounded breasts popped out from under her shirt. "Puh-lease, Mr. Officer," she whined, as she shook her breasts and gazed at me with the innocence of a doe.

"I would be jeopardizing my principles," I said in mock rebuff, "and I would never ask you to do the same."

"Fuck you!" she hollered as she pulled down her top and stormed off into the arms of her waiting boyfriend.

"If you didn't have him, I'd think about it," I said, exiting the rear door of the paddy wagon. I raised my hand in a salute and waved. "Thank you. Have a nice day."

All my partners around the paddy wagon burst into laughter and commented about her ample package.

We stood around the wagon making our deposits. Whenever we saw an attractive female, we'd offer her an invite: "Hey, how'd ya all like to come to a private party tonight at the Eleventh Street beach house?" Of course, some civilian men heard our invites after their liquor had been confiscated and pleaded, "Can we come?"

Stifling our laughter, we looked at each other, bowed our heads, and peered over our lowered sunglasses as if saying, "You gotta be kidding! It's for members only."

Later that night, after the beaches were closed and the civilians were chased away, we pulled the mobile liquor store up to the beach house and it was open-bar time. A good majority of the cops from the detail attended, some brought barbecue grills; others brought food to grill; and still others brought the women we'd met on the beaches, who, in turn, brought their friends. Music from a boom box rocked the beach house, drunken dancers reveled under the moonlit sky, and some stripped down to their skivvies for a late-night dip in the lake. The party lasted into the morning and set the tone for the rest of the summer.

It was early June when the Blues Festival packed up and left town. The next major festival in Grant Park—the Taste of Chicago, where local restaurants bring samples of their fare and the park is once again filled with music and more—wasn't coming up until the week of the Fourth of July. Without specific duties to perform other than writing up citations for open liquor, we had time to roam the beaches and entertain the tourists.

"There's no way in hell you gonna clear all four stairs."

Mike made the challenge as I stood over the seat of my ATV surveying my chances near the east steps across the street from Buckingham Fountain. A crowd of video-camera-wielding tourists had begun to assemble. Mike and I had been taking turns riding down the stairs. We became daredevils on our ATVs; we rode them with reckless abandon, flying through the open fields of Grant Park and along the lakefront, taking care not to put anyone but ourselves in immediate danger. If we ever got hurt, we knew all we'd have to do was fill out an injury-on-duty report, but we were having too much fun to think about that.

"I bet you lunch I can, brotherman," I responded, turning away from the lip of the stairs, creating a launching pad for my flight.

"Oh, you know you got yourself a deal, my man."

The tourists were primed and the anticipation mounted as I stood astride my ATV and opened up the throttle. The launching pad was roughly twenty feet long, so I was able to gain some speed.

"Holy shit!" I heard someone gasp as I cleared the first step and went airborne. My body weight shifted to the back of the seat to lighten the load up front. As my ass hit and popped open the plastic storage box on the rear of the ATV, reports and citations were sent flying into the wind. I safely landed the ATV five steps later with a neck-jerking, helmet-rattling thud. It was a new record.

"Woo-hoooo!" I screamed as I came to a stop. All the tourists were clapping and Mike was scampering around collecting the scattered papers.

"Now that's fun!" I hollered. I felt free and irresponsible; I was like a kid again with no cares in the world.

Throughout the summer, Mike and I hit every weekend neighborhood festival in uniform and on our wheels, becoming fixtures on our fun police ATVs. Our police presence was always recognized and welcomed.

"Hey," we'd hear women saying behind our backs. "It's the fun police. Can you cuff us—because we've been *real* bad?" Mike and I would shake our heads and laugh, basking in all the attention.

We soon developed acquaintances at these festivals who'd make us mixed drinks or vodka slushies in nondescript cups and invite us to back-yard cookouts. The thought of getting busted or turned in by angry citizens never crossed our minds. Our only concerns were the jealous boyfriends who looked at us with hatred in their eyes. But even that couldn't deter us in our pursuit of pleasure. It was a life I had never known—taking chances, drinking on the job, and then fading away on our ATVs in a drunken haze became our routine.

We met all different types of women at these festivals, but they all seemed to have one thing in common—an attraction to the uniform. This magnetism amazed me. Would they still be attracted to me without the uniform or would I just be another drunk in the crowd? I left each of these festivals with a pocketful of phone numbers. Mike had his share of admirers, but because he had a fiancée he had boundaries and stuck to them. I'd meet women during the day and then invite them to come get drunk with me at night. I'd feign a desire to develop a relationship, and carry on until I became bored and then I'd silently walk away. Just like the old days. I was as far away as I could get from Ana, from ten-year-old crack dealers, and from any other pain in my life. I played hard.

One day while Mike and I were talking with some women at the North Avenue beach house, Ana spotted me as she was running a few miles in practice for the Mrs. T's triathlon. She approached our small group and tried to get my attention, but I was oblivious to her presence as I was deeply immersed in trying to score another conquest. She tapped my shoulder and when I turned she gazed at me with tears in her eyes. I hadn't seen her since she had moved out of my apartment three months earlier. We had talked once or twice but never discussed reconciling. We were giving each other space, and the more space I got, the more I forgot her.

"What the fuck is going on, Juan! You're scaring me. I feel like I don't even know who you are anymore," she sobbed. "You're changing into an asshole, and I don't even think you're aware of it."

I didn't try to console her, reason with her, or even lie to her. Instead I felt a bit annoyed that she was taking me to an emotional place I didn't want to go. "I'll call you later, OK?" I said. She stared at me and then ran off. I never did call her later, and I never gave her an excuse.

The amount of attention I was getting at the lakefront and my desires for self-satisfying pleasures made it easy to forget Ana. My life as a cop and my private life began to merge into one entity. On the job I couldn't speak up when I saw injustices or mistreatment of people, so I just silenced my voice and my emotions and shut off my compassion. In my personal life, I couldn't be honest and communicate the pain I was feeling with the person I loved, so I lied to her and severed all emotions connected to her. The only relationships I wanted to enjoy now were drenched in alcohol and void of any emotional content.

While Mike and I were thoroughly enjoying our stint along the beaches, we were cognizant of the need to keep the bosses happy. As long as we did all that was asked of us—giving out citations for drinking, making an arrest once in a while, and writing some parking tickets—they'd never question us as to how we spent our days.

★ ★ ★

"Squad, we got a call of a battery victim at Thirty-ninth and the lakefront. Victim is a white male and says the offender is still on the scene," was the call over the citywide radios while we were in roll call one morning. The whole ATV team was rolling on this one, we informed the dispatcher. Heading south on the lakefront over the undulating bike trails, we crested a hill and saw a middle-aged white male flagging us down.

"There he is, there's the guy who threatened me," he told us as he pointed to a black male, about thirty years old, who was topless, shoeless, and looked like he made the lakefront his home.

"Threatened you?" I questioned as two other officers drove their ATVs toward the offender. "You called and said it was a battery. Did he ever hit you?"

"No, not really," the victim confessed. "He picked up a tree branch and started ranting and raving and swinging it around like a madman, like he was *going* to hit me."

Battery, which is a felony, is the actual beating or striking of an individual by another individual, and if it's done with a weapon, say a tree branch, it becomes aggravated battery.

"So he never hit you?"

"No."

"Did he ever threaten you in his ramblings?"

"I don't know. I couldn't understand what the hell he was saying. All I saw is what he was doing and it scared me," he said in an agitated voice. Meanwhile the offender was brought to us by the two cops who went to get him.

"Is this the guy?" Mike asked the victim as the black man looked absently to the sky.

"Yes, it is."

"What are you doing over in this part of the city?" Mike asked.

"I am a visiting professor at the University of Chicago, and I was taking a morning stroll."

I looked over at the offender. He was mumbling and cursing invisible people in his head. Then I looked back at the complainant who kept edging away from the offender.

"What do you want us to do?" Mike asked the professor.

"I want this man arrested," he declared. I didn't say a word. Mike began getting all the necessary information from the professor and had him sign complaints while I called for a squad to transfer the offender to the 21st District on east Twenty-ninth Street. The professor went on his way and we proceeded to lock this guy up for an aggravated battery. I knew it wasn't right, but went along with the crew for the sake of keeping things rolling. Mike summarized the crime in such a glorious fashion that we were awarded an honorable mention for taking such a dangerous felon off the lakefront. It was yet another injustice, but all I did was sign off on the arrest report and laugh at someone else's misfortune. I told myself I couldn't care less about some homeless bum. All I cared about was where the next party was.

I attained my quota of sexual conquests as the days of the SMU dwindled down, but I decided to pursue one last woman. I met her in the middle of August at a club called Shelter. Gerald Jackson, an officer from a mid-level team, and I had started hanging out there on Thursday nights—ladies' night.

When I first saw Karman I was sitting on a chair, talking with Gerald near the entrance of the VIP room. She walked by wearing a form-fitting red sweater and snug black pants that accentuated every curve of her gorgeous body. The allure of her perfume along with the sway of her hips enticed me to follow her with my eyes as she walked away. Her smooth brown skin glowed under the dim lights. She stood near the bar laughing and smiling with her friends. I nudged Gerald. "Check her out, bro'."

"Damn! She's fine," he said, shaking his head.

And one day she'll be mine, I thought to myself.

She picked up her martini glass, brought it to her lips and downed it in one motion. Holy shit! Clearly she was my kind of woman. She walked away from the bar and headed in my direction as I sat in my chair, mesmerized. I had to stop her.

"Excuse me," I said as she approached the doorway. "May I speak to you?"

"Sure," she replied. The mixture of her perfume and the martini created an intoxicating scent. The doorway to opportunity had opened up.

We talked long enough for me to get information on where she worked. For the next three days all I could think about was Karman. She was mysterious, spellbinding, and eight years my junior. I was inspired to write an epic three-page poem comparing her beauty to that of timeless relics. Confident my gesture would touch her, I had two-dozen yellow roses and the poem delivered to her. And I included my phone number, just in case she wanted to call and thank me for my gesture.

Later that week as Mike and I were working near Montrose harbor, I saw Marcos Sanchez, my hockey-playing buddy with a group of friends. He waved in my direction. "Hey Juan," he said, leaving his group and approached my ATV. "What happened to the tip I gave you about the board of trade?"

"My sergeant put the kibosh on it," I replied. Seeing that I was involved in a personal conversation, Mike gave us some space and drove away. Marcos and I talked a little more when I told him I wanted to come by his house for a visit and have a beer with him.

"Hell yeah, come on by anytime," he said, writing his address on a piece of paper and handing it to me.

"Is tonight all right?" I asked, glad that he was willing to spend time with me.

"Sure. You got my address," he said. "See ya later," and then headed back to his friends.

After work that night, I headed over to Marcos's house. We had a couple of beers and talked about the old high-school crowd we used to run with, laughing heartily when we recounted stories of getting high together. Remembering the effect of smoking marijuana and its ability to deaden my pain, I asked, "Do you have any weed?"

He looked at me as if I was crazy. "I ain't telling you, you're a fucking cop."

"Marcos," I began, "how fucking long do we go back? Huh, stoner? I just wanna do one hit, that's it. I need to get some things off my mind," I said. Maria and Ana had both been calling my apartment lately and leaving messages on my machine. It had been ten months since I talked to

Maria last, and a month since I had seen Ana by the lake. They both wanted to see me, but that was the last thing I wanted from either of them. The pain of hearing both of their voices was too much and I thought getting high would help me deal.

"What about your job, Juan?" Marcos asked. "Don't they test piss?" I knew they did, but I also knew that marijuana released a chemical that was stored in body fat. I rationalized that the small amount of toxins would easily be processed out of my body while I worked out.

"I won't get busted, Marcos. Come on, man, do you got any?"

He walked into another room and came back with a sweet-smelling bud of marijuana. The fragrance and texture of the bud as I held it in my hand immediately took me back to my stoner days. He packed a glass pipe and I took a hit. As the smoke filled my lungs, I instantly was transported to another world. Once the feeling hit my head, I felt free of pain. Exhaling the smoke, I laughed my ass off as I looked at Marcos, not believing I was actually doing this. As I passed him the pipe, I realized that Marcos and I had reestablished our friendship. I was amazed at how easily it was to feel reconnected to that part of my past.

I didn't care that I had just broken the law and my oath as a cop. I knew I was pushing my luck, but there was no turning back now. I even asked Marcos for a little bud to take home with me.

When I arrived home that night, Karman had called and left a message thanking me for the sweet flowers and the lovely poem. I was feeling so good, not just because I was high, but also because she had left her mellifluous voice on my answering machine. But then I realized she hadn't left her phone number. How was I going to get in touch with her? Maybe she didn't want me to get in touch with her. I guess I had to let destiny take its course.

On the last weekend before the SMU detail ended, Mike and I were hanging out at North Avenue Beach when I saw Karman riding her bike with a male friend that I thought couldn't possibly be a boyfriend. When she came over to me, I introduced her to Mike, who took the opportunity to ask what I hadn't, "Is this your boyfriend?"

She looked at her friend, chuckled, and said, "No." With that Mike walked away, giving me a wink.

"Hey, Karman, it's good to see you again," I said, amazed at how beautiful she looked in natural light. "Thanks for the message, but you never left a phone number to call you back."

She blushed and then began explaining that she didn't leave a phone number because she had a boyfriend and, while she wasn't really happy with him, she wanted to let the relationship run its course. She repeated that the poem was really special to her and that she appreciated my kindness. Playing my role, I honored her reality and didn't press the issue. I told her that we could just be friends. She seemed happy with that idea and rode off with her friend, never telling me if she'd call me back. I was smitten with her and hoped she and her boyfriend would break up soon.

"So, that's the mysterious Karman?" Mike asked, playfully slapping me in the back of the head as he walked up behind me.

"Yup." I beamed, "So what do you think?"

Mike said, "Juan, this one's trouble. You'd better leave her alone." That only piqued my interest more. Now she was a challenge and, according to Mike, a danger. I wanted her in my life. And I was willing to sacrifice everything except school to get her. I had worked too hard for too long to give up now on my academic goals.

I was entering my final year of classes to complete my MA in English, with my comprehensive test slated for the spring. I was excited to complete that task and finally have something to show after all my years of effort.

After the glorious days of summer, Mike and I went back to Narcotics suntanned and relaxed to find we'd both been transferred to the Tavern Team. It was exactly what I wanted.

32

TAVERN TEAM

IT TOOK ONE WEEK FOR ME to find out why the Tavern Team was the best-kept secret in the unit. On the sheets, we started at 8 P.M. and ended at 4 A.M., but in practice we always met at 10 P.M. because that's when most bars started hopping. I was finally going to be able to escape the ghetto and work with a different class of drugs and people. Every weeknight on a rotating basis, one team member volunteered a bar they had been watching or gotten information on and tried to work deals purchasing powder cocaine or heroin inside the establishment. Another officer would be parked directly across the street from the bar eyeballing the place, keeping us posted on the number of people coming and going. The rest of the team—all seven of us—would sit in our covert cars sleeping, reading, or listening to the play-by-play, waiting for the team member to exit. It was a perfect time for me to study.

If the team member made a deal, he'd notify us via radio once he left the bar and give us a clear description of the offender right down to the color of the person's shoes. Then they'd tell us the denomination and serial numbers of the currency used in the deal, which had to end up in the cash register as proof that the bartender knew of the deal and condoned it. We'd then call for a uniformed district car to assist us so no one would think we were robbing the joint, put on our bulletproof vests, and storm the bar with guns drawn looking for the people who dealt the dope, the currency used in the deal, and anything else we could use against the bar in our effort to shut it down. No one ever had a clue as to why we were there because our buy officer had long since left the bar and been forgotten, leaving a trail of marked money in the cash register. During the search process, we'd verify that the establishment's liquor, amusement, and vendor's licenses were current and valid. If not, we'd issue a license-violation citation. Then we'd head back to 3540 with our prisoners and begin the paperwork.

From my Iron Wedge days I was used to large amounts of paperwork in the form of many packets, but with the Tavern Team there was only one packet per buy. It was a piece of cake and would usually take us an hour or so to complete. Nobody else was at 3540 during our shift, so whatever time we left was our secret. Manko (Sergeant Mankewicz) took care of the time sheets for us and gave incentives for productivity (such as always rewarding us with two to four hours of overtime when we were successful, even if we didn't work one minute past four).

Overtime was an incredibly lucrative benefit on this team when we made a positive hit on a tavern. First, there were the OT hours granted on the night of a hit. Then a guaranteed felony court date at Twenty-sixth and California for the delivery case and an appearance at the Liquor License Commission (LLC) at 321 North LaSalle Street would follow. Each and every court appearance was OT for Tavern members because of our late-night work schedule. The OT hours kept piling up. Manko duly rewarded us when we were productive, but he loathed negatives, and a string of them could make Manko downright nasty.

If the buy officer was met with a negative, he'd return to our meet spot and give a rundown of the bar and discuss whether it was worthy of another visit. Usually, if the buy officer came out after midnight, we were to use the rest of the shift as a homework night, scoping out and visiting bars we thought were up and dealing. Coming out with a negative before midnight would result in another team member suggesting and entering an alternate bar. Then we'd go to that new location, using the nearly desolate highways as our racetracks.

The purpose of the Tavern Team was to issue citations to bars with the intent of eventually closing them down. If a licensed establishment received three citations in a one-year period, the LLC wouldn't renew its liquor license. Our team worked closely with the LLC. If there was a bar the LLC wanted investigated, we would give it a high priority. Otherwise, the members of the Tavern Team created the caseload, and Manko enforced the quota.

Manko kept his request simple: one positive tavern a week. The commander of Narcotics and Manko were friends since their early district days. They maintained an amicable relationship and were always looking out for each other. When Manko was transferred to Narcotics, Commander Boyd gave him the pick of the litter—the Tavern Team. In returning the favor, Manko gave the boss plenty of productivity.

The number of weekly positives had been slipping for six periods. Manko had to recharge the team to keep the commander off his ass, so he infused it with new blood in the form of two unproven buy officers. That's how Mike and I found our way to the team after our summer vacation along the lakefront.

My initiation as an active member of the Tavern Team took place on the second Monday after returning from SMU. I picked an alternative nightclub—Berlin—located on Belmont Avenue near Sheffield Avenue. It had enjoyed a long history of being on the wild side, catering to the freaky and depraved. It was the right place for me. The team met in the bank parking lot on the southwest corner of Southport and Belmont to discuss our plans and trade last-minute pointers.

They told me I needed to talk-the-talk and walk-the-walk if I wanted to be successful. The unit provided each officer on the team with a constantly replenished $200 stipend. We were to spend the money to purchase drinks for ourselves and prospective drug-dealing contacts, score the drugs, play pool, play music on the jukebox, or participate in whatever other diversions were available in the bar and then, at the end of the night, put in a reimbursement slip and get all that money back. The team was bankrolled by all the drug money that came into the Narcotics Unit. The official limit was two drinks, but I didn't know if I should take that limit seriously. A tight-fisted drinker won't make buddies in a bar full of strangers.

"Hey, rookie. You sure you're up to this?" Manko asked, checking my nerves and giving me shit because I was the youngest member on the team.

"How much dope you want me to get, Manko?" I shot back.

"Just give me a positive, smart-ass. Let's see if you can end our drought," Manko said, looking around at the rest of the team in disgust. "No one else seems to be doing shit! Good luck," he concluded, without breaking a smile. "Oh yeah," he suddenly remembered, "if you get in any shit, throw a bar stool out the window." This took me aback. I wondered what kind of shit I could get into that might demand that action.

I drove near the location, checked it out, and waited for the eyeball to set up on Belmont. "All right, Juan," the voice on the radio came in. "I'm parked on Belmont under the el tracks facing west. Ready when you are."

It was time for me to go to work. I parked my car on Wilton Avenue, looked at myself in the rearview mirror, adjusted my baseball hat, and made sure I had my money in two different pockets—one for drinking and the other for the marked money that had to get in the register. I got out of my car and walked past the eyeball into the bar.

Inside it was dead. Ten o'clock on a Monday night. There were only three people besides myself sitting at the bar. A flood of dread washed over me as I sat alone in the bar trying to make contacts into a drug world I knew nothing about. I knew the bar circuit, but wasn't confident buying dope. What if someone came into the bar and noticed me, I thought to myself. Would they blow my cover? Could that get me killed? How could I explain my presence in this bar? All these questions ran through my head as I sat at the bar and checked out a television hanging at the end showing male-on-male porn. Fucking great, I laughed to myself, it must be gay night. I felt awkward so I just turned my head and kept my focus on the job at hand.

"Hey, what'd ya like to drink?" a lanky male bartender, with shoulder-length black hair, dressed in all black, wearing a Johnny Cash T-shirt, asked. He then smiled, exposing a set of perfect teeth.

"Absolut cranberry," I said, taking in every inch of the place in case I had a positive and needed to write a case report. "Excuse me," I stopped the bartender when he returned with my drink. "What time does the trade come in?"

He took a step back and eyed me, "What ya looking for, sailor?"

"A little fun," I winked, "some booze, and some nose candy," I said, placing my index finger along my nose and sniffing. My teammates had told me bartenders always know who's slinging dope in their bar. I felt comfortable asking him right away since I prefaced my desire for drugs with my desire for meeting someone. Maybe he'd be willing to provide both, I reasoned.

"It'll be here later. Just kick back and relax and let me know when you need anotha drink. OK?" he said as he stood there and checked me out. I downed my drink in one motion.

"I need another drink, barkeep," I said, smiling. My plan was to get his trust by slamming down drinks.

"Damn boy, you're not playing around," he expressed, as an approving smile crossed his face. He mixed another drink and poured me a shot of Orange Stoly. "This one's on the house," he said, waving to me over his shoulder as he headed to the other end of the bar. It seemed as if my plan was working.

Man, I thought to myself, I've only been here twenty minutes and I already have a lead. How hard can this job be?

Manko informed me beforehand that I had to tie in the bar to make the buy stick, meaning the bartender had to know I was buying dope in *his* bar and my marked money had to wind up in *his* cash register. If the bartender told me to get the hell out, then that's what I'd have to do. If the bartender didn't say anything remotely discouraging, I'd stay in the bar, casting out lines into the crowd. If I had a nibble, I'd approach the bartender and ask, "Can you give me change for this hundo? I'm gonna score a forty and need some small bills." Or else, "Hey, barkeep. This guy over here is gonna sell me a forty, can I trust him?" If they helped me, then they'd be condoning the sale of narcotics in their licensed establishment. I needed their unsuspecting confidence to make it a positive and get my job done. And throwing back drinks while fabricating stories at the drop of a hat was one way to do it. It was like SMU all over again.

★ ★ ★

"So, what ya doing in town?" the bartender had returned. "I know everyone who comes into this bar, and I have never, ever seen you before." I
wasn't certain where he was heading with this, so I decided to play the
game.

"Asking all these personal questions, and I don't even know your
name," I volleyed, taking off my hat and putting it in my rear pocket.

"You can call me Ray."

"OK, Ray. My grandparents left me a bunch of cash, and I'm slum-
ming around on a coast-to-coast drunken odyssey," I began, throwing back
half my drink and kept on weaving the story off the top of my head. The
alcohol made the words flow easily and I amazed myself with my ability
to conjure up such a tale. "I'm trying to find out which states can give me
the best memories of getting fucked up. Chicago was the next stop on this
ride, so how you gonna make it memorable?" I concluded, arousing his
interest and making the story sound extremely plausible as I placed the
empty glass on the bar.

"Gimme a chance," Ray propositioned, drawling his words, "and I'll
make sure you'll never want to leave Chicago." He poured two shots of
Jaegermeister, gave me one, and proclaimed, "Bottoms up, cowboy." He
tossed the shot back and wiped his mouth with the back of his hand. Ray
turned to walk away, stopped, winked at me over his shoulder, and then
sashayed to the other end of the bar to serve another customer.

The crowd inside Berlin was getting livelier as men and women from
all different walks of life appeared and began to dance in a sort of ritual-
istic fashion. The evening waxed on and the drinks were going down
smoothly. I got up from my bar stool, navigated my way through the
crowded dance floor, looking around and wondering who was holding the
nose candy. Finally reaching the door to the men's room, I pushed it open
and entered. The pounding music rattled the mirror, distorting my image.
I had to refocus, reminding myself of the mission. Gazing intently into the
mirror, I saw an alcohol-tainted version of myself. The skin on my chin
had started to droop and my neck was starting to get fat. When the fuck
did this start happening? Was I paying for my decadence over the summer? Who the fuck was I looking at in the mirror? It was me, but yet it

wasn't. I stared harder and convinced myself I could do this shit. I splashed water on my face and headed back to the bar. I'd been there a little under two hours.

"Barkeep," I softly hummed as I walked past him, "I gots to know something."

"Yeah, sweetie, what is it you needs to know?" he said curiously, following me to my stool.

"Am I wasting my time here? My nose is getting a tad bit itchy, and I don't know how much longer I can wait," I said. "I'll tell you what, Ray, gimme another Absolut cranberry, and back it up with two shots of Jaeger, one for each of us, and when I'm done with my drink, I'm in the wind. I can't wait all night for a little sugar."

"Don't get all bunched up," he said, coming from behind the bar, sidling to the seat next to me. He picked up his shot, motioning me to do the same, "To us, and a fabulous night of meeting strangers." We threw the shots back, and then he said, "Keep your pants on just a little longer. The girl's in the bar now." I was pumped, knowing that *girl* was a street term for cocaine.

"What you want?" Ray asked teasingly. "A big one or a small one, cowboy?"

"A large one," I didn't know what it was, but it sounded right. "What do ya expect?" I replied playfully, downing my drink.

Ray disappeared in the growing crowd on the dance floor for a moment as the strobe lights flashed and the dance hall sound system made the contents of my drink vibrate. I was turning in an Academy Award-winning performance and loved the new role I had—getting drunk, buying dope, and creating lie after lie. Two hours, three drinks, and three shots had passed since I entered Berlin and the time of reckoning was near.

"Here you are, handsome," Ray said to me, placing a paper packet in a matchbook and sliding it toward me. "That'll be one hundred smackeroos."

Reaching into my jeans for the marked money, I pulled out a wad of twenties, hoping one of them wound up in the cash register, and counted out $120 and said, "Gimme another drink and two more shots of Jaeger.

It's time to party!" I saw his face light up with anticipation as he went to get the shots. "Tell me, player," I said after I swallowed the shot. "What is it you drink?"

"Orange Stoly," he informed me, taking the money and leaning over the bar getting very close. "Nice and chilled. Why do you wanna know?"

"I'm gonna get a chilled bottle and go to my place for now. Come over if you want," I said, writing out a fictitious address on the matchbook cover and putting my hat back on. Picking up my drink, I took a heavy swig and told him, "I'll save some candy for you."

"I'll see you later," he promised.

I left the bar, giddy from the alcohol and giddy from selling the story. I smiled as I passed the eyeball and tipped my hat—my sign for a positive. Jumping in my car, I got on the radio, "The rookie made the fucking deal, Manko! Listen up, dickwads!" I said laughing and definitely feeling the influence of the alcohol. "You're looking for the bartender, his name's Ray, he's dressed all in black and has on a Johnny Cash T-shirt. The cash is in the register," I said, and then gave them all the serial numbers on my marked money.

"Juarez," Manko called, "stay in the area and get some damn coffee, will ya?" I waited in my parking spot until I saw the blue flashing lights of the uniformed squad and watched as my teammates flooded the bar. Yeah! First night in a bar and I fuckin' take it down. How sweet is that? I pulled out of my spot and started heading toward the bank's parking lot.

"Juarez, you on the air?" It was Manko and he was still inside the bar; I heard the pounding music in the background. I responded in the affirmative. "Good job, kid. Listen, head into 3540, but before you do that, get everyone on the team some coffee. And plenty of cream and sugar."

"Ten-four, sarge. Did you find Ray?" I asked.

"Yeah, he's sweet as sugar. I wanna hear this story, kid."

I headed to the Dunkin' Donuts on Ashland Avenue near Wright-wood and got eight medium coffees and plenty of cream and sugar before heading into 3540. Hitting the on-ramp on Armitage and Ashland, I punched the accelerator and made it to 3540, almost ten miles away, in five minutes. I was flying high from the excessive drinking and my first-time success.

I walked up the stairs, passed Officer Martin, the same guy who was working the desk the day I got into the Unit, and entered our team's cubicle, where I started on the packet. I filled out the positive raid book, after verifying the address of the bar and the number of arrestees via the radio from Manko, who informed me they were on the way in with one arrest, and got an estimated value for the powder cocaine I had bought. Then I started on the case report when Manko called me on the radio, "We're turning onto Normal now. The prisoner's going to be coming up the stairs with the uniformed cop any second, so make sure you're in the team's room." I was in the room already, so I continued on with the case report. A few minutes later I heard Ray's voice coming up the stairs, "Honestly, officer. There has to be some mistake. I never sold cocaine to anyone."

"Tell it to the judge, sweet pie," an unknown voice told him. It must be the uniformed cop, I thought as I chuckled. The rest of the team came up the stairs as I got back to work on the report, recalling all the facts clearly, my mind refreshed by the coffee when Manko came in the room and patted me on the back. "Good job, kid. Didn't know you had it in ya."

"Manko," I said, looking over my shoulder as my teammates straggled into the room, taking their coffees, "I got some work to do. You can save your stroking for later." The room went up in laughter; even Manko laughed.

"That's a good one, kid," he said. "Keep it up and you'll be wedging tomorrow." I turned sharply from the typewriter and looked up at him. He had the goofiest grin on his face. "Gotcha," he roared.

The room became a whirlwind of precision activity. "Someone fill out the raid book," Manko delegated.

"Did it," I said as I continued typing.

"What else did you do?" he asked.

"I couldn't wait all night for you guys. I'm halfway done with my case report," I said. "Oh, and if you didn't notice, I got the coffee."

"Fuckin' kid," Manko said, shaking his head. "Mike, get an arrest report going; Paco, do the inventory."

"I already got it going now," replied Paco, as he slapped me heartily on the back. "Good job, Juan."

"All in a day's work, cousin," I said as I completed my brief but complete case report and whipped it out of the typewriter.

"Terry and Roy, you guys take the prisoner to Eleventh and State when all the paper's done." Manko looked around the room, "Who's doing the OT slips?"

"I am." Marc, the eyeball for the night, chimed in. "Hour and a half for everyone?"

"Sure, but give the transporting guys two," Manko instructed. I looked at the clock, it was 2:15 A.M. I was in line for one and a half hours of overtime and Roy and Terry, the transporting officers, were going to get two and we hadn't even ended the tour yet. Sweet!

Manko, satisfied that all points were covered, headed to the back of the office. "Follow me, kid. Oh yeah, and bring a reimbursement slip."

We headed toward the back of the floor when Manko entered the commander's secretary's office, turned around, and stuck out his hand. "Good job, kid. You keep this up and I'm going to start liking you."

I shook his hand. "Thanks, sarge. I told you I can buy dope."

"That you did. When you're done with the reimbursement slip you can head home," he said. I sat at the desk and started writing out the form while Manko did some paperwork. I removed the rest of the money from my pocket and counted out $40. Damn! I spent $160 bucks in the bar in two hours? I could account for the $100 I spent on the cocaine, but I didn't know how to explain the $20 tip and the $40 that I spent on drinks.

"Hey, sarge," I said, interrupting him. "I have to head up to the front for a second. I'll be right back."

I ran up to the front and could feel I had lost the buzz from the alcohol already. "Paco," I called out to my cousin. "Come here, I have to ask you for advice." He walked over to me with the inventory bag in his hand. "How do I fill one of these out?" I asked, holding out the reimbursement slip.

"Well, for beginners, we know you had more than two drinks, so let's start there." He suggested I inflate the price of the drinks to cover what I had to drink. "And just put down two drinks, you don't wanna jam your-self up."

"Should I do that for the drinks I bought the bartender, too?"

"Yup, and anyone else you bought drinks for in the bar."

"Thanks," I told him. "I appreciate the lesson."

"No problem," he said as he headed back into the team's cubicle and I went back to the commander's office to complete the slip and give it to Manko.

"This is a $60 bar tab," he said, counting up the numbers. "You bought three drinks for three people at five bucks a shot and you had two at $6.00 a piece?" he questioned. "That's a lot of drinks you bought for other people."

"I had to. They were all possible connects," I lied. I felt terrible for lying to him, especially after he was rewarding me with OT hours, but I had to account for all the money I spent in the bar.

"I'll sign it this time," he said. "But don't be pulling that shit any-more. I can back you up for the hundred you spent on the dope, but I can only go so far with the bar tab. Understand?"

"Yeah, sarge. I understand," I replied, looking down at the ground. "It won't happen again."

"Put the slip in the bursar's mail slot," he said as he handed me back the form. "Don't worry, kid. It was your first one. You'll learn how to make everything balance out. You did a good job tonight. Now get out of here."

I walked out of the office, dropped the slip in the bursar's slot, and headed toward the front of the building. I looked at the clock—it was 3 A.M. The team was still doing work as I said goodnight to everyone and headed down the stairs. Other than the gentle upbraiding I got for the reimbursement slip, I felt great. The liquor had worn off, I was success-ful in the bar, and I had three hours of OT coming. If this night was any indication of what I had in store, I was going to love it. I already did. It was hundreds of times better than working in the ghetto. I was getting paid to drown my pain.

Every time I entered a bar seemed like the perfect opportunity to score cocaine while getting drunk.

"Where'd ya find this kid?" Manko asked my cousin Paco. "He can buy dope like no one's business," he said after my third buy in five weeks. Manko was impressed, "This hotshot knows how to get the job done."

I didn't disappoint my new team or Manko. Over the next six periods, I was able to make six buys and take down six bars. I was on a roll. I remember going into a bar on the northwest corner of Augusta and Wood and, besides the bartender, there was only one other person there. When I radioed the positive, Manko asked for a description of the offender. I laughed and said, "He's the only one in the bar. You can't miss him." This job was easy because drinking and lying had become second nature for me.

33

AND THEN THERE WERE NONE

KARMAN WAS ELUSIVE and bewitching. When I first met her in August, she was on the verge of breaking up with her boyfriend. At the end of September, she finally did, but she told me she didn't want to get involved with anyone for a while. I could understand and respect that, but I knew what I wanted—her. So when she paged me in late October, I figured this was my opportunity. Thinking only of my desire to possess her, I took advantage of her confused emotions and put on the full press. I inserted myself into her daily life. I wanted to become the friend she couldn't live without, so I was attentive to her every need, yet I played like I was content with just being her friend. It was all part of my plan.

On weekends or nights when I got out of work early, I went to Karman's to see if she wanted to hang out. I wined and dined her. We went to bars, played pool, talked, and got wasted.

The alcohol numbed my senses and the guilt over the past, which is exactly what I wanted. I needed to live in the present. And the present was Karman. I wanted to know everything about her. She revealed that she had grown up in an abusive family—her father was a heavy drinker and physically abused her and her mother. Her parents separated before she was ten. Later in life, she found herself in abusive relationships with men that beat her and cheated on her. She had a lot of pain inside, and I was going to be the one to free her from it once she let me. I imagined loving her with gentle hands and an open heart. I wanted to let her see and feel that life was not all pain. I felt a unique kinship growing and I knew she was slowly letting down her guard with each story she told me.

She confessed that she smoked marijuana. I hadn't smoked since Marcos gave me bud, but now I had a reason to get high. I wanted Karman to trust and like me, so when she pulled out a bong, I took one hit. She thought it was cool that I was a cop who smoked weed. She asked me if I was worried about getting busted and I told her, "Fuck no!" I was willing to use every trick up my sleeve to make her want me not just as a friend, but also as a lover.

It wasn't until January 1996—six months after we first met—that she finally caved in from all my attention and allowed me to kiss her. Our lips met with the intensity of long-withheld passion. Soon our newfound fascination in each other turned to torrid lovemaking. Our desires overwhelmed us and we began having sex anywhere we could.

Since I was pretty successful on the Tavern Team, Manko gave me an undercover vehicle that I didn't have to share with anyone. It was a 1988 custom van. It had miniblinds, a bed, and a television. Karman came to work with me many nights and we'd have sex in it while a team member was in a bar. She knew I was working, but she didn't care one bit. She even got off on the fact that we were breaking the rules. It was against departmental regulations and team protocol to have civilians in an undercover vehicle, especially during work hours. But once I started breaking the rules, I figured one more wasn't going to make a hell of a difference. My desire for Karman outweighed any respect I had for my job.

I started smoking pot whenever I was with Karman. I knew at any time I could be called to take a piss test, but I trusted in my ability to get away with shit and not get busted. At first it was one-hits that I reasoned would get flushed out of my system because I was in good shape. I still had a desire to maintain a workout schedule, but as I started seeing more and more of Karman, my once regimented workouts began to dwindle. I graduated to joints and bong loads. I was free-falling into the in-the-moment party lifestyle that Karman loved and that I was willing to pay for. I needed to keep her dependent on me for her happiness at all costs. I had to keep getting high with her to make sure she stayed happy.

Then Marcos Sanchez called me up and invited me to go to Amsterdam in the fall with our group of friends from high school. I knew about the window-box hookers who invited the attention of anyone who could pay and the fountain of available drugs at hash coffee shops, and I was ready to go to this great party city by the sea. I bought my ticket.

"Are you crazy?" Karman asked when I told her about my plans. "Everyone knows what goes on in Amsterdam. What if your job finds out?"

"We're not just going to Amsterdam. We'll be traveling to Germany, Austria, and Italy," I told her. But I knew that my European vacation was nothing more than a further escape into decadence.

"That's so cool," she told me with envy in her voice, "but you're still fuckin' crazy." I didn't care; I wanted to run and hide and not deal with my past.

Ana, who had moved out of my place eight months before, was calling me and leaving messages on my answering machine that she was willing to work things out. Maria, who I hadn't seen in a year, was still leaving messages wondering what the hell had happened and where I was. Why couldn't they just accept the facts and move into the present? Friends who knew Ana begged me to open my eyes. But I didn't want to relive the past; I wanted to forget it.

Everything in my life was going down in a whirlwind of excess and abuse. I was surrounded by my lies. At work I thrived because I had turned into the barfly I had once only pretended to be. Scoring dope was easier now because the stories flowed as easily as the liquor. It also helped that I had achieved the haggard look and personality of someone who needed a cocaine remedy.

In February 1996 after I had graduated with my MA in English—how I managed to do it is still a mystery to me—Karman and I planned a trip to Puerto Rico with some of her friends. We spent the night before we left at Shelter, where we had first met and where I now reassured Karman of my feelings for her.

Earlier in the day I had driven her to UIC and when we'd arrived, she gave me a letter and then bolted out of the car without a word. I opened the letter, which informed me that she had contracted genital warts from a past lover. She explained that she was sorry for not telling me sooner. She said she felt dirty and could understand if I left her. I thought of all the times we'd had unprotected sex, and I knew what this news meant for me. I had never used condoms, but I had never contracted an STD. Now, I was branded. I should've used rubbers.

At Shelter that night I had to comfort a distraught Karman. "Come on, baby. I'd love you anyway you are," I told her. Whenever she got sad or cried, she reminded me of a little girl. "Why should this change the way I feel about you?" She continued crying as I embraced her. "Come on, baby," I said, drawing my pelvis to hers. Warts or no warts, I still loved her body. "We're gonna have a great time in Puerto Rico." I began grinding and could feel a warmth where our bodies touched. "I'm still here, so why are you crying?"

"Papa Smurf," she used her pet name for me as she looked up at me with tears in her eyes. "I just thought you'd run away, and I couldn't stand losing you." I wasn't expecting this, but I guess I had it coming. "I love you," she gushed. I longed to hear those words from her and they melted my heart. She finally admitted her feelings for me after I had been giving myself to her completely. All my work had finally paid off.

We drifted toward the rear bar and I bought two shots of tequila and two cosmopolitans. I picked up the shot, handed her the other, and proposed a toast, "To us and leaving the past behind." We clinked our glasses and threw back the shots. Then we put our empty shot glasses down on the bar, picked up the cosmopolitans, and turned to face the pool table. There was Ana in the corner with a guy.

Karman didn't know about Ana, so I wasn't worried about them seeing each other, but when Ana's eyes locked on mine, she grabbed the guy's jaw, turned it toward her, and began kissing him passionately. I could easily see that it took the guy by surprise as Ana kept looking at me for a reaction.

I thought to myself, Ana, there's no need to bring yourself down to my level— you're too good for that. I was a marked man now and I didn't care one bit what she was doing with her life. But deep in the pit of my stomach I felt like I had lost her for good and as a knot in my gut tightened, I turned my head, unable to watch. She'd be better off without me I told myself, ignoring whatever feelings I had left for her. Karman elbowed me in the ribs and caused me to spill a bit of my drink, "Wake up, stoner. Let's head up front." I left Ana in the arms of another man. I guess we were finally broken up for good.

We left for Puerto Rico the next day for a weeklong drinking and smoking binge. One night we got so loaded on rum, pot, beer, and tequila that alcohol oozed out of my pores as I slept, drenching the whole bed. I woke up soaking wet. It scared us for a moment, but it didn't slow us down. We began drinking before noon. My once streamlined body was beginning to show the effects of such a dramatic change—I billowed out from 170 pounds to a plump 205; it was all liquid. My face fattened up as my chin disappeared. My world was spinning wildly. Without question, I was out of control. Karman stood by me like a devoted girlfriend.

One night in the early spring, Karman and three of her friends met me at Sweet Alice, a bar at 11— North Damen Avenue, while I was inside trying to score dope. I had invited her earlier in the day. I'd told her that we could party all night and not pay for a thing.

We drank the city's $200 away quickly. The cosmopolitans went down without a second thought, the shots of tequila kept streaming down my throat, and I got thoroughly wasted. It wasn't my money, and the reimbursements were never questioned—who was it going to hurt? I stumbled out of the bar, got into my undercover car and told my sergeant and team members it was a negative after spending three and a half hours in the bar getting hammered. I couldn't care less that I was destroying my teammates' trust and abusing their faith in me. I was thinking solely about me, my pleasures, my problems, and my relationship with Karman.

After I radioed the negative a meet was called at the 13th District, which was south of the location, but I was so drunk and disoriented, I headed northbound and had to be intercepted by my cousin and driven back to the meet spot.

My eyeball for this bar was Mike Roberts, my partner from the rollicking summer when I first met Karman and who had told me she'd be trouble. He had recognized Karman with her friends entering the bar earlier that evening when I was supposed to be doing my job. Later that night he told me, "Boy, you better get your head on straight. You're spinning out of control."

I didn't want to get my head on straight. I was having too much fun, and who the fuck was he to tell me what to do? Since Mike and I got on the team together seven months ago, I had taken down six bars to his pathetic one.

But Mike's wasn't the only voice of concern. Tim, my mountain biking buddy, saw me one day on Lincoln Avenue when I wasn't high or nursing a hangover and said, "Jesus, Juan! You look like shit! What the hell's happened to you?" I hadn't seen him since the previous summer when we'd gotten together to ride just about every weekend. I stopped calling him once Karman became my focus. "It's like you fell off the side of the earth."

I liked Tim and thought we had become really good friends in the short time I'd known him. I needed to face the truth because I was getting sick and tired of the life I was living. I was spending all my money and time on alcohol and Karman.

"I'm falling apart, Tim. I've been hitting the fucking liquor hard, smoking weed ever since I started seeing this girl." I was surprised at how easily the truth came out.

"You're still a cop?" he asked, cocking his head in amazement. I wondered why he thought I would have quit.

"Yeah," I replied, as he continued looking at me, wanting me to say more, so I did. "I know it's stupid, but that's how it is."

"What happened to Ana? I thought you two were a great couple. Did you finally get tired of her spanking your ass in triathlons?" he asked, laughing.

He had hit a chord. The memory of those days released a flood of emotions and I felt a pang in my heart.

"We're done," I said, trying to hide my emotions as the image of her kissing that guy in the bar flashed in my head. My voice cracked. "It's over."

"Sorry to hear that," he said. "Who's the new girl?"

"Some party girl. I can't handle her pace anymore, but I can't get away from her."

"If you ask me, which I know you're not, you better drop her like yesterday. It doesn't look like she's doing you much good. Do you even get on your bike anymore, pussboy?"

That made me laugh. "No, it's collecting dust."

"I'll pick you up this weekend and we could head out to Palos to get in a ride." I looked at him like he was crazy. "Don't worry," he offered, "I'll take it easy on ya."

I thought about it for a second. "I can't, Tim. I have to be with the party girl."

"Where are your balls, man? I'm not taking no for an answer. I'll be by your apartment on Sunday at nine. Be ready to ride, sunshine."

I couldn't resist his offer even knowing I was going to pay for my winter of inactivity once I hit the trails.

"Karman," I began when I awoke in her bed after another late Friday night out drinking. "I have something to do tomorrow in the morning, so I won't be spending the night with you tonight."

She rolled over and passed her hand over her eyes, "What time is it?"

I looked at the clock. "It's 11:30."

"What do you have to do that's more important than me?" she asked.

"I'm going biking with a buddy," I told her.

"You can bike any time you want. Why do you have to do it when you need to be with me on the weekends?" she said in a whining voice. "Huh, Papa Smurf?"

The childish nickname was starting to grate on me, but I figured it was the price I had to pay for spending so much time chasing her. "Listen," I said, putting my foot down for once. "I'm going biking and that's it. How much longer are you staying in bed?"

"You don't love me anymore," she cried, turning on the manipulation I had seen one time too many.

"It has nothing to do with that," I said, feeling the anger welling up inside. "When are you getting up?"

"When I feel like it," she angrily replied, turning her back to me. As soon as she fell back to sleep, I got out of her bed, got dressed, and went home. I didn't need this stress in my life.

After four months of being intimate with Karman, I started to crash and so did my desire for her. Our sex life had suffered due to my inability to get an erection. I was tired of all the drinking and partying. I blamed it on work and drinking but she took it personally.

My productivity at work had slowed down a bit, but I was still going to bars and trying to score. I was tired all the time and had no energy. I was happy though that I was going to start graduate school in education in September. I looked forward to being in a learning environment instead of a full-time party.

It had become harder and harder for me to do things on my own. Karman was dependent on me and couldn't, or wouldn't, do anything for herself. She always expected me to do it for her.

"Karman," I said one day while we were at Portage Park, "things aren't working out between us. I need my space."

No sooner had I finished the sentence than a cascade of tears fell from her eyes. She started blubbering, "We can work it out."

That sounded familiar, but I didn't want to work it out. "Karman, I can't do it anymore," I confessed. "I can't love you the way you need to be loved."

More tears fell from her eyes and anguished cries escaped her lips as she clutched my neck and started clinging to me. "No! I can't let you go. I don't want to," she begged. "Papa Smurf, don't do this to me."

I felt guilty and watching her cry made me feel like shit. I'd chased her and caught her, and now I was stuck with her. I knew I should have listened to Mike and things wouldn't have turned out this way. Maybe things could have worked out with Ana, but she wasn't a part of my reality anymore.

I couldn't follow through with breaking it off, so I relented. "OK, Karman, we can try to work it out." But I knew it was already over.

Biking along the lakefront one day in June, I ran into Ana who was also biking. We stopped and talked for a while. She wanted to know why I hadn't called her and who the girl at Shelter was. I told her it was just a friend and she told me she broke up with the guy she'd been seeing. I looked at Ana and saw the beauty that had attracted me in the first place—eight long years ago.

"Ana, I'd like to try to work things out," I said.

She looked at me with confusion. "Why do you want to work things out?" she asked.

"Because I love you, miss you, and can't live without you." I thought the grass would be greener on the other side of the fence, but it had dried and withered after a torrid summer. I wanted to come back to where I felt safe, to where I knew the love was. I was tired of feeling like shit. Actually, I thought if anyone could pull me out of my funk, it was Ana. "Could you come by my apartment later this afternoon?"

She smiled at me and said, "Sure, I can do that."

I was elated. Now all I had to do was keep my resolve and break up with Karman. I rode home, got my car, and drove to her house. She immediately started giving me shit and wanted to know where I'd been. I suggested we head over to my apartment. I told her I had a gift for her. What I really wanted to do was give her all of her stuff she had at my apartment and then break up with her. Being on home turf would give me the fortitude I needed to get the job done. I was prepared to see this task to completion this time around.

When we got near my apartment on Roscoe and Leavitt, I saw Ana's mountain bike leaning on the front door, but she was nowhere in sight. I quickly turned around and told Karman I'd left something at her apartment, but I wasn't fast enough. Ana spied us and came running.

"Are you fucking her, Juan?" she demanded, pointing her finger at Karman. No lies could save me now, so I shut up and remained mute.

"Who is this bitch?" Karman hollered and stepped closer to Ana. A fight was imminent, I thought, but I didn't intervene with words or actions.

Ana waited through the painful silence and then shouted, "Fuck you, asshole!" as she grabbed her bike and rode away. She stopped at the corner, never turning around, and waited for me to do or say something. I was numbed and ashamed; I felt like a rat. I looked at Ana and then I looked at Karman. At that moment all I wanted was to go into my apartment and leave this whole mess behind me. Ana began pedaling east down Roscoe away from me, away from the drama, and out of my life.

Explaining anything to Karman was futile. She just wanted to be driven home, so I drove her, begging her to believe my lies. When I dropped her off at her house she slammed the screen door in my face and said, "You fucking piece a shit! Get the fuck out of here!"

"Karman," I said. "It's all a misunderstanding. I love you." The fear of being alone set in. I couldn't walk away with nothing. "Karman, don't do this."

She came rushing to the screen door. "If you want me to believe the lies you're telling me, then you better call that bitch up on the phone and tell her you're through for good. Do you fuckin' understand that?"

My head was spinning. I had to save face. I didn't want to go down like this, looking like a lying, cheating asshole. "I'll do it. Gimme the damn phone!"

She handed me the cordless. I hoped Ana wasn't going to answer but she did. I immediately pressed the end call button as if I had misdialed the number and called my house instead, beginning a conversation with my answering machine as Karman watched.

"Ana, it's over!" I began. "I don't ever wanna see you again and don't ever, ever come by my apartment!" I hollered into the phone, hoping Karman was going to buy the act. I hit the end-call button again. Then I handed the phone back to Karman with a smile.

"Good job, Juan," she said as she grabbed the phone from my hand and hit the redial button to get the last number dialed. She was livid when she heard my answering machine. "You motherfuckin' asshole!" she yelled, slamming the phone down on the kitchen counter. She grabbed a six-inch knife from the drawer. Charging the screen door with rage in her eyes, she stabbed the knife through the screen as I jumped away just in time. I stood farther away on the sidewalk now, thinking what a psycho she was as she kept stabbing the knife in the opening in the screen. I didn't need that shit in my life. I started walking away, "Don't ever fuckin' come back here, asshole!" she yelled. I got in my car, drove away. I figured at least she was out of my life now.

Three days later as I walked to my garage, I heard a car's engine revving behind me. Turning around I saw Karman behind the wheel of her Chevy Nova. She stepped on the gas pedal and drove straight at me. I had nowhere to run except behind a telephone pole, but that didn't seem to distract Karman from her mission. I thought she was going to smash into the pole, but at the last second she slammed on the brakes, skidding within inches of me.

"You motherfucker!" she screamed out her window, pure hatred in her eyes. "What goes around comes around, and when it hits your fuckin' ass, it's gonna be twice as hard, motherfucker!" Karman put the car in reverse, and maintained a death grip on the steering wheel, "Just wait, you fuckin' piece a shit! I'm gonna get your fuckin' ass!"

It was an empty threat because I wasn't scared of her. I eased my guilt by telling myself I probably deserved everything I was getting. The next day I left my apartment and noticed "Juan sucks dick!" had been keyed into my front door. I figured this was how she was getting me back. I was paying the price for fucking around with someone's heart.

I never considered that lesson long enough for it to sink in so I could learn from it.

★ ★ ★

I kept smoking pot to numb myself from the truth—I was a lying, cheating asshole who deserved everything I was getting. And then some. Work was going fine, but I had reduced my drinking and my effort for making scores. I was just going into bars for the sake of appearances, talking to no one while watching the television to take my mind off the problems in my life.

Manko had recently made lieutenant and transferred to a district. Sergeant Thomas had replaced him as head of the Tavern Team. One day during the Democratic National Convention in September 1996, Sergeant Thomas told me to go take a piss test. "Just a random test, Juan," he said. I was freaked out because I knew my piss was hot, but I fought hard to maintain my composure.

I left Manko's office, went to the bathroom, and forced myself to vomit. I then left work due to my sickness. On the way home, I stopped by a health-food store and bought a tea mixture advertising clean urinalysis results. That night I prepared it and drank it nonstop on my way to work the next day.

"Juan, you got to piss, OK?" Sergeant Thomas directed as soon as I entered the team's cubicle. "Are you feeling better today?" he asked.

"Yeah," I answered. "I just had a bad reaction to some cheese I had in my omelet." He accepted my excuse without a hint of suspicion.

I was nervous but pretty confident the tea would work. It did. My piss test came back clean and I rested easy. Now I knew I could keep getting high as long as I had a little heads-up for a piss quiz and my handy-dandy tea.

The road to destruction was the only road I knew, but amazingly it didn't seem to be hindering my academic pursuits. I wasn't getting straight As, but I was passing with Bs and was getting closer, with every class I took, to graduating with my second MA.

The majority of the education classes I had been taking at DePaul focused on the disparity and accessibility of education for minorities and members of the lower classes. I was reading and learning about the racial and class inequity throughout the public school system, but I had been living in it too; I saw it every day in the Narcotics Unit. While my devotion to the principles of the Chicago Police Department ebbed, my social awareness grew. I began thinking of my trip to Europe as a whole new opportunity. I wondered if there was a way to teach over there. That would allow me to escape everything, I reasoned.

34

WE JUST HAVING OURSELVES A LITTLE FUN

OPERATION CRACK HOTLINE was a weekend Iron Wedge assignment paid for by the federal government. This operation was strictly voluntary. I offered my services because my drinking habits were costing me loads of cash. At five to six hours of time-and-a-half pay, there were tons of volunteers. It was a time to work with unfamiliar officers from other teams. Because groups were based on rotating seniority, I was usually paired with veterans from high-level teams. I never knew what to expect working with the "old schoolers" of the Unit. I often came away with new insights.

On one particular weekend in the late summer of 1996, shortly after my thirtieth birthday, the Crack Hotline crew I was working with spent two hours on the street and secured the three requisite buys for the day. One hour ahead of schedule, we were headed into Area 4 for processing when the driver of our unmarked squad observed a parked car with three black teenagers inside kicking back, apparently listening to music.

The driver, a plump little Italian named Officer Donato, as well as the cop riding shotgun, Detective Sullivan, were both white men, members of the same high-level team, and twenty-year vets. I'd never worked with either of them before.

Detective Sullivan radioed the supervisor, "Hey Sarge, I got a suspicious car with three occupants at 6— North Harding. I'd like to do a street stop."

It didn't look suspicious to me, but then again, they were the experts. So I didn't say anything.

"Ten-four. Go on and be quick about it. Meet us at the Area. We have paper to do," the sergeant responded.

I went along, figuring a little extra activity on the twenty-four-hour sheets always looked good on Mondays when the commander checked them. Plus, it could mean more court time if they found something. In any event, it didn't matter what I thought—I was just along for the ride.

We slowly rolled up behind a flawless midnight blue 1978 Oldsmobile Cutlass that had been meticulously cared for. It was a beauty with a remarkable powder-blue-coated paint job, unique pin stripes, and silver rims. The car's trunk vibrated and rattled from the bass-heavy house music coming from inside. We exited our car and approached the occupants from the driver's and passenger's sides with guns drawn.

Donato banged on the rear quarter panel and ordered, "Shut off the motherfuckin' jungle music. All three of ya, get out of the fuckin' car with your hands up in the air! Do it nice and slow!"

"Put your fuckin' hands on your heads and walk to the back of the car!" Sullivan hollered as the music died and the occupants checked us out with blank faces. They glanced at each other and shrugged their shoulders. "Can't you fuckin' hear? Now!" And they did as he ordered.

"Cover these three monkeys, will ya, Juarez?" Sullivan said.

I had heard all sorts of derogatory terms working in the ghetto, where fellow narcs let loose with their tongues freely, but I never could accept them. I did as I was ordered as they conducted a brief but thorough search of the occupants. They possessed nothing but some U.S. currency, which disappeared into Sullivan's pocket. I looked at my watch, thinking I'd much rather be in the Area doing the paperwork and getting ready to go home.

"C'mon, my mama just gave me that," one of the teenagers complained.

"Tell her to come to 1060 West Addison if you want the money back," Sullivan replied.

The address was that of Wrigley Field, home of the Chicago Cubs. I started to grow suspicious that these officers weren't after street-level dope. I continued to cover the suspects with my gun as they were handcuffed and placed inside the unmarked squad.

Sullivan and Donato began to search their vehicle. Sullivan reached inside the car, turned the stereo back on, and started squirming around in a funky white-man dance. Donato and I bent over in laughter; Sullivan totally lacked rhythm. He was the one who looked like a monkey. The stereo remained on as Donato and Sullivan began to demolish the interior of the car by ripping the radio out of the dashboard, pulling out air vents, throwing the contents of the ashtrays all over the interior, removing inside panels of the door, and tearing the carpet from the floorboard, all the while exchanging some hearty laughs.

"Be useful," Donato said to me. "Get their information, would ya?" His words startled me. I realized that I'd just been standing there staring at them. I got in the squad and began to write up some CARs when the suspects began to make a ruckus. I looked up and saw Sullivan opening the trunk of the Cutlass and finding the source of all the rattling; it was a huge bazooka speaker along with a bass booster. The stereo in the car rivaled any audiophile's home system, and it wasn't about to escape the demolition crew.

Street-level dope wasn't even a question now. The two officers converged behind the Cutlass. Donato pulled out a pocketknife, opened the blade, and proceeded to stab and slice the paper cone of the speaker, rendering it inoperable. Donato and Sullivan moved on to the bass booster and poured some nearby antifreeze all over the accessory causing it to short circuit.

"Yo! What is that motherfucker doing to my ride? What the fuck did I do?" yelled one of the suspects.

I didn't have an answer. My heart was heavy because I could never find my voice or raise a concern when I saw something this appalling. I just went on filling out the CAR. "Ask them," I offered.

As if the electronic destruction wasn't enough, Officer Donato removed a can of Mace from his utility belt in plain sight and headed back into the besieged car as Sullivan snooped around the back of it. Donato began to mace the steering wheel. It was a practice I had seen implemented by many cops who had visions of hand-to-face contact as the driver touched the wheel and then sniffed what was on his hands. Donato maced the open air vents, too, so that the fumes would circulate in the air while the car was being driven. This trick was new to me.

Their mission accomplished, they headed toward the unmarked squad, motioning me to get out and open up one of the back doors. Donato opened the other and began to uncuff two of the fuming former suspects; while Sullivan released the other, Donato threw them their keys. I snuck back into the rear seat quickly, and we didn't linger to see their reactions or answer their questions. All I heard was Donato saying, "Shut the fuck up, will ya? Tell it to someone who cares," as the car pulled away.

Yells of protestation faded into the growing space between them and us. Donato and Sullivan knew they had absolutely nothing to worry about—they didn't wedge, and they were never in this area.

"Sarge, that's a negative on the street stop. We're coming into the Area now," Sullivan radioed in. I was glad we were finally heading in. I'd be home in an hour or so.

"Ten-four," the sergeant responded.

The caustic scent of Mace made its way to my nose and began to singe my nasal membranes.

"You guys find anything?" I asked, already knowing the answer.

Sullivan turned his head, "Fuck no! We just having ourselves a little fun."

"Those fuckin' shines don't deserve that car. It was fuckin' mint," Donato added, looking at me in the rearview mirror. "Had to be drug money. Fuck 'em," he concluded.

I rolled down my window and inhaled a cool stream of fresh air that cleared my senses and my nose. I felt instant relief and wondered why Donato and Sullivan weren't picking up on the acrid scent.

About four blocks later Donato pulled over to the side of the road as he and his partner were overcome by the vapors that were caught in the fibers of their clothing. Before the car could come to a complete stop, they had opened their doors and windows, fighting for fresh air. They got out of the car. Both of them were heaving to get their breath. Then Donato rubbed his eyes with the back of his hand, a terrible mistake. But moments later Sullivan did the same thing. Tears streamed down their faces, their eyes reddened and swelled, and they cursed a blue streak. Guttural sounds came from each of them as they doubled over, consumed by the Mace, unaware of a growing crowd of curious onlookers.

"You guys all right?" I asked, but I was laughing to myself.

I sat in the backseat as the rest of the drive went by in silence. There wasn't any joking around once we got back into the Area either. It seemed as if the more insight I got into the motives and actions of cops I worked with or came across, the more negative my view of cops became. It seemed that the code of silence was there to assist those officers who wanted to abuse the system, indulge their prejudices, and feel superior to everyone else. I began to question whether I wanted to remain a part of this brotherhood of corruption.

35

MISTAKEN IDENTITY OR IGNORANCE: "HEY, I DON'T WANNA LISTEN"

IN THE EARLY FALL OF 1996, I was doing homework one night after we had been cut loose. I decided to visit the hip nightclubs Shelter and Elixir after being tipped off that they were hot spots for "E" or Ecstasy, a dangerous new designer drug. Shelter had once been my stomping grounds, so as I entered the curtained vestibule, a flood of rich memories—good and bad—filled my head. Recalling the night I'd met Karman there brought a smile to my face, but I also remembered the night I saw Ana kissing another man—thank God all that was behind me now. As I walked around the club, I saw plenty of people I knew, but I didn't give a shit about the place after my fallout with Karman. If I caught them dirty, the bar was going to get nailed; unfortunately, my investigations yielded nothing.

I left at 2 A.M. I walked down DesPlaines Street, an industrial street, which, except for a number of parked cars, was desolate. I entered my undercover vehicle and turned the ignition. I was pulling away when I noticed headlights approaching rapidly in my rearview mirror. Stopping at the traffic light at Lake Street, I signaled and proceeded to make a right-hand turn when the lights behind me began to flash. It was a tactical unit from the the 12th District apparently doing a street stop.

I thought these officers recognized me and were goofing around, but when I saw the two, unfamiliar mustachioed faces in my rearview mirror, I knew I was wrong. My next thought: What was their probable cause? My car was properly licensed and I hadn't committed any traffic violations. One of the cops approached the driver's side window with his gun drawn and ordered me to turn off the car, step out, put my hands on my head, and walk backward toward their squad. Now I really wondered what they were up to. Did they just see me as a Mexican with a close-shaven head and a goatee—a stereotypical gangbanger coming out of a nightclub? Surely they didn't see me as a college graduate with an MA under my belt and another almost finished?

"Hey guys, what's—"

"Shut the fuck up! Don't say a fuckin' word unless we tell you to!" commanded a voice behind me. I was perplexed because I knew this misunderstanding would be over in a second once I said the three magic words.

"Hey, Rambo. Take it—"

A light blinded me. "Shut the fuck up, asshole!"

I did as I was commanded.

One of the officers ordered me to place my hands on the back of the car and then he began to search me. He was a short, stocky Hispanic with an I-ain't-taking-no-shit attitude. After completing his search, he stepped back. His chest rose high as he unholstered his gun, covering me with his flashlight while the other officer began to search my covert car. The other officer was a white thick-necked military type. They appeared to be straight out of the academy.

I had had enough. Six years on the job should afford me some leeway. "Officer, what did—?"

"Shut the fuck up, asshole!" the Hispanic cop demanded, interrupting my question as he adjusted to a more aggressive stance and moved in closer. I was watching the flashlight in his hand—it can be a pretty good weapon, too.

"There's no need to do this, I'm a—"

"Asshole! Didn't I say to shut the fuck up?" he asked, slapping the back of my neck hard with an open hand.

"Where's your license, shithead?" questioned the other cop, who stuck his head out of my car.

Simultaneously, I removed my hands from my head and started again to identify myself and make this ugly episode stop. "Hey, I'm—"

"What the fuck do you think you're doing? Didn't I tell you to shut the fuck up?" I was cut short once again as the Hispanic cop trained his gun on me. "And put your hands back on your fuckin' head, asshole!"

"I was just—"

"What the fuck! Are you deaf and stupid?" screamed his white partner, who stopped searching the car and stood up. "Cuff him and throw him in the back of the squad!" he ordered his partner as he stepped back and unholstered his gun. "Go on, I got him," he said, pointing it at my face while the Hispanic cop cuffed me. This incident, according to the use-of-force chart (a police procedures chart), did not call for this reaction. If I had been threatening their physical safety, then they'd be justified in physically restraining me, but I was presenting no threat. Instead, they should have been using verbal direction to get me to do what they want.

It was useless to attempt a conversation, so I gave up, shook my head, and kept my mouth shut as a flood of thoughts came to me. The stop didn't appear to be racially motivated and there's no way it could be me personally. I was still smoking weed, but they didn't know that and I wasn't stupid enough to ever have any in my police car. What had I done? According to the chart, I was still a passive resister who could be calmed by the verbal instructions of a trained officer, but these cops had escalated this incident to epic proportions. The Hispanic cop was about to put me in the back of their squad, but I wanted to give them one more chance to do the right thing. All they had to do was open their ears.

"Hey, listen—"

"No! You fuckin' listen! Shut yer trap and get in the back of the car, asshole!" he said, tightening the cuffs, which began to cut into my wrists. My hands started throbbing from the sudden loss of blood.

This was beyond my comprehension. How could they justify their actions? Besides having a badge, what gave them the right to do this? Their ignorance was a total violation of my constitutional rights as a citizen of the United States. Then I flashed back on my whole career, from Locallo to Franco to Donato, and I suddenly knew why they did it. They did it because they could.

I got in the back of their squad and watched as the two ransacked my car. I'd like to know what went through their minds when they found my wallet, my badge, and my ID. I thanked God that I had been unsuccessful in the clubs that night. My situation would have become really interesting if there had been some drugs in the car. I wouldn't want to even imagine that scenario. They walked back to their squad, red-faced.

"Why didn't you tell us you were one of us?" the Hispanic cop asked. A faltering smile crept across his brown face as he pulled me out of their car.

"You told me to shut the fuck up, so I did! What the fuck, dickhead? Take these fuckin' cuffs off me!" He did, and my hands slowly came back to life.

The once-vociferous Hispanic cop couldn't find any words now, "Well . . . uh . . . um . . ."

This was going to make an excellent office story. I was over the drama, but I figured I'd get their names to bring the story to life.

"We don't have to tell you," the white cop said curtly, crossing his arms.

To minimize the chance of a renewed verbal attack by being a passive resister, I glanced at their plates and made a mental note. "Fine. You guys have a good night and maybe next time you'll think and listen before you act."

"You should listen to your own advice. Don't worry about us."

That left me scratching my head. I couldn't find any sense in it at all.

I got into my disheveled car and drove away as the interior flap of the passenger's door hung limply from the handle. I had been physically and verbally assaulted, handcuffed, thrown into the back of a police car, released without an apology, and, to top it off, my undercover police car was in total disarray.

I recalled all the abuses of authority I had seen since my first day on the job with Steve Tyler. I thought back to the time I had slapped around a kid to get the truth about a stolen bike when I worked in the 14th

District. I thought about when Franco beat up on the wrong guy and I pictured what Donato and Sullivan had done to those kids and their car because the music was too loud. In every case, we did it because we could. And we did it with the comfort of knowing that it was highly unlikely that there would be any repercussions from these abuses.

I was suddenly thoroughly disgusted at being a cop. But there was a huge difference between most abusive cops and me. I had only committed physical abuse once. Though I had stepped over the line and abused my authority in other ways, I didn't find it necessary to kick some kid's ass for the sake of my ego.

★ ★ ★

The next night at work, I related my experience to Sergeant Thomas who said, "Don't worry about it, Juan. I'll take care of it."

I didn't really want him to take care of it; I'd sooner forget about the whole ordeal. But what the heck, he offered. Besides, I wanted to see the power of clout work its magic.

Two weeks later while at court, an acquaintance from the 12th District informed me that the two tactical officers who'd shaken me down had since been dumped to a beat car. I also heard I was the "motherfuckin' asshole" responsible for their fall in the ranks. Guessing I must have been the only cop from Narcotics they fucked around with, I was happy they got what they deserved. But it was obvious from the comments I heard that they couldn't own up to their actions and were looking for someone else to blame.

36

LAST CALL

IN SEPTEMBER 1996 the Tavern Team started working earlier hours (4 P.M. to midnight) because the LLC was getting complaints of open drug trafficking in Mexican taverns, especially during happy hour. I began hitting the bars near Eighteenth and Twenty-sixth streets, Forty-seventh and Ashland, and Damen and Blue Island pretty hard.

It had been more than three months since I'd last seen Karman behind the wheel of her car, aiming to make me a hood ornament. It had been about the same amount of time since I had talked to Ana. I had decided to take a break from women. I had breakfast with my dad and stepmother one morning, and I told them that I was in over my head—I was in debt to the tune of twenty thousand dollars.

"Why don't you move in with us until you get your feet back on the ground?" my stepmother asked. I looked at my dad to ensure the offer was real.

"Yeah, you can have back your own room," my dad confirmed. I took them up on the offer and moved in as I began yet another fall quarter at DePaul.

It was weird to find myself, at almost thirty years old, moving back in with my parents, but I didn't care about images anymore. I just wanted a place to rest and think about what the hell I was going to do for the next year. I was only four classes away from finishing my second master's. I figured these last few credits were going to take me another two years if I kept taking one class a quarter. I wasn't in too much of a hurry because the Department was still paying my tuition. But teaching was looking better all the time. I found myself beginning to think of leaving the force once I graduated; police work was beating me into the ground.

I found myself in Pilsen with the Tavern Team, slowly coming back to life as a buy officer and a drinker—a moderate one this time—so I had things under control. I volunteered to work a bar on the northwest corner of Eighteenth and Damen. As usual, I quickly began made a connection with the bartender and let him know I was looking for coke. I ordered one beer and a shot. I didn't find it necessary to start slamming the alcohol, but if it came down to it, I would. It was 6 P.M. The after-work crowd was starting to straggle in. The bartender called me over and asked if I was still interested in some cocaine. When I said yes, he introduced me to two Mexican American guys. Their names were Guillermo and Frank, and they both seemed like good potentials. One of them worked for the city's Streets and Sanitation Department and the other was a union ironworker. I stayed in the bar for a while and got to know them. We played pool and I bought them rounds of drinks while I nursed my beer. The conversation began to flow and my story began to take shape from their initial question.

"Why you up in this 'hood?" Frank asked, chalking up his cue.

"I got a *chiquita* over here, and she loves to party. Once she gets high on the flake, she lets the freak out." They both lifted their eyes from the pool table and laughed. I was back to creating stories off the cuff and it felt good to make these guys laugh and to laugh with them.

"I knew some freaks like that," Guillermo stated, "but they're all toothless skanks now."

"Like the one you're married to," Frank capped and we all howled.

After buying them two rounds in less than two hours, I took the opportunity to cast my line. "You guys know where I can score some flake?" I felt the rust begin to fall off my delivery. Over the last couple of months I hadn't really been trying to score in bars, but now I was ready to try anew.

They looked cautiously at each other and then eyed me, "We don't use that shit, bro'."

"Sorry, man. I was just asking," I quickly replied. "It ain't really for me, it's for my lady, bro'."

"Someone might be around later, but he usually pokes his head in here 'round midnight," Guillermo stated as he sank one of the balls on the pool table. "Why don't you stick around and hang out?"

"I'd love to, bro', but duty calls and by that time I'll be slamming hips," I testified, knowing full well I didn't want to hang out in the bar another four hours. I didn't want to get caught up in having to drink beyond moderation. (Liquor had lost its luster now that I had a huge debt I had to manage.)

"Why don't 'cha come back next Tuesday around six and we'll see what we can do for you, bro'," Frank suggested.

It was a week away; I could wait.

"Sounds good to me. I'll just have to keep her begging." We all laughed. Could this job be any easier? I thought to myself as I clinked bottles with my unsuspecting offenders. I realized that I hadn't lost my touch, and it felt good.

I hung out in the bar another hour, continuing to buy Frank and Guillermo another round and two shots of tequila.

"How come you're not drinking, bro'?" Frank asked.

"I had a long weekend and had one too many," I said, but then he ordered me a beer. When I went to the men's room a few minutes later I dumped it in the urinal. We played another game of pool and shot the shit for a little while longer. It was fun. I left the bar at 10 P.M. and informed Sergeant Thomas of the news. It was nice working for my old boss again. He listened to the rundown and we put the bar on the back burner.

It was the fourth week of September and I had seven weeks to go before my trip to Europe, but I had to keep my mind on work for the time being. I was excited—not because of the bar, but because of my looming vacation. I had been talking to an English professor at DePaul who came from

Italy. When I told him of my desire to teach in Europe, he said, "Let me put in some calls, and I'll have a list of connections for you before you leave." This further heightened my anticipation for my time away.

The next Tuesday, I went back to the bar at 6 P.M. and met up with Frank and Guillermo, who told me, "The guy with the coke'll be by later. Why don't you hang out and play some pool?"

We drank, talked, laughed, and played pool to pass the time. We never talked about cocaine, but instead discussed our jobs and lives. Guillermo told me about his wife and family, and how he got the job with the city. "If it wasn't for my teacher at Juarez (High School), I'd probably be doing some bullshit work or hanging in a gang right now. He changed my life."

"No shit, bro'. I'm a teacher, too. I teach at a school on the North Side," I responded, amazed at how easy it was to envision myself in that role. Even so, I knew I'd be changing Guillermo's life too, and not in a positive manner. "How did he change your life, bro'?" I asked.

He began nodding his head as if recollecting that very moment. "He must've liked me because when I was a senior I was gonna get suspended for some bullshit fight. He stuck his neck out and talked to the principal. They made a deal and put me on a super-tight probation. After I graduated, he made some calls and hooked me up with a summer job with the city." Guillermo sat back in his stool and put his arms on the bar. "I haven't looked back since then. It's nice to know there are people out there who'll help when you need it." It felt funny to hear him say that because that's exactly what I had aspired to do, from my first day in uniform, six-and-a-half years ago. And I knew I hadn't accomplished this except for the one day I helped that woman in the 14th District get her sons' bikes back.

"Damn straight, bro'," I shot back. "By the way, where is this buddy of yours with the flake? My lady keeps on paging me and I gotta jam." Looking at my watch, it was 10:30 P.M. and I thought about my team outside in their parked cars.

"I don't know. He's probably caught up in some shit. If you gotta jam, tell me what you need and I'll pick it up for you."

"I'm just looking for a twenty. Ain't nothing big," I casually affirmed. "If you need the cash now, I'll give it to you."

"That's cool, bro'," Frank, who was sitting with us at the bar, jumped in. "You're straight. We'll float ya the ducats if we see the guy. Why don't ya come back tomorrow night? Maybe we'll have it for ya by then." I already knew the bartender had consented to the deal by making the introductions; getting my money in the cash register would just be a formality.

I swallowed the last of my beer, thanked them for helping me out, and then left the bar. Sergeant Thomas thought I had a positive since I was in the bar for almost five hours, but when I told him the story he seemed a bit annoyed and sent everyone, except me, home.

"Juan," he began, shaking his head in disapproval, "You've been in there all night. I hope you're not fuckin' around."

I assured him I wasn't and gave him the complete rundown, telling him I'd probably be able to work these guys for larger quantities of cocaine. I lied to protect myself, but also to have him send me in the bar again. He agreed to give me one more night there.

It was October and Chicago was experiencing an Indian summer. When I went back to the bar the next night, a full-out barbecue was taking place in the yard next to the bar and Frank and Guillermo were there grilling carne asada and hamburgers. Frank had his two daughters, ages three and five, with him, and Guillermo had his four-year-old son. Guillermo said he had the dope and we made the transaction, but I stood around to enjoy the festivities because these guys reminded me of some family friends on Eighteenth Street I had while growing up. It also made me flash back to the warmth of Ana's family and the barbecues they invited me to share. I felt sad that I was now out of that circle.

As luck would have it, Mark, her brother, had recently made sergeant and was detailed to Narcotics. It was a bit awkward seeing him on the second floor and I wondered just exactly how much he knew about what I had done to his younger sister. He was cordial enough, but I couldn't look him in the eyes.

"Hey," Frank called across the yard, hoisting his younger daughter on his shoulders as she laughed. "Why don't you come over to the crib on Sunday so we can watch the Bears game?"

I had never found myself in this situation before, but there was no way I could get personal with these guys. I had to keep up the lies. "Oh man, I can't make it. I told my sister I would help her move this weekend."

"That's cool, bro'. We can do it some other time. How'd you want your carne asada cooked?" Guillermo asked.

As the night continued and the party grew, I looked at Frank and Guillermo's children and began to feel guilty because they were family men. What would their children's lives be like with their fathers in jail? Frank and Guillermo weren't gangbangers who had nothing better to do with their lives than sell drugs, and they weren't deadbeat dads who impregnated girls and then left them to raise the kids on their own.

Through our conversations I found out they were both in their mid-twenties, and had married their high school sweethearts. It had been a challenge for them just to finish school and stay out of gangs, which were ever-present in Pilsen, and they were doing their best to provide for their children. Neither of them did drugs, and they definitely weren't bad guys.

I had to think about this. My conscious was battling hard—should I fuck these guys' lives up for some bullshit dope? In essence, I'd be throwing them in jail for being too nice and trusting me too much. I had already learned from my experience with Karman what it was like to mislead people once they've taken you into their trust. I didn't want to do it again.

I went back to my sergeant, turned over the dope and created fictitious names when it came time to divulge who the offenders were. I lied to him again when I told him they'd promised to get some bigger weight the next week. I just wanted to go back and hang out with these guys because they were civilians and they were cool to me. I was getting tired of hanging out with cops all the time and sucking up the cop mentality. Frank and Guillermo provided me with a different perspective.

Sergeant Thomas let me run with it, but I had no intention of fucking with these guys' lives, their families, or their livelihood. Once you're given the title of felon, it's nearly impossible to change the way people see you. These guys didn't deserve that. I had seen it happen too many times to nameless faces, but these faces had names and they let me in to their lives.

The next week I went back, and, sure enough, they were there. They asked me how the move with my sister went and then informed me I didn't miss much because the Bears game sucked anyway. Frank extended the invitation again for the following weekend. We drank, exchanged more personal stories—some more truthful than others on my part. We got to know each other even better. I was determined to let them skate when, after three beers, I went to the men's bathroom and gazed in the mirror, trying to find the courage to make a decision I could live with. I found it hard to look myself straight in the eyes. It wasn't as easy as it was at Berlin.

I left the bar and went to my covert car. I called Sergeant Thomas and told the team to head to the meet spot. During the debriefing, I told them the two wanted offenders hadn't shown up. I told them the same thing for the next two weeks as the pressure to take the bar down increased. Warrants were then drawn out for the two fictitious names I created, but I knew they would never be executed. It made me happy. My job conscience finally surrendered to my social conscience. The War on Drugs the Narcotics Unit was fighting made no sense to me.

I had taken my first step toward extracting myself from the police brotherhood.

Luckily, my escape was on the horizon—my vacation. The night before I left for Europe I decided to call Karman up and to see if she'd like to go out for drinks and play some pool. Five months had passed since I'd seen her last and I thought she would be over the pangs of the relationship. I was lonely and I wanted company and, in truth, I really had enjoyed her company before she went ballistic on me.

Things were changing for me. I was getting back into shape by swimming at Shabona Park on Addison Avenue near Harlem Avenue. I was drinking moderately and losing weight. I had started biking a bit more with Tim. I had time to think and clear my head during the two months I had been living at my parents' house. I was moving forward, and I hoped that Karman was too. At any rate, she agreed to meet me at a bar near Shakespeare and Leavitt called The Charleston.

I was excited because I was leaving the moral battle of being a cop behind, and I was going to research the teaching connections my professor at DePaul had lined up for me. When I saw Karman, I couldn't conceal my happiness. She looked just as beautiful as she had the first time I saw her at Shelter. She smiled at me, but she seemed a bit distant. I had to give her some leeway—just because I could easily move forward and forget the past didn't mean everyone else could.

"Hey Karman, what's going on?" I asked. "You still drinking martinis?"

"I sure am." I ordered two martinis and two shots. We played some pool and made small talk. Over the course of an hour Karman became a bit more amiable and asked, "You still heading for Amsterdam?" while she put on her coat.

"I sure am," I said, mimicking her earlier words.

"I got a favor to ask you, Juan," Karman said innocently. "First, let's go out to your car and spark up." Just like old times. We left the bar and entered my car and she lit up a joint. "You know what I would really like from Amsterdam?" she asked.

"I need you to ask me, Karman. I can't read your mind."

"Hash, Juan. I would really appreciate it if you brought me back some hash."

Karman didn't seem to be holding any grudges about our past, so I said, "Sure," making it sound as friendly as possible. I took a drag on the joint and passed it to her. "I'll try to bring you back a little package."

When the joint was done, she got out of my car and went on her way. That didn't go too badly I said to myself. I was looking forward to seeing her when I got back.

The next day I left for Europe. I was free!

37

THE AIRPORT STORY

As the seven-hour trans-Atlantic flight from Italy touched down silently on the runway at O'Hare International Airport, my head snapped to attention. The jarring motion of deceleration slammed me back to the present—I was back in Chicago.

I had gotten wasted every day in Amsterdam, visiting coffeehouse after coffeehouse, sampling the very best buds, and smoking hashish like there was no tomorrow. By the time we got to Rome, I was ready to get to work. I pulled out the list of phone numbers and names of contacts my DePaul professor had provided me and made sure to call on each of them. When I went to see them at their respective schools, I was amazed by how eager they were to help me find a teaching position. They were very impressed with my resume, but they all had the same advice when I walked out of their doors: "Move to Rome. That's the easiest way to get a job here."

I was so excited that I extended my trip five days longer than planned so I could visit more schools. As I said goodbye to my friends at the Spanish Steps, I rejoiced at my good fortune in having the chance to explore Rome all by myself. I had fallen in love with the eternal city. Around every corner I was greeted by monuments to historical events that I'd only read about in books. I was enamored with the slow ease with which Romans walked, the beauty and majesty of the architecture, and the glorious fountains that dotted the *viae*. I knew this city would be the perfect place to relocate.

There was nothing holding me in Chicago. As I flew home I began planning how to make this new dream a reality. I had three classes to finish in order to graduate with my second master's and earn my teaching certificate. The only lingering questions concerned work.

The flight back to Chicago gave me plenty of time to consider my options. My first option was to take a leave of absence from the job. By doing this I could leave open the possibility of returning to the police force if I didn't like teaching. My second and preferred choice was simply to quit the force. If I did this I would have to commit myself completely to being a teacher, which was a bit daunting. I would have to finish my remaining classes as quickly as possible to move ahead with this plan. Career changes can be tricky, but, once I thought about it, I realized there was nothing to fear. Anything was better than where I was.

"Attention all passengers," the flight attendant announced as the plane taxied to the terminal. "Please have your passports in hand when getting off the plane."

Since I was nearest the door, I'd be the first one out. I stood up, stretched my legs, and hoisted the backpack onto my shoulders. I reached into my jacket pocket for my passport as the plane's door began to open.

I was immediately greeted by an eager German shepherd, which was being restrained by a grim-faced United States Customs agent wearing black fatigues. As the door fully opened, a second agent with another menacing dog appeared. One of them snatched my passport from my hand. I was dumbfounded. Glancing at my picture then at me, he grabbed the shoulder strap of my backpack and yanked me through the door of the plane. The agents and their drug-sniffing dogs escorted me down the Jetway, ducking down some stairs before we reached the terminal. I hesitated, leery of where they were taking me.

"Follow him, Juan!" the customs agent said sharply, jutting his chin toward his partner in front of us.

"I'm a Chicago police officer," I informed the agent as my shock diminished. His dog started to sniff my shoes at the bottom of the staircase.

"You got something there, boy?" he questioned, not even willing to respond to my assertion. It was obvious that they were looking for something, but I wasn't sure if he was asking his dog or me. The idea of me, a Narcotics agent, trying to smuggle dope into this country was hilarious. If I wanted any drugs, I could just take them from the streets of Chicago. I had fully enjoyed my vacation in the hash bars of Amsterdam's red-light district, but I hadn't brought any souvenirs home.

"Sure, I do," I responded in a wry and exhausted voice. "I got some smelly feet." The customs agents didn't find any humor in that. "What's going on?" I asked,

The agent beside me remained stiff-necked and tight-lipped, peering at me from the corner of his eye. The one in front of me stopped abruptly and got in my face, "We'll ask the questions here, OK? What were you doing in Amsterdam?" he demanded as they resumed escorting me down a long corridor in the international terminal.

"I was on vacation, checking out teaching jobs," I said. Then I added, "Is that OK with you?"

"Is that all you were doing there?" he persisted as we entered a room at the end of the hall. He shut the door behind me. I noticed there were three other agents standing around a table in the center of the room.

"Yes, that's all I did," I blurted out, concerned by the growing number of adversaries surrounding me.

"Is that all of your luggage?" one of the agents asked, pointing at my backpack on the folding table.

"Yes, it is. I travel light." They began searching the contents of my bag, throwing them carelessly on the table. Another agent began systematically searching me.

"Strip!" the agent ordered when he didn't find anything.

"What?" I asked, remembering I wasn't wearing any underwear. "What the fuck's going on?"

"Didn't I tell you before not to ask questions!" barked one of the agents who had taken me off the plane. "What part of strip don't you understand?"

I did as I was ordered. I pulled off my shirt, kicked off my boots, and began removing my pants when one of the agents shoved me in a chair.

My pants gathered at my ankles and the agent grabbed my sock-encased feet. I smelled them clearly now and made sure the agent got a noseful of the pungent scent as I brought my feet up to his face.

"You see anything there?" I asked. The sarcasm was as thick as the fumes emanating from my feet.

"Take your stinky-ass socks off," he sneered. I did. He threw my feet down disgustedly and glared at me. Now I was annoyed and frustrated; I just wanted to get home. In the back of my mind, I began to suspect a set-up; clearly they had been expecting me to be smuggling something. I looked over at the contents of my backpack strewn on the table and sighed.

"He doesn't have any other luggage," scratched a voice on their radios.

"All right," said the agent who'd made me strip, "get dressed and get the fuck out of here!"

"Are you gonna put my stuff back in my bag like it was when I got here?" I asked, as I slid my pants up. Their derisive chuckling was my answer. I proceeded to dress and repacked my bag. I was pissed off. What the fuck did I do to deserve this treatment? I wasn't going to ask any questions though. I knew when I had gotten away with something. I had bought a marble hash pipe in Amsterdam and they hadn't found it in a zippered pouch on the side of my backpack. Fucking amateurs. After leaving the room and passing the baggage claim area of the international terminal, I headed toward the sliding glass doors to freedom.

"Juan," a female voice behind me called. I turned and saw Officer O'Ryan, a cop from Narcotics I had worked with on a couple of operations. She had left the unit and gone to IAD.

Before I could ask what she was doing there, she said, "You need to come with me. You're under investigation."

"Investigation for what?" I looked O'Ryan straight in her eyes. "You've got to be joking! I was just strip-searched by Customs and they didn't find shit. What the fuck's up?" She turned her head, averting her eyes.

"Someone dropped a dime on you," she informed me under her breath as we walked down another long passageway to a room full of cops.

"I fucking knew it," I muttered. My head spun and I wondered who had set me up.

"I'm Sergeant Hyde," said the middle-aged, slightly overweight cop at the end of the table. "You are hereby informed of an investigation brought upon you by a complaint received by IAD. Here's your copy."

He reached out his hand and gave me a yellow piece of paper from a triplicate form set. I couldn't read it. My eyes lost focus. Everything around me took on a red tint as anger replaced my frustration.

"Complaint number one," he said, "is that you went to Amsterdam for the intent and purpose of smuggling contraband. That's why we're here." That complaint didn't hold any water, but I kept silent, gritting my teeth and shaking my head as my anger kept building.

"Complaint number two," he continued, looking around the room, "is that you went to Amsterdam to smoke hashish and marijuana. You'll need to submit a urine sample or face immediate suspension." He waited for my response.

A flood of dizziness slammed my head, making it spin in every conceivable direction as my vision narrowed to the sealed plastic cup on the table.

"What?" I barked. "I refuse!" This was a knee-jerk reaction. I couldn't believe I had been snitched on for something so trivial—smoking hash on vacation seven thousand miles away from my job.

"As a sergeant of the Chicago Police Department, I command that you submit a urinalysis or face immediate suspension for failing to heed the commands of a superior officer." He smiled and held out the cup. "Do you understand?"

I felt my anger dissipate through my fingertips and feet, only to be replaced by resignation. "Yes, I do," I mumbled, as reality conquered the nausea and I realized the full extent of this investigation. I wasn't getting out of this one.

"So, will you submit a sample?"

"Sure." My whole career as a cop began to pass before my eyes in a collage of rapidly moving pictures and faces.

That was Friday, December 13, 1996.

38

FACING THE MUSIC

"Report to your commander on Monday at 10 a.m.," Sergeant Hyde informed me as I handed him the still-warm cup of my piss. I realized that I'd have all weekend to think about my hot piss, which was now in the possession of the Chicago Police Department. I left the interrogation room at O'Hare and headed toward the glass doors where my father was waiting for me. This time I made it.

"What the hell was that all about?" asked my father as I came through the doors.

"Nothing," I said, still pissed off about my experience.

"So who were they? I know they were coppers, but where were they from?" he persisted.

"They were IAD," I conceded, knowing I wasn't going be able to keep this from him. We walked out to his car, which was parked in front of the international terminal. My stepmother was behind the wheel.

As soon as we got in the car, my father spoke out. "IAD was waiting for sonny boy when he got off the plane. I saw it through the glass doors. They interrogated him for over an hour."

Dale looked at me in the rearview mirror, "What did they want, Juancho?"

"Somebody told them I was smuggling some dope," I offered. "When they didn't find anything they made me take a piss test."

"What?" my father exclaimed.

"Listen," I began. "I got to be honest with you two. While I was in Amsterdam I went into the coffeeshops where there were tons of people

270

smoking pot. There's a good chance I got second-hand smoke in me and I think it's going to show up on the piss test. The results will be in on Monday and I have to go see Commander Griggs first thing in the morning."

"How can they jam you up for secondhand smoke?" Dale asked.

"It doesn't matter," my father said. "A hot piss test is a hot piss test. Don't worry, Juancho, I'll check around and look for a solution."

"Didn't Green piss hot and then get a lawyer to fight the case?" Dale asked my father, referring to someone in their district.

"Yeah," he responded. "She claimed someone put something in her food while she was in Aruba and was able to beat the case."

"There's hope for you yet, Juancho," Dale said.

I wish I had the same amount of hope she did. I knew I had to pay the piper and it made me feel like shit that I lied to them, but there was no way I was going to admit to smoking pot. It would disappoint them beyond words and it wasn't really necessary. There's no way they'd find out about the investigation since IAD was running it. The inquiry was confidential and wouldn't leave the IAD office. We got home and I went into my bedroom, wondering what the hell had happened.

I spent the weekend trying to piece together the fragmented clues that would lead to the person who'd snitched on me. I was furious that someone could alter my life so swiftly—and so severely. An anonymous tip—bullshit! I was filled with disturbing visions of retribution, fueled with fear of losing my job in such a defaming fashion. After a while, time and common sense smothered that burning rage. Still, I prayed that Monday would never come. But it did.

The Monday morning drive into 3540 was numbing; dread engulfed me and I came to the realization that I had no idea where life was taking me.

Sergeant Thomas was in our team office, sitting at his desk doing paperwork as I came in. "Damn, Juan. If I could've warned you, I would've. Some funky shit has been going down around here since you been gone. Griggs (Narcotics' new commander) really wanted to nail you," he sadly informed me. "C'mon. Griggs is waiting for us."

He got up from his seat and we began the long walk to the commander's office. I felt as if I was a dead man walking. We passed numerous cops who knew me and had worked with me. They all lowered their heads as I passed by. Where was the brotherhood now?

"What the fuck, Billy! How come no one's even looking at me?" I was hurt; there was no support here. A friendly nod would have gone a long way.

"In times like this, you'll find out real fast who your friends are, Juan."

The commander's secretary was sitting at her desk, typing some reports. "Go on in, he's been expecting you."

We entered his office, taking our seats, while he quickly walked to the door, said something to his secretary, and abruptly slammed it, rattling all the windows lining the room. I'd had no previous contact with Griggs, but I knew he didn't like the Tavern Team or Billy. He made Billy account for every minute of our time and called the Unit to make sure we were working every night until four. He also gave Billy shit when we weren't productive. When he had come into the Unit, a huge buzz had preceded him. There was a rumor that he had been snared twice in a prostitution sting called Operation Angel. Because of his stature in the department, the arresting officers had let him slide, but no one could keep it from hitting the department rumor mill.

"Juarez!" he began, in an agitated voice, folding his hands on his desk and nodding his head. "You pissed hot!"

I was expecting that. I knew I'd be immediately suspended and removed from service on the second floor of 3540. I looked over at Billy, raised my eyebrows as if to say sorry. I think that expression pushed some of Griggs's buttons.

"You're a fuckin' disgrace to this job, you piece of shit!" he yelled. He unfolded his hands and pointed his finger at me accusingly. "You've brought shame to me and this unit! You fuckin' piece of shit! You're going down! Now get the fuck out of my office!" I wasn't expecting this harsh brevity, and neither was Billy. We both sat in our chairs stunned.

I slowly stood up on rubbery legs, wondering what it was I did. I just smoked some pot and hash, yet Griggs seemed to take it so personally.

"What the fuck was that all about, Billy?" I asked, once outside the commander's office. He looked at me and shrugged his shoulders.

"Juarez," the commander's secretary called out. There was too much smoke in my head from the caustic attack I had just endured, so it took me a brief moment to realign my focus. "Juarez, I need your raid jacket, radio and charger, and your undercover driver's license before you leave. Remove the lock from your locker, and see Sergeant Jones; he's got some paperwork for you to complete," she stated without emotion. "You're being reassigned to callback."

Billy touched me on the shoulder and brought me back to reality. I wondered how long I had been standing there in the same spot with my mouth slightly open, stunned, not believing what was going down.

I turned to Billy. "What's callback?"

"You're going down to Eleventh and State, answering phones until the department decides what to do with you."

It turned out I was being sent to 1121 South State Street, a section where all the officers who were being investigated by IAD were known as prisoners of war.

"What are their options?" I asked.

He looked at me and raised his eyebrows, "They can either fire or suspend you."

"Fire me! What did I do that was so wrong?" I felt my anger rise. "I was on fuckin' vacation. It's fuckin' legal in Amsterdam and so is prostitution. Maybe I should tell Griggs about that so he can have a field day there without the fear of getting busted," I spat out.

Billy started laughing and it made me relax a bit. When he was done he said, "I know. Come on, let's head back to the office."

"It's fuckin' bullshit, Billy," I protested as if it could change the reality of what was happening. When the anger passed, shame filled me and I hung my head as we began walking down the hall.

"That was strange, Juan," Billy continued, shaking his head. "Never in my twenty years have I ever seen a reprimand like that." It was beyond me too—the callous nature, the unprofessional tone, the personal attack. It all seemed out of line from such a high-ranking public official.

"I gotta take a piss, Billy," I said as we approached the door to the bathroom. "I'll meet you back in the office." Standing at the urinal, I watched my piss stream onto the pink tablet, slowly dissolving it. My piss must still be hot, I mused and zipped up my pants. I heard the bathroom door open and turned my head. It was Gerald Jackson, a fellow cop I had hung out with a lot at Shelter. He was with me the night I met Karman.

"Yo bro', what's going on?" he asked.

"I've seen better days, that's for certain, my brother," I replied, beginning to wash my hands.

"I don't know if this will help at all," he began, looking me squarely in the eyes. "But I saw Karman up in here two or three times since you've been gone."

"What the fuck was she doing here?"

"I don't know, bro'. But every time she was here, she went into Griggs's office."

"What the fuck! Do you have any idea what went down?"

"People speculating that she told him you beat her and put a bug in his ear about you going on vacation to Amsterdam."

"Get the fuck outta here. Why did she come more than once?"

"It's just a rumor, but I heard they got physical and she had sex with him."

My jaw dropped. "No fuckin' way! You can't be serious."

"You know Griggs's track record. I wouldn't put it past him."

"I wouldn't put it past him, either. But why would she fuck him?"

"She must've had a hard-on for getting you busted."

"Well, she got that mission accomplished, that's for sure." I said, devastated. "Thanks for the tip, Gerry,"

"Hey, good luck to you, college boy," he said, as I slapped his extended hand and shook it. I left the bathroom armed with an epiphany: Karman was the snitch! Spotting the nearest phone, I picked it up and dialed her number.

"Hello," I heard her once-sweet-sounding-to-my-ears voice answer.

"Hello, Karman," I didn't know what to say, so I went back in history. "It's me, Papa Smurf. How you doing?"

She hesitated. "Oh, I'm fine. How was your trip?"

The fucking nerve of her! "It was a trip all right! I got busted at the airport smuggling hash!" I lied. "Hash I brought back for you!" I thought I heard her stifling laughter on the other end, but she didn't say a word. "I got one question to ask you, Karman."

"What is it, Juan?" she asked nervously.

"I've heard rumors you've been seen at the Narcotics building, talking to the commander."

Dead silence and then she blurted, "I didn't tell anyone anything, so don't blame me, motherfucker!"

"Take it easy, Karman. I never blamed you for anything. I just asked a question."

"Fuck you, asshole! I told you what goes around comes around! Don't you ever call here again!" she screamed as she slammed the phone down.

Holy shit! I held onto the receiver and stood mute, thinking about what she had just revealed. I was so pissed I could have strangled her right on the spot.

"Juan," Sergeant Jones, the administrative sergeant, said behind me. "Go to your locker and get your things." Fuck it, I thought, my anger wasn't going to get me out of this hell I found myself in. So I listlessly walked down the hall, going straight to my locker and went to collect and turn in my raid jacket, license, radio, and charger.

I walked back to Sergeant Jones's office. He closed the door once I got in. He went over to his desk and pulled out a file folder, removed forms from it, and placed them in front of me. I was too devastated by the bomb Karman had dropped to focus on the task at hand, but I listlessly filled out all the forms in triplicate.

"You are hereby being notified that you are no longer permitted to enter this building. Your presence will get you arrested for trespassing. Do you understand?"

"Yes," I mumbled. I was getting kicked out of the club.

"You have been reassigned to callback at 1121 South State Street, on the thirteenth floor," he informed me. "You are to report to Lieutenant Brown on the first watch, starting tomorrow night. Do you understand?"

"Yes, I do," I repeated, feeling the life being drained from my body, heart, and spirit. The game had ended.

I walked down the hall and went in to see Sergeant Thomas. "Well, Sarge," I said. "It's been heaven working for you and I am glad to have had the opportunity." I stuck out my hand to shake his.

"Juan, keep your head up," he suggested as he shook my hand. "This isn't the end of the world. I know it seems like it is, but this is only a job." I looked him in the eyes and he continued offering me encouragement.

I had met Billy on my first day in the unit and here he was, on my last day as well. What a coincidence. "Why the hell did you do all that schooling anyway? You'll land on your feet," he said. I tried to really believe what he was saying. "The Lord must have bigger plans for you."

A handshake wasn't going to do him justice; I had to give him a hug.

"Thanks, Billy," I said, hitching my bag on my shoulder.

"Hey, Juan," he said as I began to leave. "You got my home number and my pager, feel free to give me a call any time you want. I'd love to hear how you're doing."

"Will do, Sarge," I said. "Thanks again for your words of support."

"Remember this: things could be worse," he proclaimed. I nodded and left the room. This chapter of my life on the second floor of 3540 had officially come to an end.

39

PARTING WAYS

On April 13, 1997, I resigned from the Chicago Police Department after spending four months as a prisoner of war—a term given to officers who are under investigation for committing infractions against the code of ethics the police are sworn to uphold. My crime: pissing hot. I was thirty years old and had spent a total of seven years as a Chicago police officer.

I had stopped getting high and concentrated on getting back in shape, mentally and physically, by reading motivational books, swimming, and mountain biking. I had to get my life back in order. I had to control where I was going.

It was during those four months working the phones at 1121 South State Street that I took inventory of myself and what I was doing with my life. Initially, I was devastated and filled with vengeance toward Karman, the CPD, and the whole fucking universe for throwing me a curveball. It was bullshit that I got singled out when there were plenty of cops out there who were committing much more heinous violations and getting away with them. I was consumed with the notion of finding out for certain who had ratted on me. Then my saving grace appeared in the face of a friend I met during the summer of 1996.

Her name was Lyn Turbin. I met her one day after Karman tried to run me over. She was sitting on the sidewalk with my upstairs neighbors on the corner of Roscoe and Leavitt. We started talking and immediately became friends. She was an artist and had a perspective on life that was unique and refreshing. Lyn was the first woman who captivated me that I didn't want to have sex with. Not that she wasn't beautiful—she was—but we had a relationship that transcended physical attraction. Sex would have cheapened our bond. She had an incredible passion for her artwork, which was fed by a voracious reading habit. Once I was reassigned to callback, I started hanging out with her at her apartment and we talked about poetry, music, art, politics, and metaphysics, which was something I never heard about before.

"Juan," she said as we sat in her small front room while she painted. "You gotta understand that everything happens for a reason. The things that we're experiencing and the challenges that confront us in this lifetime are lessons from previous lifetimes that we haven't yet conquered."

"So you believe in reincarnation?" I asked.

"It's not so much reincarnation as it is karmic," she clarified. "Did you ever hear of what goes around comes around?"

"Yeah," I said, remembering that's what Karman told me as she put her car in reverse and drove off in a tizzy. "I've heard of it before, but I never believed in it. I mean how in the hell do these things follow us around? Are we magnetized and the shit we haven't dealt with are little metal shards that stick to us?"

Lyn laughed lightly. "Sort of, but not really. I believe there's a vibrational grid that we're on and the higher vibration we resonate at is dictated by how much stuff we're carrying."

She was losing me now. "Maybe I should do one hit so I can understand you better?" I joked.

She looked at me, shook her head, put her paintbrush down, and went into her bedroom. She returned with a book that she presented to me. "The *Bhagavad Gita?*" I asked.

"Read this book. You've got a master's in English. You should know how to deconstruct symbols and metaphors," she said, piquing my interest as she started painting again. I was captivated by what was forming on the canvas—the strokes were unique and blended into the other colors magically. "The moral of the stories are allegorical, which means—"

"I know what it means," I said. "The story has two meanings and could be interpreted through symbols."

I started to read the book as soon as I got home and read it every night at callback. I loved the simplicity of the moral in one of its chapters; it was just as Lyn said: everything happens for a reason. It further espoused that it's up to us to find that reason through the silence of prayer and meditation, which was also new to me. But I tried it and was happy to find a hint of peace in the silence of sitting. I asked questions of myself, and a little voice inside began to give me the answers.

Here I was blaming others for everything that had happened to me and never once had I acknowledged that I was the creator of all my misery. I slowly accepted the fact that knowing who snitched on me couldn't change the present. I realized that this wasn't the end of the world. I had something the Chicago Police Department had paid for and couldn't take from me—my education—and it was time to use it.

However, I had some lingering fears and doubts about the immediate future because, after all, my world had been turned upside down. Since I was reinventing myself, I had to tell my father and Dale the truth that I smoked marijuana and hash in Amsterdam. They were initially perturbed that I had lied to them, and when I told them the truth about Karman and getting snitched on, they briefly blamed her for my misfortune. My father was more upset than Dale, but when he opened his eyes, he said I had made a stupid choice. He never brought it up again, knowing full well we couldn't change the past. He consulted his connections and found a lawyer who specialized in defending officers accused of pissing hot. I spoke to the lawyer and he assured me there was no way I would be fired because I had been on vacation and the drugs were consumed in a country where they were legal.

But the real question now was whether or not I wanted to remain a cop. I had been reassigned and was under investigation so I still had the choice to be reinstated if cleared of all charges. My father told me the decision was mine alone to make and that he would accept my choice without question.

After all I had seen during my career and after all I had reflected upon during those four months as a POW, the answer was no. My spirit was telling me I wasn't happy with the life I had been living.

I would be able to resign with a confidential exit—meaning future employers could only be told that I had resigned from the job—and use the seven years as a cop on my resume, and I would still receive my full pension and benefits. What did I have to lose?

I saved the exit report I wrote first, which stated this reason for resigning: "R/O (reporting officer) resigns due to the fact that the inherent deracination of subjectivity from years of being privy to the basest of society has taken its toll. R/O no longer wishes to participate in the perpetuation of such rigors that exact, from the conscious, the essence of egalitarianism which, subsequently, leads to a life of apathy."

I didn't think the administration would understand that, so I wrote: "R/O resigns in order to seek new employment." I did just that and left the police world behind me.

EPILOGUE

AFTER APRIL 13, MY LAST DAY as a Chicago police officer, the fortitude and resilience that prayer and meditation had provided suddenly evaporated. As I walked away from the job I had once loved, I felt as if an enormous burden had been lifted off my shoulders. Strangely, this had the effect of making me think I had a free pass to party as hard as I could. Physically marked and internally shamed by the fact that I had an STD, I decided that women wouldn't play a part in this chapter of my life. This trip was meant for one.

After cashing in my pension and deferred-compensation accounts, which totaled a little more than fifty thousand dollars, I immediately set about feeding my whims and fancies. I bought a two-thousand-dollar mountain bike, a laptop computer, the latest snowboard gear—even though I had never snowboarded in my life—and a used 1988 BMW K75S motorcycle. I was living extravagantly, unconcerned about the future. I spent absolutely no energy on finding a new job. For the first time in more than twelve years, I found myself uninterested in school, even though I still needed three more classes to earn my master's in education. I reasoned that I already had one advanced degree and I was able to obtain my teaching credential so another advanced degree could wait. Until when? Who knew? I was too caught up in my new passions.

In June with half of my retirement funds already spent, I traveled to Jamaica for a week and then spent the rest of the summer mountain biking in Southern California where my sisters, Lee and Marie, had moved years earlier. Alternating between the two of them, I crashed at their houses to gain unlimited access to the Santa Monica Mountains. Earning my keep was easy—I just bought the food I planned to eat and I treated my sisters to restaurants whenever I felt like it.

When I returned to Chicago in September, I continued living way above my means—eating at fine restaurants, staying out all night with friends, getting high, and listening to music. By then the initial euphoria of leaving the police force had worn off; reality set in; my life seemed pointless and uninspiring.

I had no one to cherish, no one to call, and no one to fall asleep with. Deep inside I knew that I had let my father down, even though he never mentioned it. I had disgraced him by getting fired for smoking pot. I kept up all appearances of being happy, but I was miserable, knowing I had all the money I needed but no one to spend it on or with. And without the security of my police job, I wasn't confident about my future. Teaching in Europe, which had once been my dream, now seemed impossible. I lacked the courage to start a new life in a foreign country.

When I began teaching in the Chicago Public Schools, the schedule proved problematic because it was a hindrance to my late-night lifestyle. I half-heartedly completed ten weeks of student teaching at Foreman High School. After my student teaching ended in mid-November, I somehow managed to get a permanent substitute and swimming-coach position at the school. I was excited to get back into sports, but this revitalization was as short-lived as the swim season. I didn't want to be a substitute, going from room to room, facing ornery and disrespectful kids, but I grudgingly kept the job, hoping it would lead to a full-time position the next school year.

At the end of November I flew back to Amsterdam in an attempt to revisit the decadence I had enjoyed a year earlier. This time I was going with my pockets lined with cash. I visited prostitute after prostitute but was dismayed to find that I couldn't maintain an erection. The storefront hookers took my money anyway. Mind-altering therapy was only a coffee-house away, and I got lost in the heavy, pungent clouds of hash that offered a form of temporary salvation. When I returned to the United States, I went on a traveling frenzy with some friends during my Christmas break from school, looking for the purpose and direction I had lost and hoping to find myself on a mountaintop.

We visited world-class ski resorts in Colorado and Utah while I lavished time and money on my new passion, snowboarding. I made sure I always had a healthy stash of the best marijuana money could buy.

My partying and excessive living came to an abrupt halt on April 27, 1998, shortly after the one-year anniversary of my resignation from the police force and one month after I moved out of my parents' house. I hadn't been planning to end my fast-living lifestyle, but in the end it wasn't my choice. After a late night of smoking joint after joint, I awoke the next morning to find the entire left side of my body paralyzed and my sense of balance diminished. I attributed the temporary paralysis and loss of balance to my decadent behavior, but it probably saved my life. This physical shutdown, diagnosed as a muscular disease, did something for me that losing my job, Ana, Maria, and Karman had not—it forced me to think through my actions and my life, because for the next two months all I could do was lie in bed and think.

During my illness, which forced me to rely on crutches just to get around my apartment, my sister came to my rescue. Marie, who was studying spiritual psychology in a school in Santa Monica sent me a book about the origin of diseases, which connected them to past behaviors. I inhaled this book and arrived at the conclusion that my life was fucked up because of the way I had treated people, especially women. Now, I was paying a spiritual price for my behavior. As I lay in bed, the ghosts of my past came back to haunt me—and eventually provided the genesis of this book. I had to revisit relationships and see things with clear eyes and an open heart if I wanted to understand my past. If I tried to do otherwise, my conscience slapped me and asked: are you going down the road of denial again? what are you so fucking afraid of? My answer: pain.

I didn't want to feel the pain or admit that there was pain in my life. But as bedsores began to appear, my mind focused on my childhood. I saw how hard I'd fought to keep from acknowledging the fact that my family was as dysfunctional as they come. I had long tried to cover up the fact that I had been sexually abused and that, to some extent, I had enjoyed this abuse because it was the only chance for human warmth I'd had during my childhood.

Once these feelings arose, there was no way I could deny them. I didn't want to accept responsibility for my part in the abortions or for the fucked-up way I had treated Ana and Maria. I didn't want to think about the way I tried to escape all that shit by playing with Karman's head and heart. I didn't want to accept my accountability for all the years of police abuse I witnessed and even participated in; I'd stood by, silently pledging my allegiance to the code of silence. I didn't want to admit my part in a futile War on Drugs that seemingly did nothing more than fill the prisons across America with young black men. The lost gaze of David Thomson, the ten-year-old kid I busted for selling crack, disturbs me to this day and I wonder if he's alive or if he wound up just another statistic in a book—dead or in prison.

I vowed to break my pattern of denial and escape. I have, through writing this book, found the truth behind my actions. I acknowledge the truth regardless of how harmful, hurtful, and heinous it may have been. Acknowledgment is the first step on the road to any type of reform, and yet it may be the most difficult step to take because it involves so much pain. But I truly believe there is one certainty in my journey: the truth shall set me free.

One of the greatest gifts of life is that, once in a while, you have an opportunity to rectify past mistakes and change destructive patterns. Although I once found it impossible to speak out due to my lack of self-esteem, I can no longer hold back. I have found my voice. I realize that my feelings are valid, and I must honor my connection to humanity. This what I hope to achieve by sharing my story with you.

★ ★ ★

Since leaving the police force, I have found peace of mind away from drugs, alcohol, and Chicago. I'm not perfect. Once in a while I regress and fall back into old habits, but changing life patterns requires diligence and a strong desire. I feel blessed by the crosses I bear because if I didn't have them, I wouldn't have moved on in my life and away from the lies I once lived.

My being open to the truth has rewarded me with a sweet wife who helps me maintain a balance. With her I have learned to appreciate the beauty in life. She fans the flames of my optimism. I feel as if a lifetime has passed since I was a cop, but in reality it has been only seven years.

I once read that the only constant in life is change—seasons change, people change, beliefs change, and I've changed. I hope that one day the Chicago Police Department's treatment of minorities and inability to punish abusive cops will change as well. But it hasn't happened yet. In 2001 and 2002 there were 112,163 people arrested for narcotics violations in the city. Of those, only 8.3 percent were white. In these same two years, citizens filed 5,446 claims of police brutality and 2,555 civil rights violations. A mere 310 (less than 6 percent) of police brutality claims and 22 (less than 1 percent) of the civil rights violations were substantiated. Where is the public outcry? Has injustice become so thoroughly enveloped in the arms of authority that it's become institutionalized and accepted by the general public?

★ ★ ★

I now live in California, where minorities make up 66 percent of the prison population but only 37 percent of the total state population. Here I'm finally putting my twenty-five years of education to good use and I feel I'm making a difference. I teach at-risk students in a middle school in which the majority, 98.3 percent, are Mexican—my people, my blood. It's fulfilling to give the underprivileged youth of society hope and the necessary skills to compete in the world rather than extinguish their spirits and dreams by throwing them in prison. I know it's an uphill battle, but this is one war I am proud to be a part of. I have gone from being a cop to being a teacher. The youth of this country need education, not incarceration. As Mahatma Gandhi said, "You must be the change you wish to see in the world."

I am.

THE DIRTY TRUTH
BY THE NUMBERS

FROM CHAPTER 6

Initiation

Only 9.1 percent of graduating seniors at Clemente High School, in the heart of the Humboldt Park community, read at or above grade level from 1991 to 1995, while a staggering 58.3 percent of students dropped out during these same years. (The future doesn't hold much promise when only 46.3 percent of Humboldt Park residents graduate from high school and 26.9 percent of teenage girls get pregnant. But the real social problem in this community is poverty. According to the Community Area Health Inventory 1996–1998, a report by the Chicago Department of Public Health, more than 67,000 people lived in the Humboldt Park area in 1990, and 57.8 percent lived *two times* below the national poverty level.)

FROM CHAPTER 12

Crossing the Line

The Office of Professional Standards (OPS) documented a trend when dealing with complaints of official misconduct and excessive-force beefs lodged by the general public that increased over the years. This trend favors cops. This is especially true in minority-populated districts, where some cops maintain order by instilling fear of a beating.

So who polices the police? OPS? Hardly. David Fogel, the chief administrator of OPS, said in a 1987 memo: "The troops love OPS. It actually operates to immunize police from internal discipline, increases their overtime, leads to an enormous 'paper storm,' and has institutionalized lying. I have come to the conclusion that OPS gives the appearance of formal justice but actually helps to institutionalize subterfuge and injustice." Fogel was quoted in John Conroy's book *Unspeakable Truths, Ordinary People.*

A hefty 91.5 percent of the cases pertaining to excessive force are deemed unfounded. In most cases, the officer, as well as the department, is found not liable by OPS. In 1996, 1997, and 1998 there were 9,110 excessive-force complaints filed in the city and only 772 were sustained (meaning it was determined that the cop had indeed done something wrong). Those numbers cannot be logically explained; worse, this leniency communicates that police officers can and will receive impunity while violating codes meant to check and balance their authority. Regardless of the severity of the violation or the injuries, cops usually walk.

FROM CHAPTER 16

Welcome to Paradise

Initially, I was astounded that a city with some three million inhabitants could have such a small Narcotics Unit. Later in my career Sergeant Moore told me why he thought this was the case. He said it's much easier to stay out of the spotlight of suspicion when fewer cops knew exactly what the Unit is doing, be it legal or not. Fifty or even one hundred twenty members could be managed very easily. And officers who didn't go along with the program, refusing to adhere to the directives of a supervisor, quickly find themselves on the outside looking in.

The tight bond of the Narcotics Unit veterans probably would have remained intact, he revealed to me in confidence, except that downtown (administration) sent a directive to expand the Unit. Rumors about dishonest cops in the Unit stealing cash, drugs, and personal property began circulating around city hall. The rising numbers of complaints seemed to support that rumor. The notoriety brought on by this spotlight was not welcome at 3540. Something had to be done. The directive to add more cops to the Unit was given "official" justification having been sponsored by President Bush's War on Drugs. This more than doubling of the Unit's members was partially designed to cover up any allegations of official misconduct, Sergeant Moore surmised. But then the war gained public support, and talks of unit efficiency began to replace rumors of old-school corruption. The new members were more than welcome in the Unit—as long as they knew their place and kept the secrets of the Unit a secret.

FROM CHAPTER 17

Is the Court System in Cahoots?

The most appalling injustice against society happens, ironically, in the very place entrusted to secure justice—the Cook County Court House at Twenty-sixth and California.

While I worked in the 14th District, I hardly went to court outside of my key court dates as an arresting officer and state's witness. When I arrived at 3540 South Normal Street, my attendance increased dramatically because of my case-officer duties and the fact that we arrested so many people. Consequently, I became quite familiar with that building—those halls of justice—and I began to notice the relentless pursuit of individual gain, driven by greed and the desire for power at the cost of someone else's freedom. If the Police Department operates as the bottom-feeder in the prison economy by fueling the engines, I believe the court system tends and stokes the fire by condoning and enforcing the lopsided presence of minorities behind the bars in the Department of Corrections. I offer the following facts and evidence and suggest that society take a long, hard look at the prison economy.

FACT 1: There are at least three groups of professionals who benefit from the relentless pursuit of jail sentences: police officers, state's attorneys, and judges.

Off-duty cops immediately benefit by making good pocket money on court appearances because they earn three hours of overtime (salaried time and a half) as long as they spend at least fifteen minutes in court. Or if the cop chooses, overtime (OT) can be put on the books as compensatory time to be used any time or to be paid upon retirement. An officer in a district is assigned a key—a specific date that changes every period—and with that key he receives three automatic court dates per period. Each and every felony arrest translates into extra court dates. For aggressive cops, OT could be a profitable venture. But in the Narcotics Unit or any other specialized unit, it's not uncommon for an officer to be in court three, four, or five days a week. For that matter, there were plenty of officers in the Narcotics Unit whose OT checks were more than their biweekly paychecks. I alternated between these every month—one month I'd take the overtime in cash and the next month I'm take it in time that I'd either use for vacation or let it build so that I could cash out with it at retirement. It was a nice bonus either way, but it was all made possible by being in the right unit.

That, for me, was one of the greatest fringe benefits of being transferred to Narcotics. As part of Iron Wedge, my overtime was greatly hampered by my work hours, as my schedule and court times would overlap. But when I hit the Tavern Team, every court appearance was money in the bank because we worked 8 P.M. to 4 A.M. and court appearances in the Liquor License Commission were at 9 A.M. and 1 P.M.

The secrets of working the system for overtime were passed on from one generation of cops to the next, and many cops abused the system. Eventually, this caused the administration to crack down. In 2001, the department limited OT for coppers in districts and members in specialized units unless approved by the watch commander. This measure came years and years after the city's Treasury Department had been pilfered by the Chicago Police Department.

The second group of professionals who benefit from the vast number of people Narcotics prosecutes and convicts are the state's attorneys. They glean rewards by ascending the prosecutorial ladder and earning respect while showing diligence and efficiency. All state's attorneys start at the bottom and then graduate to more prestigious assignments as their conviction rates increase. They are looking after their futures, and some have high expectations and lofty agendas. Richard Daley started off as a state's attorney and went on to become the mayor of Chicago, while many others have gone on to judicial seats and political positions. Being a state's attorney is indeed a doorway to many possibilities.

The judiciary profession comes next. It thrives on the prestige and honor that accompanies the constituency approval won through efficacy. Prestige and honor open doors to infinite possibilities—the opportunity to become a partner in a venerable law firm or make the big leap into politics, for example. The combination of zeal and greed with a firm and resolute personal agenda in these three cogs in the court system fans the flame of the prison economy.

FACT 2: The incredible explosion of prisoners, not just in this county but in counties all across the nation in the last two decades, has led to the war cry to build more prisons.

The rate of incarceration grew from 80,000 in 1925 to a high point in 1939 of 120,000—a growth of 50 percent—and back to a manageable 100,000 by 1970. It then tripled by 1980 when 300,000 people were incarcerated in the United States prison system. And as of 2000 there were two million prisoners in jail (*Bureau of Justice Statistics, Sourcebook of Criminal Justice Statistics 2000*). That is a 660 percent increase over 20 years, compared to a 124 percent rise in population. If the trend continues, there will be more than 13.2 million people in jail by 2020. According to the National Criminal Justice Commission, if this trend continues, 63.3 percent of *all* black men between the ages of eighteen to thirty-four will be behind bars.

The prison economy is a money-making business, which is where all the problems in the court system and the government begin. It's a business, and all businesses thrive on expansion. And what makes up the prison economy? Contracts. Contracts for building the facilities. Contracts for providing the inmates with supplies they need: beds, sheets, clothing, food, books for the prison libraries, and mail services. It is a never-ending process in which people are making money at great expense to state and federal taxpayers.

FACT 3: The United States Congress passed the Anti-Drug Act and the Omnibus Act simultaneously in 1986. These laws gave police departments all over the country the power to wage a war on drugs, and the official race to incarcerate was on. Anyone in possession of five or more grams of crack or caught dealing any amount of crack—no matter how small—to an undercover police officer faced mandatory five-year prison terms. And anyone who was connected to the delivery of crack could be snared by the same web. This only applies to crack cocaine. Punishment for possession of powder cocaine, on the other hand, is a bit less severe. It takes five hundred grams of powder cocaine to warrant felony status and five hundred grams in a delivery case to get the same five-year sentence according to the laws set down by Congress. The explanation for this discrepancy is that powder cocaine is too expensive for the junkies in the ghetto.

In the Narcotics Unit where I worked, there was a disturbing and completely profitable practice of arresting as many people as possible connected with delivery cases in Operation Iron Wedge. It's called *sandbagging*. It's a discriminatory practice based on meeting and surpassing the weekly quota. We were expected to make three to four transactions a day, bringing in four to ten arrestees a day, and twenty to fifty arrests a week. Because of the competitive nature of the Unit and the laws of the U.S. Congress, sandbagging was a contest to see which team could amass the most arrests for weekly, monthly, and yearly productivity in unit. There were no rewards other than bragging rights. Narcotics led the department in arrests every year I was there.

To give a full picture of the powerful 1986 acts in detail, here is an example of what happens to someone who possesses powder cocaine. This example is from 1996.

Reese Robbins, an officer on the Postal Team, informed me that a kilo of powder cocaine was detected in the mail and the mailing address was on the Northwest Side of Chicago. The Postal

Team went through with the delivery of the package and arrested the individual who received it. He was a Polish kid, and he was charged with possession of one thousand grams of powder cocaine. When he went to court, he took a plea bargain and was sentenced to seven years' probation. Later in the week, Reese went to court on a delivery of .10 gram of crack, and the offender got thirteen years in jail. "Justice, the American way," Reese told me sarcastically.

This discrepancy may not make much sense, but it was all legal according to the judicial and legislative branches of the U.S. government.

FACT 4: The number of arrestees who flowed in and out of my team's clutches was quite large, and the act of identifying arrestees was simple. But it unquestionably violated their rights.

Regardless, it was a unitwide practice. We would snap two Polaroids of the arrestees within minutes of having placed them into our custody—one for the case officer and the other for the buy officer. The purpose was to put a face on the case because we needed to positively identify these individuals when we went to court two to three months after the deal had gone down. With the daily influx of new cases, it would have been impossible to remember each case and the corresponding offender. Hence, the photos were taken and then attached to the paperwork peculiar to that case.

I remember going to court once, arriving with my file complete with the photos, when a state's attorney notified me that such a practice violated the rights of the offender and that I was not to let the defendant's lawyers see them. He further added that it was a necessary and good, albeit illegal, practice "because all the offenders looked alike." The bottom line is this: if a state's attorney knew that the Narcotics Unit's practice was illegal and he never raised an issue about it, I submit that the courts were willing accomplices in this violation of civil rights.

FACT 5: Because of the large numbers of arrests during Operation Iron Wedge, buy officers sometimes could not recognize an offender even with the use of the instant Polaroids.

When this realization was brought up in the courtroom, usually during the pretrial conferences in the witness room, the state's attorney would subtly imply that if the offender was arrested, then he or she must have been the one involved in the case. The defendants were, in some state's attorneys' eyes, guilty until proven innocent.

The state's attorney would then coach the officers involved, request that they just go along with their questioning, and do the best they can when testifying. The onus of responsibility then falls on the officer to do the right thing, either professionally or morally. But because incarceration was known to be the winning strategy in the War on Drugs and the state's attorney wanted convictions, the professional motives a cop considers can usually conquer any moral waffling.

In my four years as a Narcotics officer, I never once hear a state's attorney opt to halt the proceedings because of an arresting officer's inability to positively identify an offender.

FACT 6: Different justice is available for different folks. It was my third year in the Narcotics Unit when we arrested some white kid for selling crack cocaine near Jonquil and Paulina in the 24th District. I was the case officer and, as my name was on the paper, I had to go to court. When I received the subpoena, it informed me that the trial was in the Skokie branch of the Cook County Court System. I had been there once before and wondered about the change in location because when our team had worked the north end of Rogers Park before, all the cases were sent to Twenty-sixth and California.

While we were in the pretrial stage, the state's attorney made a deal with the offender. It called for a guilty plea in exchange for a 1410 probation. I had never heard of this type of judgment, so when I got back to the Unit, I asked Sergeant Moore what this was. He informed me that a 1410 probation included, upon successful completion, expunging the arrest record of the offender. Expunging a felony? I hadn't known that was possible. In essence, this type of probation would leave the offender with a clear record, as if the arrest never took place. The white offender was granted an opportunity for securing decent employment, enlisting in the armed services if he desired, receiving educational grants and scholarships, and eventually being able to jump right back into mainstream society without the black mark of a felony to stunt his growth and development. In all my years of going to court, I had never heard of 1410 probation. When I conveyed this to Sergeant Moore, he chuckled. "Maybe the black mark is meant for black folks."

FACT 7: The only individuals risking anything of importance are the offenders.

These individuals lose their freedom and their ability to be a part of mainstream America—although many offenders don't believe they were ever a part of it to begin with. Laws governing the rights and privileges convicted felons lose vary from state to state. Being a convicted felon strips them of their right to vote for the rest of their lives in fourteen states. Forty-six states deny the right to anyone imprisoned, and thirty-two restrict voting privileges for those on probation or parole. The laws in many states hold that a person convicted of a drug offense may lose or have heavy restrictions placed upon grants and other federal benefits, such as welfare, social security, retirement, health insurance, disability, and public housing access. Federal felons may also be restricted in their choice of profession. All convicted felons are denied enlistment in any branch of the armed forces, and depending on the nature of the crime, felons who are veterans can lose their pension, disability, and Veterans Administration benefits. In short, felons are denied the opportunity to change. Instead, they remain locked up within the system even after they leave prison.

Cook County is spending 83 percent of its drug-war money on incarceration and persecution while education gets 3 percent of the funds earmarked to fight this war. Real change is needed there.

After seriously reviewing these seven facts, I can only conclude that convictions fuel the legal system in an effort to drive the prison economy, which is flourishing in Chicago, in Cook County, and across this country. Prisons provide a way to rid society of an unwanted underclass.

FROM CHAPTER 20

It's Just a Numbers Game

The City of Chicago's Annual Police Report shows that in the mid-1990s the total number of people arrested for narcotics violations increased, from a total of 51,005 in 1995 to 54,679 in 1997. In each of these years blacks comprised 80 percent of all arrestees. During this same period, blacks made up less than 40 percent of the city's population.

On the Chicago Police Department's arrest reports, blacks are given the numeric identity of *1* in the offender box. Many officers in the Unit prepared preprinted arrest and case reports with the race of the offender already marked with a *1*.

In January 2000 Roosevelt University's Institute of Metropolitan Affairs conducted a study on the allocation of local, state, and federal funds earmarked for the War on Drugs in Cook County, which includes Chicago, and found that out of an aggregated $1.2 billion:

- 83 percent goes toward the prosecution and incarceration of violators. That's $996 million focused on putting people, mostly blacks, in jail.
- 14 percent is marked for treating drug abuse.
- 3 percent is spent on prevention through educational programming.

Members of the public surveyed in this study think that drug addicts are to be blamed for their problems—drug addictions are seen purely as substance abuse and not a social health issue. Unfortunately, our country's attitude toward drugs is conservative, maintaining that addictions are a social problem solved by punishment rather than through prevention or treatment. Enforcement and incarceration take precedence over treatment and education. Is the City of Chicago and Cook County, and perhaps the whole country for that matter, afraid of an educated minority?

FROM CHAPTER 24
A World Apart

The dilemma in this country is that we can't admit that the nation is waging a War on Poverty by making poor people's lives virtually intolerable. Driving down the streets where minority kids walked, lived, and learned gave me insights I will never forget. I saw anger on the faces of kids as we drove through their neighborhoods. I saw neglect on those same faces; they were starving for attention and compassion. Children were caged up in the projects, afraid of playing outside because the chance of getting struck down by random bullets was real. I arrested young men who left schools without graduating, unprepared to participate in mainstream society, and others who read at only a fifth-grade level in high school.

I knew random gunfire in the projects was common, but I had no idea how prevalent it was. I was an outsider, free to come and go as I chose, and I was grateful for that. That perspective changed when my father had a firsthand experience, getting caught in the middle of a gang fight at Cabrini Green, and was forced to lay on the floor in a stairwell as a storm of bullets hit the cinderblock wall above his head for fifteen minutes. I started to ask myself what my reality would be like if every second of every day, I had to live in fear of a bullet flying through my front window? In such a reality, I would be forced to board the windows up, blotting out the sun, to feel a sense of protection. Better yet, how could my kids thrive when walking down the streets to school makes them target practice? Taking a circuitous path through gangs, street dealers, and junkies when walking home isn't any easier.

In the areas we hit the hardest, Chicago Public Schools statistics revealed that less than 10 percent of graduating seniors could read at or above grade level (*Chicago Public School Data Book, Tests of Achievement and Proficiency Reading, 1991–2002*). Where is the other 90 percent, and why are they left behind? Where do they go when their options are so limited? Many join gangs, sell dope, and wind up in jail because they can make more money in an hour selling dope than they can flipping burgers or bagging groceries for a week. I know drug dealing is an individual's choice but generation after generation of oppressed children are becoming involved because they lack choices and opportunities. It makes me sad that children have to pay the price. When drug dealers, junkies, whores, thieves, and recidivists are children's role models, all of society pays.

While I worked in these blighted areas, in school I was reading about Maslow's hierarchy of needs, a theory formulated in the 1960s. It uses a pyramid to describe the four levels of needs an individual must fill to fully understand qualities such as truth, order, justice, beauty, and uniqueness. Maslow argues that a person needs to achieve one level before he can ascend to the next. A person's development becomes arrested or halted if they never make it to the next level because they'll live a life mired in issues in that stage.

The bottom level of the pyramid describes basic needs: food, air, shelter, and clothing. Attaining these rudimentary needs, one moves to the next level: safety. This is where one feels safe within their own body, home, and environment. This is also the level that addresses whether or not an individual is nurtured at home and in their environment, learning appropriate behavior, morals, and consequences. Moving up to the next level of development involves achieving self-respect, self-worth, pride, and respect for others. Finally, there is self-actualization, living life to one's full potential.

I'm not making a generalization when I say that the neighborhoods where I worked in Narcotics weren't safe for developing children. While many of the children in these impoverished areas had their basic needs met, the second level of Maslow's hierarchy was unattainable for them. How could they feel safe and secure when rampant violence—in their houses or on the streets—was exploding all around them?

Drive around these parts of the South Side of Chicago and see desolation, hopelessness, and lack of spirit. There are blocks and blocks spotted with dilapidated and abandoned buildings—havens for junkies, prostitutes, rapists, and gangs. People sit on stoops with blank stares; others walk aimlessly. In the vast spaces in between buildings there are rubble-filled and refuse-laden lots, overgrown and unsafe. Where are the playgrounds and parks? How can a kid be a kid here?

As I drove around the South Side near our targeted areas, I was always amazed by the billboards. These eyesores bombarded poverty-ridden neighborhoods, screaming out the message that consumers should eat fast food, smoke cigarettes, and drink liquor.

If these billboards hawking alcohol and cigarettes were as prolific on the North Side—say Lincoln Park, Edison Park, or even Rogers Park—there'd be a community uproar. But on the South Side it's all right to promote these negative images and values. Why is that?

In 1989, three years before I began working in those areas, Reverend Pfleger, a pastor and a crusader for the underclass, asked the same questions as he waged a war against advertising. He uncovered many startling statistics. Upon surveying the ten blocks around his church at 1210 West Seventy-eighth Place, he counted 118 alcohol and tobacco billboards. When he did the same survey in a North Side neighborhood, he found only 3. "When you target a particular race of people with ads for 2 of the nation's top killers, that's genocide," Reverend Pfleger claimed.

In 1990 the Chicago Lung Association decided to investigate Reverend Pfleger's revelations and found that 86.4 percent of all billboards in Chicago are in minority areas. Asserting, with support from medical professionals, that alcohol and tobacco products are legal drugs that often lead to illegal ones, Reverend Pfleger started a national campaign against billboards. He had petitions signed, legislation proposed, and protest marches organized. He even had the ear of Bush's drug czar, William Bennett. It didn't help. The industry refused to meet with him to discuss these obvious discrepancies. Finally exasperated and beyond talking, Pfleger was arrested on July 10, 1990, for defacing billboards. Reverend Pfleger hit 'em where it hurts—their pockets. The industry finally bowed to pressure from the storm of adverse publicity created by Reverend Pfleger's arrest, which had begun to affect sales. The numbers of billboards in minority areas decreased. These changes were made in 1990. Yet as I drove through these ghetto areas in 1993, it was hard to see any evidence of change.

Even the corner stores were scary. I remember many instances when I went into a store for a bottle of water or a pack of gum only to find empty shelves and a clerk behind a bulletproof partition. A miniature revolving door on the counter allowed the clerk to pass products and money through. There was no self-service here because the store was behind the clerk. All the consumer products, neatly stacked and shelved, were protected by the shield. If you wanted anything, you had to ask the clerk to get it. I've never seen that on the North Side. I wonder if the kids who go to those stores on the South Side think the whole world is like this.

Shopping malls, restaurants, coffeehouses, quaint little sidewalk cafes, and other luxuries that flourish on the North Side are few and far between in all of the areas we worked on the South and West Sides. There were no stores such as Whole Foods, Jewel, Dominick's, Crate and Barrel, Starbucks, Home Depot, Lettuce Entertain You Restaurants, or The Gap. It was tough to find conveniences and amenities such as dry cleaners, shoe-repair stores, tailors, or safe parks. These things are commonplace on the North Side. It was startling to me to see just how segregated Chicago was.

FROM CHAPTER 30

The Youth Shall Pay

Since Congress signed the Anti-Drug Abuse Act of 1986, there has been an 80 percent increase in the federal prison population from 1986 to 1995, according to the U.S. Department of Justice, Bureau of Justice Statistics 2000. Furthermore Marc Mauer's *Race to Incarcerate* documents that 95 percent of those incarcerated for selling crack cocaine were *not* high-level drug dealers. More than 60 percent of them were street dealers who had only one or two grams of crack in their possession when they were busted. Ninety percent of all crack cocaine cases that were brought to trial involved blacks. So it's no wonder the prison systems are overloaded, the court docket is severely backed up, and many black inner-city communities are lacking father figures.

Operation Iron Wedge was an extremely successful operation if judged by measure of putting people in jail. But it failed in its purpose to keep drugs off the streets; as soon as one corner was vacated by an arrest of a small-time dealer, another would take his place, and business would resume.

Every other month the department held Hammer Downs, or special operations. Hammer Downs were a unit-inclusive operation, lasting ten to twelve hours a day and designed as a hyperaggressive Iron Wedge day where 180 arrests were conceivable. The truth of the matter is that the Narcotics Unit put vast numbers of people in jail without putting a dent on the narcotics trafficking in the city.

The taxpayers pay for the internment of the prisoners. The first year of imprisonment costs $78,154 per prisoner for their initial trial and sentencing according to the *Bureau of Justice Statistics 1999—Justice Expenditure*. The cost then goes down to $43,971 per year if a prisoner has to keep going to court while in jail, due to transportation needs and security measures. Once the prisoner has exhausted all chances in court, the cost of imprisoning him or her hovers around $26,134 a year. Couldn't taxes be used to combat the source of the problem instead of warehousing people while creating even bigger problems?

Society needs to open its eyes and admit there is a problem. Instead of letting the poor and uneducated drown, we must teach them to swim by creating neighborhood programs that educate and offer awareness of a drug-free life; sports programs that keep the youth occupied and channel aggression in constructive ways; literacy programs that bolster reading skills; parental classes that support parents in raising kids; alcohol-abuse classes that teach the dangers of alcohol; and programs that teach marketable skills such as auto repair, carpentry, electrical and plumbing skills, and computer programming. Finally, if they have real employment opportunities, the poor will learn to swim on their own.

Poverty has become a national epidemic. According to Harvard sociologist Julius William Wilson, "In 1975 one third of Americans had incomes below 50 percent of the amount officially designated as the poverty line; in 1992, 40 percent did so. And among blacks, the increase was even sharper from 32 percent in 1975 to nearly half—about 49 percent—in 1992."

GLOSSARY

Area: a police district used as a hub for the surrounding districts

Area 1: located at 5101 South Wentworth Avenue, serving Districts 1, 2, 3, and 21

Area 2: located at 727 East 111th Street, serving Districts 4, 5, 6, and 22

Area 3: located at 3900 South California Avenue, serving Districts 7, 8, and 9

Area 4: located at 3151 West Harrison Avenue, serving Districts 10, 11, 12, and 13

Area 5: located at 5555 West Grand Avenue, serving Districts 14, 15, 16, 17, and 25

Area 6: located at 2452 West Belmont Avenue, serving Districts 18, 19, 20, 23, and 24

beat cop: uniformed district police officer who works a regular demarcated area known as a "beat"

beef: a complaint lodged by a citizen against a cop regarding brutality and/or theft of services or money

box: station

CAR: contact arrest report; a sheet used to write down information about an arrestee such as name, address, phone number, and school

Chinaman: someone with clout who could sponsor a promotion or a rise in rank

Choch: abbreviation for *chocha* in Spanish; translates as "pussy" in English

clout: political or departmental connections

come-along hold: a hold taught in the police academy for controlling subjects. Standing alongside the suspect, a cop slides his arm between the suspect's arm, locking the people together. With the subject's arm locked, the officer quickly places subject's elbow in the pit of the officer's stomach with his free hand while raising subject's forearm straight up and in toward the officer's chest. This action keeps the elbow firmly in the cop's stomach. The cop then bends the wrist of the subject's locked arm with both hands and presses downward. If done correctly, the subject will be rendered helpless; if the cop applies too much pressure, the subject's wrist will snap like a pencil.

Confidential Informant (CI): a snitch who gets paid for information

drop a case on you: fabricate a charge such as disorderly conduct or any other trifling crime

drop a dime: snitch or provide information that will lead to an arrest

Estimated Street Value (ESV): a price determined by law officials that estimates how much drugs are worth on the street (usually higher than the actual purchase price)

Field Training Officer (FTO): veteran police officer who volunteers to teach recruits the duties of a cop on the streets. FTOs are compensated with a slight increase in pay.

1505 funds: money gathered from an illegal drug deal that is confiscated and added to the unit's coffers to be used in the War on Drugs

first watch: a work shift; early cars work 11:00 P.M. to 7:00 A.M.; late cars work 12:00 A.M. to 8:00 A.M.

forty: street term meaning a half gram of cocaine (usually costs $50)

411: information

Frank: code for a type of police action taken

full-boat: full price

furlough: vacation time, usually twenty-eight days

half-boat: half price

holding: in possession of narcotics with the intent to sell them

General Offense Case Report (GOCR): a police report used to record virtually all crimes

girl: street name for cocaine

going around the clock: changing work shifts with each changing period

hype: drug user; more specifically someone who uses hypodermic needles; someone who uses drugs heavily

Internal Affairs Division (IAD): a division in the Chicago Police Department in charge of investigating alleged official misconduct committed by police officers

john: a man who patronizes prostitutes

lieutenant: a supervisor above the rank of sergeant and below a captain

office: slang for officer, usually used by fellow cops

Office of Professional Standards (OPS): a civilian-employed branch of the Chicago Police Department that investigates alleged abuses by police officers; considered ineffective and a joke among cops

Paul: police code for peace restored

period: a twenty-eight-day segment divided equally into two parts: A and B. There are thirteen periods over the twelve calendar months. With each new period comes a watch change.

pinches: arrests

Records Division number (RD#): a number obtained from a radio dispatch that is used to officially document a case when a report is filed

Glossary

redline: when a police officer fails to answer a call from the dispatcher after three consecutive attempts; consequences vary according to the supervisor

second watch: a work shift; early cars work 7:00 A.M. to 3:00 A.M.; late cars work 8:00 A.M. to 4:00 P.M.

sergeant: a supervisor above the rank of police officer but below a lieutenant

sling: sell narcotics

specialized unit: a unit of police personnel that specializes in a certain area of crime, e.g., prostitution, narcotics, or gang crimes

squad: a police car or the radio dispatcher

steady watch: working the same watch period after period

Street Narcotic Impact Program (SNIP): formed in the late 1980s with undercover officers and methods to combat narcotics in the Areas. In the early 1990s, it coalesced into the Narcotics Unit to begin Operation Iron Wedge.

Summer Mobile Unit (SMU): a unit composed of police personnel from districts and units to patrol the beaches from the day they open to the day they close

tactical unit (tac): district cops who work in plain clothes and unmarked vehicles; they are usually more aggressive than beat cops

takedown: the act of enforcement officers converging on a drug-dealing suspect after he or she has sold narcotics to the police

10-4: code used by a two-man squad when acknowledging an assignment

10-99: code used by a one-man squad when acknowledging an assignment

third watch: a work shift; early cars work 3:00 P.M. to 11:00 P.M.; late cars work 4:00 P.M. to 12:00 A.M.

to-from-subject report: a report that explains an action or requests permission, usually written by a police officer to a supervisor

twenty: a street term meaning a quarter gram of cocaine (usually costs $25)

undercover vehicle: vehicle used by an undercover officer that has no outside markings or plates identifying it as a police car

unmarked squad: vehicles of the same make and model as police squad cars but void of police markings; used by supervisors in specialized units or district tac teams

watch party: party thrown by a certain watch to celebrate the end of a period

SOURCES

Abramsky, Sasha. *Hard Time Blues: How Politics Built a Prison Nation*. New York: Thomas Dunne Books, 2002.

Chicago Department of Health. *Community Area Health Inventory, 1996–1998*.

Chicago Public School Data Book. "Tests of Achievement and Proficiency Reading, 1991–2002."

City of Chicago Annual Police Report, 1995–1998.

Conroy, John. *Unspeakable Acts, Ordinary People*. New York: Alfred A. Knopf, 2000.

Donzinger, Steven. *The Real War on Crime: The Report of the National Criminal Justice Commission*. New York: Harper's Perennial, 1996.

Mauer, Marc. *Race to Incarcerate, The Sentencing Project*. New York: The New Press, 1999.

Padilla, Felix. *Puerto Rican Chicago*. Notre Dame: University of Notre Dame Press, 1988.

Pfleger, Rev. Michael. "St. Sabina Church Press Release," December 1993.

Roosevelt University, Institute of Metropolitan Affairs, January 2000.

United States Census Bureau. http://www.census.gov.

United States Congress. Anti-Drug Abuse Act of 1986.
http://thomas.loc.gov.

United States Department of Justice. *Bureau of Justice Statistics, Justice Expenditures, 1999.*

United States Department of Justice. *Bureau of Justice Statistics, Prisoners 1996.*

United States Department of Justice. *Bureau of Justice Statistics, Sourcebook of Criminal Justice Statistics 2000.*

Wilson, Julius William. *When Work Disappears: The World of the New Urban Poor.* New York: Alfred A. Knopf, 1996.

"WLS-TV News Release," October 14, 1992. Staff writer.